U0164806

西域古法七貫拳

西域天山派武学秘籍系列（一）

献给恩师杨公耀钧（义父）诞辰 120 周年

Dedicated to the 120th anniversary of the birth of Yanggong Yaojun (foster father)

中华无形道

天山派第七代掌门 董纲成硬功展示

原宁夏回族自治区武警，特警武术总教练。
现上海国防教育进修学院，武术研究中心
上海交通大学客座教授

前　言

孩提时，吾与纲成弟同在家父杨耀钧指导下练功习武。六月忘暑，严冬感春，四时各有其趣。他练功认真，习武刻苦，三十余载饶有“武痴”之别号，其武其功均有大成，后因工作各奔东西，惜别十几载又相聚，观其言行仍似以往，事亲以孝，守身以节，待人以义，处事以诚。练功习武仍孜孜以求颇有心得，达到相当高的境界。其德其品令人欣慰，吾深深佩服家父当初的眼力。纲成弟子的家父武学之隐微，不负所望，终有今天之成就，想必家父了无身后之蹙矣！

上古圣人之垂教，礼仪威仪犹居家。家有严有慈，治国有赏有罚，然人道之于文武技艺，必亲有修持，非以信手拈来。今阅纲成吾弟所著凡密技绝学、功夫之道，皆能忠实传承吾父所教，全面且有心得，堪称练功习武之佳范。

欣闻大作即将出版发行，切望该书能为弘扬中华文化之遗产、强健中华儿女之体魄做出贡献。孜孜以求之精神，努力进取，练功习武，保家卫国，惩恶扬善，振我中华之雄风，是为至盼。为此跋语。

杨华增

一九九二年三月于上海

Foreword

When I was a child, I practiced Wushu with my brother Gangcheng under the guidance of my father Yang Yaojun. The summer is forgotten in June, and the harsh winter feels like spring. The four seasons have their own characteristics. He practiced earnestly and worked hard in Wushu. For more than 30 years, he has the nickname of "Wu Chi". His Wushu achievements and Wushu skills have achieved great success. Later, because of his work, he said goodbye to each other for more than ten years. When he came back, his words and deeds are the same as before, with filial piety for relatives, keeps etiquette for others, treat others with righteousness, and act with sincerity. He keeps practicing Wushu and he has lots of experiences while still diligently seeking for a higher level. His virtue and quality are gratifying, and I deeply admire my father's original vision of choosing him. The Wushu of the disciple of Gangcheng's father is faint, but he has lived up to expectations. With his achievements today, presumably, his father will have no trouble behind him!

The teachings of ancient saints, the etiquette and majesty are like being at home. There is strictness and kindness in the family, and rewards and punishments for governing the country. However, humanity must be practiced in the civil and martial arts, not by any easy methods. Today, my brother Gangcheng's esoteric skills and Wushu can be faithfully inherited from my father's teachings, comprehensive and knowledgeable, and can be regarded as a good example of Wushu.

I am delighted to hear that the masterpiece will be published soon, and I hope that this book can contribute to the promotion of the heritage of Chinese culture and the strengthening of the physique of Chinese children. I deeply looking forward to the spirit of diligence, strive for progress, hard practicing of Wushu, defending the family and the country, punishing evil and promoting good, and revitalizing China's glory, therefore I wrote this for all of you.

Yang Huazeng

In Shanghai in March 1992

序　言

中华拳术是国技，先贤言传身教，世代相续，源远流长，为古今士庶所钟爱。因门类繁多、方法各异，教学传承颇费心力，然万变不离其宗。古往今来，是拳家多囿于门派之间，极为保密，理论与技法双全者甚少，故能表述其真谛之书亦如凤毛麟角，历代文献罕见佳作。

本人自幼喜好武术、气功，尤嗜技击。八岁受业杨耀钧恩师门下，并被恩师收为义子，传武传德视为己出。时恩师已年逾半百，正蜚声武林，承买师祖衣钵，勤修苦练，技艺超绝，在河南派心意拳门中首屈一指，号称“豹子头林冲”，古法心意拳第三代掌门人，亦是杨家本门汤瓶七式拳、回回十八肘第六代掌门传人。

杨耀钧先生是回族人，享年九十一岁（1900 年 12 月 1 日—1991 年 2 月 1 日），1926 年入党曾做过董必武贴身保镖、地下党。国家离休干部，曾兼任中华全国中医学会宁夏分会顾问。出身于岐黄武术世家，几代行医习武，居河南周口，皆精于心意拳。师祖买壮图家传其子买鸿斌师爷，师爷买鸿斌亲授女婿杨耀钧吾师、师娘买文英、师叔买文俊。买鸿斌不仅是得承师祖买壮图正脉的一代心意拳大师，还是清末商丘、周口一带悬壶济世的有名中医，与丁兆祥、宫宝田、安大庆、袁风仪、袁长青、铁志豪、吕金樑、陈英重，李风洲等拳家齐名。后来又涌现出杨殿卿、尚学礼、卢嵩高、宋国宾等知名拳家。

初稿 1992 年 5 月完成于宁夏银川，定稿 2019 年 7 月完成于南京牛首山西麓书院（历时 27 年）。

董纲成

Preface

Chinese boxing is a national skill, taught by the sages by words and deeds, and has a long history. It is beloved by ancient and modern scholars. Because of the variety of categories and different methods, the teaching inheritance is quite laborious, but it never changes in root. Throughout the ages, many boxers have been confined to sects, and they are extremely secretive. There are few who have both theory and technique. Therefore, books that can express their true meaning are rare and rare in historical documents.

Since I was a child, I like Wushu and Qigong, especially boxing. I was accepted by my teacher Yang Yaojun at the age of eight and was accepted as an adopted son. He taught me etiquette and Wushu skills. My teacher was nearly a hundred years old, and he is well-known in Wushu field, he has bought his master's mantle, diligent and hard-working characteristics, and has superb skills. He is second to none in the Henan School of Xinyiquan. He is also the sixth generation of the head of the Yang family's Tangping seven styles boxing and

Mr. Yang Yaojun is a Hui nationality from China. He was 91 years old (December 1, 1900-February 1, 1991). He joined the party in 1926 and worked as Dong Biwu's personal bodyguard and underground party. At the time when the national cadre retired, he once concurrently served as a consultant for the Ningxia branch of the China Association of Chinese Medicine. Born in a family of Qihuang Wushu, he has practiced medicine and Wushu for generations, and specialized in Xinyiquan in Zhoukou, Henan. The master of his master Mai Zhuangtu raised his master Mai Hongbin, and Mai Hongbin taught his son-in-law Yang Yaojun, my teacher, his wife Mai Wenying, his senior Wenjun. Mai

Hongbin is not only the first generation of master Xinyiquan who have inherited his ancestors, he is also a famous Chinese medicine doctor in Shangqiu and Zhoukou in the late Qing Dynasty. He is as famous as the boxers such as Ding Zhaoxiang, Guan Baotian, An Daqing, Yuan Fengyi, Yuan Changqing, Tie Zhihao, Lü Jinliang, Chen Yingzhong and Li Fengzhou. Later, famous boxers such as Yang Dianqing, Shang Xueli, Lu Songgao and Song Guobin emerged.

The first draft was completed in Yinchuan, Ningxia in May 1992, and the final draft was completed in Nanjing Niushou Mountain Xilu Academy in July 2019 (which lasted 27 years).

Dong Gangcheng.

目 录

第一章 …… 001

西域天山派传承人物…… 002

武有汤瓶七式拳 董纲成

——访武林中人、中华无形道创始人董纲成大师…… 023

文有汤瓶八诊医 杨华祥…… 030

亲力亲为始传承 孜孜不倦为众人

——记汤瓶八诊第七代传人杨华祥 …… 031

心意六合起源…… 044

心意门西域古法气功大师传略…… 054

西域古法心意拳风格…… 059

西域古法心意六合拳习技体练习秘要…… 071

第二章 …… 109

静功十段（功法练习） …… 110

动功十八势(功法练习) …… 113

神勇六合功…… 117

第三章 …… 131

古法心意六合拳十大形的单练法…… 132

十大形的练法…… 137

第四章 ······ 255

汤瓶心意四把捶 ······ 256

回回十八肘拳法解释 ······ 275

汤瓶七式拳 ······ 281

穆氏汤瓶七式拳天山派汤瓶七式拳 ······ 288

第五章 ······ 295

汤瓶八诊介绍 ······ 296

不忘初心 传承有序 ······ 301

后记 ······ 326

西域天山派秘籍书籍 ······ 333

第一章

西域天山派传承人物
武有汤瓶七式拳 董纲成
文有汤瓶八诊医 杨华祥
心意六合拳起源
心意门西域古法气功大师传略
西域古法心意拳风格
西域古法心意六合拳习技体练习秘要

西域天山派传承人物

第一代

西域古法心意拳七代传承人为北宗名将杨继业，杨家将后裔杨明公（1730--1850）出身于中医武术世家，自幼酷爱中医武术，武术技法是养生修炼也是回族汤瓶功法早期传承人，据家谱记载明公长寿活到120岁，壮年时曾中武举。刀剑拳棍皆通，晚年执掌杨氏武馆，有杨老太公之称。教门颇深，悟性极高。精通武医之道。对中国古代医学和内经学表有钻研。花甲之年得按在教门规础上延续并创始和发展了伊斯兰汤瓶功法。

First generation

The seven-generation inheritor of the Xiyu Ancient Method Xinyiquan method of the Western Regions is Yang Jiye. Yang Minggong (1730-1850), a descendant of the Yang family, was born in a family of traditional Chinese Wushu. He loved traditional Chinese Wushu since childhood. According to the family tree, Ming Gong lived to be 120 years old and had a Wushu exercise in his prime. He specialized in all knives, swords, fists and sticks, and he is in charge of the Yang family Wushu Center in his late years, and is known as Yang Laotaigong. The teaching is quite deep, his savvy is extremely high, and he is proficient in Wushu. He has studied ancient Chinese medicine and internal classics. In the Sixtieth Year, the Islamic Tangping Gongfa was established and developed on the basis of the religious rules.

第二代

杨振山（1744--1844），杨明之子，曾应试中举，为继承父业，转而研究医道，尤其精通周易，五行认及中医的经络学说，医技绝伦，接管杨氏武馆，其间依然恪守教规，同时广泛义诊德艺双馨。

Second generation

Yang Zhenshan (1744--1844), the son of Yang Ming, had taken the Chinese traditional exam. In order to inherit his father's career, he switched to the study of medicine. He was especially proficient in Zhouyi, the Five Elements Recognition and the meridian theory of Chinese medicine. He is still abide by the rules, but and at the same time he is extensive free consultations on morality and art.

第三代

杨万运（1780--1879），明公之孙，痴迷于汤瓶功以及回族医学，40岁时已经闻名中原，凭汤瓶功和汤瓶八诊济贫行医教武，对弘扬和发展回族武功医学卓有贡献。

Third Generation

Yang Wanyun (1780--1879), the grandson of Ming Gong, was obsessed with Tangping Gongfa and Hui medicine. At the age of 40, he was already well-known in the Central Plains. He taught Wushu for the poor by using Tangping Gongfa and Tangping Eight Diagnosis, which has made great contributions to the promotion and development of Hui nationality Wushu medicine.

第四代

杨岭云（1825--1928），杨万运之子，6岁起随父亲练功习医，掌握汤瓶七式,以精湛武功而享誉中原,并学汤瓶八诊后因性情孤僻,便立八子杨瑞堂执掌家门。并与心意巨匠买壮图常来常往,视为好友。

Fourth Generation

Yang Lingyun (1825--1928), the son of Yang Wanyun, started practicing Wushu and medicine with his father at the age of 6, mastered the seven styles of Tangping, and was famous in the Central Plains for his exquisite martial arts. After he learned Tangping Eight Diagnosis, due to his withdraw temperament, he made the eighth generation Yang Ruitang the head of the family, and he visited the master of Xinyi Mai Zhuangtu frequently, and treat him as friend.

第五代

杨瑞堂（1863--1950），重点研究汤瓶八诊回族养生修炼法擅长针灸，有“神技武师”之誉，为同乡义诊分文不取，颇有先祖明公之风。与买壮图儿子中医外科买鸿斌是世友，与心意大师杨殿卿是亲兄弟。

Fifth Generation

Yang Ruitang (1863--1950) focused on the study of the Tangping Eight Diagnosis of the Hui nationality's health maintenance practice. He is good at acupuncture and moxibustion, with a reputation of “master of Wushu with magical skills”. He treats fellow villagers without any fees, which quite suits the style of Ming Gong. He is a family friend of a Chinese medicine surgeon, Mai Hongbin, who is the son of Mai Zhuangtu, and his brother is Yang Dianqing, the master of Xinyi.

第六代

杨耀均（1900--1991），私塾深造融先祖大成，是心意师祖。买壮图孙女婿将中华回医回药进一步推动发展，多年来一直义务以汤瓶武功、八诊重病施治系统整理，并挖掘汤瓶七式拳。西域古法心意拳，回回十八肘回族三大古战争保家卫国拳法，以及为汤瓶诊的传承竭尽余力，做出巨大贡献。

Sixth generation

Yang Yaojun (1900-1991), went to a private school for further study and achieved a integration of ancestors, is the ancestor of Xinyi. The grandson-in-law of Mai Zhuangtu further promoted the development of Chinese medicine of Hui nationality and for many years, he has been obliged to organize the system of treatment of serious illnesses with Tangping Wushu, Eight Diagnosis Method, and excavate Tangping seven styles boxing. The ancient method Xinyi Quan of the Western Regions, eighteen cubits of the Hui nationality, and the three ancient wars of the Hui nationality, and He made great contributions to the inheritance of Xiyu ancient Xinyiquan, the three ancient wars of the time-and-again 18 elbow-on-elbow method for defending the country, and the Tangping diagnosis.

第七代

杨华祥教授自幼承袭回族武功，医学汤瓶八诊。1986 年创造中国宁夏伊斯兰医疗康复中心，即回民医院，任中心主任兼院长、副主任医师传统医学教授。早年深造于广州学院，是中国回医回药汤瓶八诊，国家级非物质文化传承人、宁夏医科大学汤瓶八诊培训学院院长。

Seventh generation

Professor Yang Huaxiang inherited the Wushu of the Hui nationality since childhood, and learned the medicine Tangping Eight Diagnosis. In 1986, he created the Ningxia Islamic Medical and Rehabilitation Center in China, namely the Hui Nationality Hospital, and served as the director and dean of the center, as well as the deputy chief physician and the professor of traditional medicine. In his early years, he studied in Guangzhou College. He is the national inheritor of intangible culture Hui nationality medicine Tangping Eight Diagnosis, and the dean of the Ningxia Medical University Tangping Eight Diagnosis Training College.

第七代

董纲成，自幼八岁拜恩师义父杨耀均与长子杨华增次子杨华祥教授一起学武习医，得到真传，不负所望曾被邀请担任宁夏武警部队武术教官，被国外称为神州大侠，是国内回族三大古战场保家卫国拳法之一、汤瓶七式拳西域古法心意拳，回回十八肘第七代传承人之一，青海形意拳研究会顾问，新疆乌鲁木齐昊龙武馆高级顾问，国家非遗西域天山派第七代传承人。

Seventh generation

Dong Gangcheng, who learned from his master and adoptive father, Yang Yaojun, and his eldest son, Yang Huazeng, second son, Professor Yang Huaxiang, since 8 years old, he learned Wushu and medicine together and got the true inherit. He lived up to expectations, was invited to serve as a Wushu instructor of the Ningxia Armed Police Force, and was called a Chinese hero by foreigners. He is one of the three ancient battlefields to protect and defend the country, one of the seventh generation inheritors of Tangping seven styles boxing Xiyu Ancient Xinyiquan, time-and-again 18 elbow-on-elbow method, consultant of Qinghai Xingyiquan Research Association, senior advisor of Haolong Wuguan in Urumqi, Xinjiang, the seventh-generation heir of the Xiyu Tianshan School of the National Intangible Cultural Heritage.

第八代

马泰鑫，1962 年出生青海西宁人，中国武术六段，一级裁判员、一级教练员，国家级社会体育指导员，青海武术院副院长、青海省武术协会形意拳研究会会长、中国形意拳尚字辈、孔门拳 12 代传承人、孔门拳非物质文化遗产项目传承人，格尔木市武术协会副主席、湟中县武协副主席。

马泰鑫积极投入到武术传承与发展工作中，在弘扬武道、传承中华武学方面做了大量卓有成效的工作，还担任形意拳 (国际) 大联盟副主席、宁夏散打协会名誉副会长、湖北省武当太极拳协会名誉顾问、《武魂》杂志社编辑部委员、华武功夫杂志编辑部武术策划。

世袭于武术世家馬云甫之孙，自幼耳濡目染，喜爱盘练拳脚，60 年代继承家传孔门拳、心意六合拳、查拳、长拳，后拜青海名家田登双为师，在师父的教导下系统学习了八卦掌拳械系列内容，形意拳械系列内容，通备拳、劈挂拳、翻子拳、金钢拳、盘龙棍、大刀、铡刀、双刀、双钩、苗刀、双手剑、绨袍剑、西北缠海鞭杆等各种器械，经过深造后，他对拳术的历史、文化、内涵进一步进行了挖掘。

多篇论著在相关知名刊物发表并获好评，书籍《中国当代武林

人物志》、《当代中华武术人物大典》、《中华民间武术名人录》、《中国武术文化传承人物》、《当代西北武林人物风采》《2020 武术家风采》、《2021 中国武术家》发表。

2017 年被马来西亚体育总会聘为"中国马来西亚武术文化传播大使"，并受吉隆坡武术总会特邀在"名师讲坛"主讲"西北鞭杆"被评为武术名家，

《中华武术》杂志 2016 年第 12 期 拳种探秘版发表《回族武术简介》。

《中华武术》杂志 2019 年第 08 期 学术版发表《浅论形意拳的形意精髓》。

《武魂》杂志 2021 年第 1 期 学术版《西北鞭杆》。

《武魂》杂志 2021 年第 4 期 功法明旨版《练习内家拳的功法与健康养身功效》。

2018 年 8 月参加国家体育总局中国武术协会举办的第三届全国武术科学大会，参加论文答辩会，荣获三等奖。

2019 年 11 月国家体育总局杭州萧山湘湖论坛，参加论文答辩会，荣获三等奖。

结合实际，整理撰写了多部著作，有《追魂密肘》、《苗刀》、《龙头大铡刀》。参与副主编书籍有《当代西北武林人物风采》、《西域古法心意拳》、《西域天山五大绝技》、《昊龙双节棍技法大全》、《丁氏流星锤》、《临夏武术》、《八门拳》、《西北马祥禄人物风采》。"武术进学校"活动特聘武术辅导员。

同时不断拓宽领域，培养社会、学校、企业等行业领域优秀武术人才，推动武术向着正规化、系统化、科学化发展，共同担负传统武术的传承使命，让更多人可以了解并体悟传统拳术，通过学习达到防身健体、体悟生命的目的，借助互联网的帮助，推动武术的体育化进程，倡导和推动武术交流。

Eighth generation

Ma Taixin, born in Xining, Qinghai in 1962, Chinese Wushu sixth stage, first-class Wushu referee, first-class coach, current vice president of Qinghai Wushu Academy, president of Qinghai Wushu Association Xingyiquan Research Association, deputy of Golmud City Wushu Association Chairman, inheritor of Confucian Boxing Intangible Cultural Heritage Project.

Ma Taixin actively participates in the inheritance and development of Wushu, and has done a lot of fruitful work in promoting and inheriting Chinese Wushu. He also served as the vice chairman of the Xingyiquan (International) Major League, the honorary vice president of the Ningxia Sanda Association, and the Hubei Province Honorary consultant of Wudang Taijiquan Association, director of the editorial department of "Chinese Wuhun" magazine, and Wushu planner of the editorial department of Huawu Gongfu magazine.

Many articles have been published in related well-known journals and have been well received good feedbacks. The articles were published in the books "Chinese Contemporary Wushu Figures", "Contemporary Zhonghua Wushu Figures", "Zhonghua Folk Wushu Famous Figures", "Chinese Wushu Cultural Heritage Figures", "Contemporary Northwest Wushu Figures", "2021 Chinese Wushu".

In 2017, he was hired by the Malaysian Sports Federation as the "Chinese-Malaysian Wushu Culture Dissemination Ambassador", and was specially invited by the Kuala Lumpur Wushu Federation to give a lecture on "Northwest Whipstick" at the "Famous Teacher Forum" and was named as a famous Wushu expert.

"Chinese Wushu" magazine Issue 12, 2016, Types of Boxing

Exploring Edition published "Introduction to Hui Nationality Wushu".

"Chinese Wushu" Magazine Issue 08, 2019 Academic Edition published "A Brief Discussion on the Essence of Xingyiquan".

"Wu Hun" Magazine Issue 1 of 2021 Academic edition published "Northwest Whipstick."

In August 2018, he participated in the 3rd National Wushu Science Conference organized by the Chinese Wushu Association of the General Administration of Sports, he won the third prize with his paper "talking about the 'Xing' and 'Yi' in Xingyiquan" in the contest.

In November 2019, at the Hangzhou Xiaoshan Xianghu Forum of the State Sports General Administration, the paper "The Development of Chinese Wushu" participated in the defense meeting and won the third prize.

Combining the actual situation, he has compiled and written many books, such as "Xiyu Tianshan Soul Chasing Mizhou", "Xiyu Tianshan Soul Chasing Miaodao" and "Xiyu Tianshan Dragon Head with Big Blades". Participating as the deputy editor of the books are "Contemporary Northwest Wushu Characters", "Xiyu Five Stunts in Tianshan", "Haolong Nunchucks Techniques", "Ding's Meteor Hammer", "Eight Gates Boxing", "Northwestern Ma Xianglu Characters". He was also specially hired as a Wushu instructor for the "Wushu in School" activity.

At the same time, he continues to broaden the field, cultivate outstanding Wushu talents in the fields of society, schools, enterprises and other industries, promote the development of Wushu to be standardized, systematic and scientific, and jointly takes on the mission of inheriting traditional Wushu, so that more people can understand and appreciate traditional Wushu. Through learning to achieve the goal of self-defense, fitness, and understanding of life, with the help of the Internet, promote the physicalizing of Wushu, and advocate and promote the exchange of Wushu.

第八代

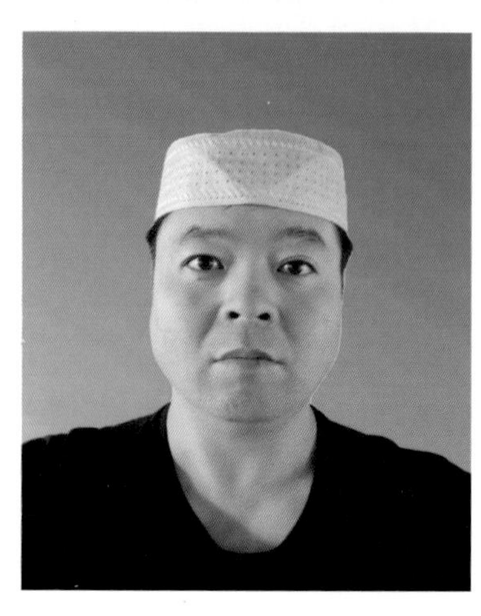

马原子，回族，生于 1977 年，甘肃定西人，现籍临夏市。西域天山派汤瓶门第八代传承人，中国武术段位六段、中国武术协会会员、中国武术段位制指导员、考评员、国家一级裁判员、国家一级社会体育指导员、国家体育行业初级武术指导员、国家中级保健按摩师、高级气功格斗师。

现任中华民间传统武术国际交流促进会执行会长、中国昆仑武学研究院常务副院长、甘肃天马武道影视文化发展有限公司董事长、临夏州公安局特警支队特警教官、临夏市武术协会主席、临夏市星光公益协会常务理事长、中国武术协会段位考试点主任、甘肃省八门拳研究会副会长、中国武当山武当拳法研究会特邀研究员、宁夏国际语言学校武术客座教授。曾任中央电视台《高手在民间》栏目系列片武术指导顾问兼制片主任、河南电视台《翰墨春秋》栏目副导演、《搏击》杂志编辑记者、北京《武魂》杂志策划指导兼副主编、定西市武术协会常务副主席。

自幼世袭武术，练得梅花拳、梅花棍、天山派汤瓶门回回十八肘、昆仑派武学门八分拳、星月拳、登霄鞭杆、星月子母圈、昆仑玄幻太极手、追魂大刀、阴阳十三把、玄武扇、三环大枪、双刀、双钩、

双锏、双斧、单鞭、双鞭、玄武剑、七式剑、梢子棍、三节棍、少林棍、双手剑、绝命十三刀、连环铲、子母鸳鸯钺、铁筷子、脱手牧羊鞭、五味铁手劲内功等本门功法。

2012年开始在全国武术段位套路推广和普及中做了很多工作。被甘肃省武术协会、定西市体育局、定西市武术协会授予“先进个人”“先进工作者”，入选《中国当代双节棍人物》《中华武术30年》《榆中县武术志》《中国当代武术人物辞典》《走向世界的中国学者》等，被并荣登《搏击》《武魂》杂志封面；曾被中国《武汉》期刊交易博览会演武大会评为“武林百杰”称号；第五届华夏武状元国际争霸赛组委会聘任为副秘书长兼裁判长，并被授予“国际武术文化传播大使”；2015年5月24日应邀参加了甘肃电视台少儿频道的《欢动甘肃、六一晚会》节目录制，节目《中国功夫》获金奖，个人被评为“优秀指导老师奖”，2017年被马来西亚科学技术部副部长授予“国际武术养生传播大使”称号。

2012年10月18日--20日在定西成功举办了“天马武道杯”定西市首届全省武术馆校暨西北棍术、散打邀请赛，2014年举办了首届“东南杯”西北国际武术节暨陇南市传统武术、散打邀请赛；2018年11月成功举办了第二届西北武术节，2019年1月份举办首届临夏市民间传统武术邀请赛三级武术裁判员、体育指导员培训班，6月份举办了“梦之星”世界青少年体育会预选赛、8月份总决赛，2019年6月份在临夏州体育局主办下组织培训了武术二级裁判员，10月份担任了首届宁夏银川功夫文化节武术套路裁判长工作，11月份应邀出席并担任首届中华武术健康大会裁判工作。

通过多年整理和编辑，出版了《八门统备武艺》《当代西北武林人物风采》《昊龙双节棍技法大全》《西域天山追魂密肘、五大绝技、西域天山追魂苗刀、西域天山龙头大铡刀》和《丁氏流星锤》等著作。

Eighth generation

Ma Yuanzi, with a Hui nationality, was born in 1977, a native of Dingxi, Gansu, and is currently from Linxia City. He is the eighth-generation inheritor of Xiyu Tianshan Tangping School, Chinese Wushu eight stage, member of Chinese Wushu Association, Chinese Wushu Stage System instructor, assessor, national first-level referee, national first-level social sports instructor, national sports industry junior Wushu instructor, national intermediate health masseur, senior Qigong fighter.

He is the current Executive Chairman of the Chinese Folk Traditional Wushu International Exchange Promotion Association, the Executive Vice President of China Kunlun Wushu Research Institute, the Chairman of Gansu Tianma Wudao Film and Television Culture Development Limited Company, the Special Police Instructor of the Special Police Detachment of Linxia Prefecture Public Security Bureau, the Chairman of Linxia Wushu Association, Executive Chairman of Linxia Starlight Public Welfare Association, Director of Stages Examination Center of China Wushu Association, Vice President of Gansu Bamenquan Research Association, specially invited Researcher of China Wudang Mountain Wudang Boxing Research Association, Guest Professor of Wushu at Ningxia International Language School. He served as the Wushu Guidance Consultant and Production Director of the series of "Folk Master" series of CCTV, the Deputy Director of the "Han Mo Chun Qiu" column of Henan TV, the Editor and Reporter of "Wu Hun" magazine, the Planning Director and Deputy Editor of Beijing "Wu Hun" magazine, Dingxi Executive Vice Chairman of the Municipal Wushu Association.

He has inherited Wushu since childhood, practiced Meihuaquan,

Meihuagun, Tianshan school Tangping time-and-again 18 elbow-on-elbow method, Kunlun school Wuxuemen Bafenquan, Xingyuequan, Dengxiao Biangan, Xingyue Zimuquan, Kunlun Xuanhuan Taijishou, Zhuihun dadao, Yinyang Shisanba, Xuanwushan, three-ring spear, Double knives, Double hooks, Double maces, Double axes, single whip, Double whips, Xuanwu Jian, Seven styles sword, Shaozi stick, Three-section stick, Shaolin stick, Two-handed sword, Thirteen deadly knives, Serial shovel, Son and Mother ono, Iron chopsticks, Shepherd's whip, Five-flavored Iron hand with internal strength, etc.

In 2012, he started to do a lot of work in the promotion and popularization of the national Wushu Stages Routines. Awarded as "Advanced Individual" and "Advanced Worker" by Gansu Wushu Association, Dingxi Sports Bureau, Dingxi Wushu Association, and was selected as "Chinese Contemporary Nunchucks Figures", "30 Years of Chinese Wushu", "Yuzhong Country Wushu History", "China Contemporary Wushu Figure Dictionary", "Chinese Scholars Going to the World", etc., were also featured on the cover of "Bo Ji" and "Wu Hun" magazines; once named "Wulin Hundred Masters" by the China "Wu Han" Periodical Trade Fair Performing Wushu Conference; and was appointed as the fifth generation deputy secretary-general and chief referee by the organizing committee of the China Wushu Champion International Championship, and was awarded the "International Wushu Culture Communication Ambassador"; on May 24, 2015, he was invited to participate in the "Happy Gansu, 1st June Evening Party" program recording, the program "Chinese Kungfu" won the gold award, and the individual was named "Excellent Instructor Award". In 2017, he was awarded the title of "International Wushu Health Communication Ambassador" by the Deputy Minister of Science and Technology of

Malaysia.

From October 18th to 20th 2012, the "Tianma Wudao Cup" was successfully held in Dingxi City. The first provincial Wushu school and Northwest Club and Sanda Invitational Tournament was held in Dingxi City. In 2014, the first "Southeast Cup" Northwest International Wushu Festival with Longnan City Traditional Martial Arts and Sanda Invitational Tournament was held; In November 2018, the second Northwest Wushu Festival was successfully held. In January 2019, the first Linxia Citizens Traditional Wushu Invitational Tournament Level 3 Wushu Referee and Sports Instructor Training Class was held. In June, "Dream Star" World Youth Sports Association qualifiers, and the August finals competition was held. In June 2019, the auspices of Linxia State Sports Bureau organized and trained martial arts referees of level 2, and served as the head referee of martial arts routines in the first Ningxia Yinchuan Kungfu Culture Festival in October. In November, he was invited to attend and serve as a referee in the first Chinese Wushu Health Conference.

After years of sorting and editing, published "Bamen Wushu", "Character style of Contemporary Northwest Wushu", "Haolong Nunchuck Techniques", "Xiyu Tianshan Soul Chasing Mizhou", “Five great stunts”, “Xiyu Tianshan Soul Chasing Miaodao”, “Xiyu Tianshan Dragon Head Big Blade" and "Ding's Meteor Hammer" and other works.

第八代

童嘉昊，1979 年出生，西域天山派第八代传承人，从小习武至今，有丰富的教学经验。赐道号“铁腿神拳”。对道家内丹道术医学、针灸十二经络有独特见解。跟随天山派汤瓶门第七代传承人董纲成、杨华祥习练古法心意六合拳、汤瓶七式拳等、天山派气功养生专家。整理编辑出版了《天山游龙剑》《昊龙双节棍技法大全》《天山五大绝技》《天山龙头大铡刀》《天山追魂刀》《天山追魂密肘》《天山气功》《无极玄空十二指》《吐纳十二桩》《无极玄空手》等。

曾任新疆建设兵团副主席，中国武术六段，中国武术协会会员，国家一级社会体育指导员，国家一级保健按摩师，一级气功格斗师，国家一级武术裁判员，一级散打裁判员，高级教练员，天山派市级非物质文化遗产立项传承人，中国昆仑武学研究院新疆分院院长，新疆双节棍功夫研究会会长、新疆精武研究会副会长、青海省形意拳研究会副会长、宁夏散打协会名誉副会长、湖北省武当太极拳协会名誉顾问、中华民间传统武术联盟副主席、昊龙武道创始人，宁夏硬汉格斗形象代言人。2006 年日本双节棍实战冠军。2007 美国双

节棍实战冠军。2009年香港双节棍实战冠军，赢得“世界棍王”称号。2013年广东佛山国际双节棍争霸赛获得单棍、双棍、功力、实战全能冠军。2014年首届武汉国际棍王挑战赛获得单棍、双棍、功力、实战全能总冠军，并获得“棍王”称号。2016年4月参加河南新乡举办的中国武术国际交流会荣获拳法、棍法两枚金牌。2016年参加第七届华夏武状元国际武术争霸赛，在国内国际比赛中获得金牌108块，等等，2016年5月荣获国际武术文化传承人。新疆第一位将双节棍推广到公安和学校，成为防身、自卫、防暴总教官。新疆规范化双节棍教学及推广第一人。多次受到央视，新华社、新疆电视台等，媒体报道和采访。童嘉昊自传承天山派以来，秉承师训，严以律己，无私奉献，积极参与社会各界的武术活动，并致力于传承后人，向广大群众传播健康的理念与方法。立志将新疆天山派武术这一非物质文化遗产传承下去，在未来我们将依托载体，进一步传承和弘扬天山文化，不断扩大天山派武术对外影响力！

Eighth generation

Tong Jiahao, born in 1979, is the eighth-generation heir of the Xiyu Tianshan School. He has been practicing Wushu since childhood and has rich teaching experience. He was named as "Iron Leg with Magical Fist". He has unique insights into Daoist inner alchemy, Daoism medicine, and the twelve meridians of acupuncture and moxibustion. Follow Dong Gangcheng and Yang Huaxiang, the seventh-generation inheritor of Tangpingmen of the Xiyu Tianshan School to practice ancient Xinyi Liuhequan, Tangping seven styles, etc., as well as Xiyu Tianshan School Qigong health experts. He organized, edited and published the "Xiyu Tianshan School Dragon Sword", "The Encyclopedia of Haolong Nunchuck Techniques", "The Five Great Stunts of the Xiyu Tianshan School", " Xiyu Tianshan Dragon Big Blades ", "Xiyu Tianshan Soul Chasing knife", "Xiyu Tianshan Soul Chasing Mizhou", and "Tianshan Qigong", "Wuji Xuankong Twelve Fingers", "Twelve Spit Nap", "Wuji Xuankongshou" and so on.

He is the sixth stage of Chinese Wushu, member of Chinese Wushu Association, National First-Class Social Sports Instructor, National First-Class Health Masseur, First-Class Qigong Fighter, National First-Class Wushu Referee, First-Class Sanshou Referee, Senior Coach, Tianshan City Class Intangible Cultural Heritage Project Inheritor, Dean of Xiyu Tianshan Wushu Research Institute, Director of Xinjiang Branch of Kunlun Wushu Research Institute of China, Chairman of Xinjiang Nunchuck Kungfu Research Association, Vice Chairman of Xinjiang Jingwu Research Association, Qinghai Province Vice President of Xingyiquan Research Association, Honorary Vice President of Ningxia Sanda Association, Honorary Advisor of Wudang Taijiquan Association

of Hubei Province, Vice Chairman of Chinese Folk Traditional Wushu Alliance, founder of Haolong Wudao, Ningxia tough guy fighting image spokesperson. He is the 2006 Japanese nunchaku champion in actual combat, 2007 American nunchuck combat champion, 2009 Nunchaku champion in actual combat in Hong Kong, won the title of "King of the World of Sticks ". In 2013, he won the single stick, double stick, Gongli, actual combat all-around champion Foshan Guangdong International Nunchaku Championships. In 2014, he won the championship of single stick, double stick, skill, and actual combat all-around in the first Wuhan International Stick King Challenge, and won the title of "King of Sticks". In April 2016, he participated in the Chinese Wushu International Exchange Conference held in Xinxiang, Henan and won two gold medals in boxing and sticking. In 2016, he participated in the 7th China Wushu Champion International Wushu Competition, won 108 gold medals in domestic and international competitions, and so on. In May 2016, he was awarded as the international Wushu cultural inheritor. He was the first in Xinjiang to promote the nunchuck to public schools, became the chief instructor of self-defense and riot control. He was also the first person to teach and promote standardized nunchuck in Xinjiang. He has been reported and interviewed by CCTV, Xinhua News Agency, Xinjiang TV Station and other media many times. Since inheriting the Tianshan School, Tong Jiahao has been adhering to teacher training, self-discipline, selfless dedication, actively participating in Wushu activities in all walks of life, and dedicated to inheriting future generations and spreading healthy concepts and methods to the general public. He is determined to inherit the intangible cultural heritage of Xinjiang Tianshan school Wushu. In the future, he will rely on the carrier to further inherit and promote Tianshan culture, and continue to expand the external influence of Tianshan school martial arts!

武有汤瓶七式拳　董纲成

——访武林中人、中华无形道创始人董纲成大师

他是一代武林高手、中华无形道创始人；

他曾经与香港著名导演唐季礼交流武术并受到对方大力赞扬；

他被马来西亚总理私人保镖称为师爷并视为座上宾；

他只用三次交手就打赢享有泰拳之王的海外高人；

他对高傲的日本武士说，这就是打败你们的中华无形拳；

2009 年北京，他在中国全民健身节上表演，中央电视台曾专题报道。

……

带着敬慕之情，与武林高手、中华无形道创始人董纲成先生再次谋面。依旧是穿透心肺朗朗洪亮的声音、炯炯有神的双目，以及沉稳矫健的步伐，一招一式，彰显出练武之人的阳刚与威武。

董氏，名纲成，字天籁。“穆氏汤瓶七式拳天山派”第五代掌门人、“买氏心意六合拳”第四代传人、“杨氏天山派汤瓶功”第七代传人；上海回族武术协会主任兼秘书长；中国宁夏回族自治区武术协会顾问；中国伊斯兰汤瓶功研究会特邀常务委员兼总教练；西夏精武国术馆长兼总教练；等等。

董大师，自幼酷爱武术略露天赋，八岁时遇河南派心意六合拳天山派汤瓶门高手杨耀钧老先生（原中国气功科学研究学会宁夏回族自治区武术协会顾问），深得杨老先生厚爱，纳为义子并在膝下习艺。杨老先生乃杨氏名门后代，一代宗师、武林泰斗，又是心意大侠买壮图亲孙女婿，其妻买桂英，为家传汤瓶七式拳、杨氏阴阳母子回回十八肘第六代传人，心意六合拳第八代嫡系传人，在家乡

素“有豹子头林冲”之美名。为弘扬中华武术文化，摒弃门户俗见，老先生倾其所学，将濒临失传的天山派西域绝技等功夫传授与董纲成，以免失传之虞。董纲成勤学武艺，终于不负恩师所托，同师门学子及杨老先生次子杨华祥教授，将传统武术精华积极推广，发扬光大，功德无量。

在担任中国人民武装警察部队宁夏总队特邀教官时，董大师传授武术气功，短时间就能掌握头、拳、指、胯和脚击石破砖，且能掌握金钟罩、铁布衫等硬气功夫，能忍受身躯各处防卫抗打技能。他指导的部队曾经多次在大比武中获得好名次，为维护宁夏地区社会治安的稳定，打击犯罪分子做出了杰出贡献。

中华武术，博大精深。“回回十八肘”“汤瓶七式拳”和“心意六合拳”，被武林界称为三大绝技，然董大师有缘受于三种拳法及内家功法的真传。近十年来，董纲成大师潜心研究，博采众长，融合民间传统武术内家拳和外家拳为一体，以有形为无形、刚柔并进的综合拳法；以心意六合拳、汤瓶七式拳、回回十八肘三大拳法为主，以太极八卦、自然门、咏春、气功、迷踪拳法等为辅，终于独创出“中华无形道”，即无形拳。此拳法，是运用掌握的绝技拳法和超前意念，反应敏捷，身手矫健，交手诡异，眼到拳到，其最大秘诀就是七分在脚、三分在手，来无影去无踪，行进中动作快、狠、准。此拳法一经问世，轰动武坛，更得到同门交口称赞。

董大师曾多次受邀走出国门与国际武林界交流，在切磋武艺交流中，大师运用无形拳，分别与泰拳、跆拳道等派系高人交手，以后发制人、虚实结合、柔刚并兼等绝技，连连战胜对方，被中外人士赞为一代“神州侠怪”，董大师走遍大半个中国，深山寺庙，闯五关陆码头，吃过洋葱大蒜头，遇到过无数高手，在切磋与交流中深度的验证武学，得以弘扬。

目前，董纲成大师正潜心培养弟子，传授无形拳之绝技。他说，恩师曾教诲我们，练武之人，首先要秉承武德，心无旁骛。练武成

就三种人：一种是保家卫国的骁将勇士；一种是自娱自乐的爱好者；另一种则是走歪门邪道之小人。因此，他挑选徒弟很有讲究。

也借此，大师呼吁国人都来关注传统武术，唤起国人对练武之人的尊重与支持。同时，他还透露一个心愿，想通过国内外诸多武术比赛等活动，发现和吸收一批有志传承中华绝技的年轻人。他说，老祖先留给我们的宝贵财富不能丢啊，这是义不容辞的责任。

董纲成大师一直投身于对少儿武术的培训，也经常受聘为一些大专院校做武术指导。尤其是少儿班的教学更具特色，以少林童子功秘籍做开蒙教学，通过动、静、呼吸、运气、用气等独到之处的传教，让学员练就一套秀如猫、抖如虎、行如龙、动如山、声如雷的技能，并掌握一般的防身抗力之法。通过武艺与文化相结合的教学方法，有利于激发孩子们学武术的热忱，有助于提高青少年的综合素质，对传承、弘扬中华国粹和民族精神具有深远的意义。

董大师至今 72 岁，弟子无数，简单提几位不同阶段、有影响的徒弟：馬泰鑫、马原子、童嘉昊、杨庆宝、张吉生、洪新忠、朱光华、杨俊峰、赵 华、刘胜利、刘旭晨、盛友春、袁小建、古小辉、海洋、朱向东、孙文、王学军、张青路、李培青。 家父在宁夏除全面传授我与蒋红岩外也曾传授过：王新武、张全乐、张新乐、于承慧、袁济生、杨建军、吴尚、杨天柱、指导过杨俊峰，但这些人主要是由我代父传承的。

Chief Editor Dong Gangcheng

——Interview with Master Dong Gangcheng, the man in Wulin and the founder of China Invisible Daoism

He is a generation of Wushu masters and the founder of the Chinese Invisible Daoism;

He once exchanged Wushu with the famous Hong Kong director Tang Jili and was highly praised by the other side;

He was called a master by the personal bodyguard of the Prime Minister of Malaysia and regarded as a guest of honor;

He only used three matches to defeat the overseas expert who named as “the king of Muay Thai”;

He said to the proud Japanese samurai, this is the Chinese Invisible Fist that defeats you;

In 2009 in Beijing, he performed at the China National Fitness Festival, which was specially featured on CCTV.

...

With a feeling of admiration, I met again with Mr. Dong Gangcheng, a master of Wushu and founder of China Invisible Daoism. He was still having the bright and loud voice that seems to break through my heart and lungs, the piercing eyes, and the calm and vigorous pace, one by one movements, showing the masculinity and mighty power of the Wushu master.

Dong's name is Gang Cheng, and the word is Tian Lai. He is the fifth-generation head of "Mu's Tangping Seven styles Boxing Tianshan School", the fourth-generation heir of "Mai’s Xinyi Liuhequan", the seventh-generation heir of "Yang's Tianshan School Tangping Gong"; concurrently Director and Secretary of Shanghai Hui nationality Wushu Association; Consultant of the Wushu Association of China's Ningxia Hui nationality Autonomous Region; specially invited Standing Committee Member and

Head Coach of the Chinese Islamic Tangping Gong Research Association; Director and Head Coach of Xixia Jingwu Guoshu; etc.

Master Dong, has a passion for Wushu since he was a child and showed his talent. When he was eight years old, he met Mr. Yang Yaojun, a master of the Henan School of Liuhequan and Tianshan School Tangpingmen (formerly the consultant of the Chinese Qigong Science Research Society Ningxia Hui nationality Autonomous Region Wushu Association), and he was deeply loved by Mr. Yang. He was accepted as a righteous son and practice Wushu under his knee. Mr. Yang is a descendant of the Yang family, a master of the Wushu generation, a master of Wulin Taidou, and a grandson-in-law of the hero of Xinyi, Mai Zhuangtu. His wife, Mai Guiying, is a descendant of the sixth generation of Tangping seven styles fist, and the Yang's Yinyang Son and Mother time-and-again 18 elbow-on-elbow method, and also the eighth generation of Xinyi Liuhequan, and she is known as the "Lin Chong with leopard head" in her hometown. In order to promote Chinese Wushu culture and abandon popular views, his master devoted his knowledge and taught Dong Gangcheng the skills of the Xiyu Tianshan School, which was on the verge of loss. Dong Gangcheng studied Wushu diligently, and finally lived up to the entrustment of his master. His fellow students and the second son of his master, Professor Yang Huaxiang, actively promoted the essence of traditional Wushu, and carried it on with immense merit.

When serving as a special instructor for the Ningxia Corps of the Chinese People's Armed Police Force, Master Dong taught Wushu Qigong. He was able to master the head, fists, fingers, hips, and feet to break bricks in a short time, and he was able to master hard-breath Gongfu such as golden bells, iron cloth shirts, etc. He can endure the defense and anti-fighting skills of every part of the body. The troops under his guidance have won many places in the competition and made outstanding contributions to maintaining social stability in Ningxia and combating criminals.

Chinese Wushu are broad and profound. "Time-and-again 18 elbow-

on-elbow method", "Tangping seven styles fist" and "Xinyi Liuhequan" are known as the three great stunts by Wushu circles. However, Master Dong is predestined to receive the true transmission of the three types of boxing and the inner family fist. In the past ten years, Master Dong Gangcheng has devoted himself to research, learn from others' strengths, and integrate the traditional folk Wushu internal boxing and external boxing into one. Intergrating the tangible to the intangible, and the rigidity and flexibility go hand in hand. Time-and-again 18 elbow-on-elbow method is the main three methods, supplemented by Taiji Bagua, Ziranmen, Yongchun, Qigong, and Mizongquan, and finally created the "Chinese Invisible Daoism", that is, invisible boxing. This boxing method is the use of mastered special skills and advanced ideas, quick response, vigorous skills, weird fights, and the best punches. The biggest secret is that the seven points are on the feet and the three points are in the hands. The action is fast, ruthless and accurate. Once this boxing technique came out, it became a sensation in the Wushu world, and it was even more praised by the same door.

Master Dong has been invited many times to go abroad to communicate with the international Wushu community. In the exchange of Wushu, the master uses invisible boxing to fight against the masters of Muay Thai and Taekwondo. He defeated others again and again, and was praised by Chinese and foreign people as a generation of "Shenzhou Chivalry". Master Dong traveled to most of China, deep mountain temples, rushed to the five-pass land wharf, met countless masters, and was in discussions and exchanges with in-depth verification of Wushu can be carried forward.

At present, Master Dong Gangcheng is devoting himself to training his disciples and teaching the invisible fist skills. He said that our mentor taught us that Wushu practitioners must first uphold the Wushu ethics and have no distractions. There are three kinds of people in Wushu: one is the brave warrior who defends his family and the country; the other is the self-entertaining enthusiast; the other is the villain who walks in the

wrong way. Therefore, he is very particular about choosing apprentices.

In this way, the master appealed to all Chinese people to pay attention to traditional Wushu and to arouse Chinese people's respect and support for Wushu practitioners. At the same time, he also revealed a wish that through many Wushu competitions in his country and abroad, he wanted to discover and absorb a group of young people who aspired to pass on Chinese stunts. He said that the precious wealth left to us by our ancestors should not be lost. This is an unshirkable responsibility.

Master Dong Gangcheng has been devoted to the training of children's Wushu, and is often employed as a Wushu instructor for some colleges and universities. In particular, the teaching of the children’s class is more distinctive. It uses the secrets of Shaolin Tongzigong to do enlightenment teaching. Through the unique teaching of movement, calmness, breathing, and use of energy, students can practice a set of skills that looks like beautiful cats but trembling tigers; walking like a dragon, moving like a mountain, and sound like thunder, and master the general method of self-defense resistance. Teaching methods that combine Wushu and culture will help stimulate children's enthusiasm for learning Wushu, help improve the comprehensive quality of young people, and have far-reaching significance for the inheritance and promotion of the Chinese national quintessence and national spirit.

Master Dong is 72 years old and has countless disciples. Simply mentioned a few influential apprentices at different stages: Ma Taixin, Ma Chito, Tong Jiahao, Yang Qingbao, Zhang Jisheng, Hong Xinzhong, Zhu Guanghua, Yang Junfeng, Zhao Hua, Liu Shengli, Liu Xuchen, Sheng Youchun, Yuan Xiaojian , Gu Xiaohui, Haiyang, Zhu Xiangdong, Sun Wen, Wang Xuejun, Zhang Qinglu, Li Peiqing. Besides teaching me and Jiang Hongyan in Ningxia, my father also taught: Wang Xinwu, Zhang Quanle, Zhang Xinle, Yu Chenghui, Yuan Jisheng, Yang Jianjun, Wu Shang, Yang Tianzhu, and Yang Junfeng, but these people were mainly passed on by my father.

文有汤瓶八诊医　杨华祥

杨华祥 宁夏医科大学回族汤瓶八诊培训学院院长、
中国汤瓶国际健康连锁机械董事局主席

杨华祥，回族，国家级非物质文化遗产——汤瓶八诊第七代传人，1952 年生于上 海一个医学武术世家，于上世纪 70 年代支边宁夏，从此落地生根。1987 年创办宁夏 首家伊斯兰医疗康复中心 (回民医院)，1992 年应邀赴马来西亚传播汤瓶八诊，客居至今。现任宁夏医科大学回族汤瓶八诊培训学院院长、中国汤瓶八诊国际健康连锁机 构董事局主席。

亲力亲为始传承 孜孜不倦为众人

——记汤瓶八诊第七代传人杨华祥

杨华祥教授，男，回族，1952 出生于祖传的医学武术世家，中医学副主任医师、传统医学教授，国家级非物质文化遗产项目回医药回族汤瓶八诊疗法国家级传承人；于上世纪 70 年代从上海支边来到宁夏。1987 年创办中国首家伊斯兰气功医 疗康复中心任主任，期间当选为宁夏回族自治区第五届、第六届政协委员。1991 年应邀 赴马来西亚客居至今，创办了马来西亚均恒（国际）医药有限公司、华祥生命保健有限公司；2005 年被宁夏伊斯兰国际经济文化友好促进会聘请为顾问、2006 年被宁夏回族自治区人民政府聘任为宁夏政府驻马来西亚经济贸易联络处主任；2007 年被宁夏医科大学回族医学研究所聘请为高级特邀研究员；2009 年被宁夏回族医学研究所聘请为顾问；现任宁夏政府驻马来西亚经济贸易联络处主任、宁夏汤瓶八诊保健按摩有限公司（中国汤瓶八诊国际健康事业连锁机构）董事局主席、马来西亚均恒国际医药有限公司董事主 席、宁夏医科大学回族医学研究所特邀研究员、宁夏医科大学回族汤瓶八诊亚健康疗法 职业技术培训学院院长等职务。

汤瓶八诊 中阿医学文化的结晶

说起汤瓶八诊的由来，杨华祥一直认为它是中医文化和阿拉伯医学文化互相交融的产物。早在 1300 年前，很多中东穆斯林商人通过丝绸之路来到中国，长途跋涉中，为减轻和消除旅途疲劳，他们在驿站洗浴和歇息 时，自创了一种保健方法——通过揉脚和按摩身体的某些部位来消除旅途的劳顿。随着大批穆斯林先民来到中国，伊斯兰医药文化也随之 传入，他们又汲取了传统中医的经络理论、

腧穴理论、脏腑理论之精华，经过长期探索、总结和完善，形成了具有中国回族特色的自然疗法—末梢经络根传法，这就是汤瓶八诊的雏形。但末梢经络根传法最初只是对手、脚、耳等身体部位进行的捏、推、点、揉等手法，并不十分完备。明末清初，出生于回族中医世家的杨明公，也就是杨华祥的祖辈，他在末梢经络根传法的基础上，从穆斯林的宗教礼仪、生活习惯中得到启发，发现了人体的异经奇脉，又提炼出转五围的自我保健方法。这种保健方法在杨氏家族世世代代的传承中不断完善，逐步形成了“头诊、面诊、耳诊、手诊、脚诊、骨诊、脉诊、气诊”这八大诊疗方法，这就是汤瓶八诊名称的由来。

打破家规 公开传授汤瓶八诊法

杨氏家族世世代代承袭着汤瓶八诊养生疗法的精髓，并不断完善和发扬。1952 年，杨华祥出生在上海医学武术世家，从小就跟随父亲学医习武。他的父亲杨耀钧是汤瓶八诊第六代传人，他常年坚持以汤瓶八诊为重病患者施治，并系统挖掘整理了汤瓶八诊养生疗法，也使他从小耳濡目染父亲的医德和医术。上世纪 70 年代，他

支边来到宁夏，从此 在这里落地生根，与回族医学结下不解之缘。1986 年，他牵头创建了宁夏伊斯兰医疗康复中心，也就是当年的回民医院，并担任康复中心主任兼医院院 长，推广回族医学和汤瓶八诊。后来，为了使汤瓶八诊这一回族医学文化瑰宝发扬光大，他在银川开办了“汤瓶八诊养生坊”，并打破了“传子不传女、传内 不传外”的家规，公开传授汤瓶八诊疗法。2008 年 1 月，回族汤瓶八诊疗法入选国家级 非物质文化遗产名录。杨氏家族近 200 年的代代相传和坚守得到了肯定，这也使得杨华祥更加有信心和毅力，把这份文化遗产发扬光大。

广泛传播 奥运会世博会显身手

2008 年北京奥运会与残奥会期间，汤瓶八诊受邀入驻国家奥体中心，通过奥运祥云小屋这个载体，为各国官员、运动员提供康复理疗服务。汤瓶八诊立即引起了参加奥运会各国来宾的浓厚兴趣，许多人慕名而来，了解和体验汤瓶八诊的功效。奥运会闭幕后，北京残奥会组委会又要求汤 瓶八诊的工作人员继续留下来，在祥云小屋展示 汤瓶八诊高超的技艺。为了更好地在北京奥运会 期间宣传汤瓶八诊，让更多的人了解宁夏回族医学，杨华祥将公司得力员工安排在祥云小屋，继续为大家服务。2009 年 8 月 7 日，正值北京奥运会举办一周 年，许多市民集中在北京国家奥林匹克体育中心，再次重温一年前的热闹场景。在这样一个提倡全民 健身的日子里，汤瓶八诊康复理疗中心的员工们在 奥体中心现场表演起汤瓶功；同时，中心的杨华祥 教授现场介绍和讲解了汤瓶八诊。一年前曾经到奥运村参观过“中国故事 · 祥云 小屋”的人们不难想起，汤瓶八诊正是当时代表宁 夏回族自治区参展的项目。在去年的展示中，包括北京市市长郭金龙和许多教练员、奥组委的官员等许多人都当场体验过汤瓶八诊，认为它“不但有文化底蕴，还有实用价值”。据汤瓶八诊康复理疗中心 运营总监郭宏杰介绍，当时有几个摔跤运动员在比

赛中肌肉拉伤，需要紧急处置，就用上了汤瓶八诊。赛后的体检证实，汤瓶八诊对于运动员伤势的恢复确实发挥了作用。因此，奥运会后，奥体中心就跟宁夏的参展代表协商合作细节。今年 6 月 17 日，汤瓶八诊从宁夏来到北京，正式进驻奥体中心。 从国家奥体中心的汤瓶八诊康复理疗中心正式成立到现在的两个多月，凡是做过诊疗的人纷纷 给予好评。2009 年国家竞走队在奥体中心集训期 间，全体队员接受了汤瓶八诊康复理疗中心提供的训后康复调理，国家体育总局田径管理中心主任杜兆才对汤瓶八诊非常关注，体验后决定采纳汤瓶八诊为国家田径运动员助力。 最近，国家竞走队队员王浩也在汤瓶八诊康复 理疗中心得到了有效诊疗。郭宏杰说：“王浩的胸椎有些变形，走 20 公里以后会影响他的呼吸，所以我们就为他做理疗。这次看到王浩获得世界田联锦标 赛 20 公里竞走银牌，我们也由衷地高兴，希望以后我们能更好地为运动员服务。”

内病外治 八诊的奇妙传奇之处

如果把这个占地面积 1700 余平方米、总投资超过 2000 万元的汤瓶八诊康复理疗中心当做一个普通的按摩店，那就错了。汤瓶八诊是国务院、文化部认定的国家级非物质文化遗产保护项目，它有着深厚的文化底蕴和实用价值，不仅为人们治疗病痛，还传承着回族的传统文化。那么，汤瓶八诊究竟是什么？它如何达到保健效果？汤瓶八诊包括头诊、面诊、脚诊、气诊、脉诊、骨 诊、手诊、耳诊，千百年来一直以口传心授、言传身带的方法在民间流传。养身疗法采用民间的按摩、 刮痧、火罐、放血疗法和穆斯林洗“阿布代斯”过程 中的自我按摩，经学者们的相互交流，形成了较为完整的回族保健理疗方法——汤瓶八诊。 杨华祥强调：“回族医学的总体原则是‘内病外 治’。汤瓶八诊通过非药物疗法，激发调动人体潜能、疏通经络、平衡阴阳，并根据不同人体肌能而采取不同的方式进行

保健康复治疗，这是它与普通按 摩疗法最大的区别。”人体经络就像交错复杂的道路，气滞成病、血滞成疮，气血能平衡才能正常运营、保证健康，汤瓶八诊就是通过内病外治的手法 舒经活络，调动激发自身的潜能，促进正常代谢，维护健康。

External Treatment of Internal Disease
The Wonders of the Eight Treatments

It would be wrong to regard this Tang Ping Eight Treatments Rehabilitation Physiotherapy Center, which covers an area of more than 1,700 square meters and has a total investment of more than 20 million yuan, as an ordinary massage shop. Tang Ping Eight Treatments is a national intangible cultural heritage preservation project recognized by the State Council and the Ministry of Culture. It has profound cultural heritage and practical value. It not only treats people's ailments, but also maintains for the future the traditional culture of the Hui nationality. So, what exactly is Tang Ping Eight Treatments? How does it achieve health effects? Tang Ping Eight Treatments include head, face, foot, qi (energy), blood, bone, hand, and ear treatments. For thousands of years, it has been taught by word of mouth and so spread amongst the people. The therapy uses folk massage, scraping, cupping, bloodletting therapy, and self-massage from the “Abu Dys” Muslim cleansing procedure. Through mutual exchanges between scholars, a relatively complete method of health care and physiotherapy for the Hui nation has been developed – Tang Ping Eight Treatments. Yang Huaxiang emphasized: "The general principle of Hui medicine is 'external treatment of internal disease.' Tang Ping Eight Treatments uses non-drug therapy to stimulate the human body's potential, clear the meridians, balance Yin and Yang, and adopts different methods for health care and rehabilitation according to different human muscle energies. This is the fundamental difference

from ordinary massage therapy." The meridians of the human body are like a complex pattern of intertwined roads. Stagnation of the qi leads to disease, stagnation of the blood leads to sores. Only when qi and blood are in balance can you operate normally and ensure your health. Tang Ping Eight Treatments uses external treatment of internal diseases to relax the meridians and collaterals, mobilize and stimulate your own potential, promote normal metabolism, and maintain health.

洗身洗心 汤瓶奇疗效传文化

除了八诊以外，另一个关键之处就是汤瓶。“汤瓶”的命名更是中国特有的：唐朝时期，当波斯、中东的穆斯林对中国经济的繁荣有所贡献的时候,唐朝皇帝李世民为了对其表彰,按照穆斯林洗“阿布 代斯”的习俗，打造了一只瓶状的“洗壶”，命名为“唐壶”，其意为穆斯林“洗大净”和“洗小净”的水 壶。壶内装有热水，古时热水称之为“汤”，故易名为“汤瓶”。汤瓶是穆斯林具有代表性的专用器具。杨华祥说：“洗‘阿布代斯’是伊斯兰教的宗教仪式。洗脸，就是以崭新的面貌面对人；洗耳朵，就 是不听坏话；洗嘴巴，

就是不说脏话；洗脚，就是走正路……这个仪式包含净化心灵的意义。汤瓶八诊的文化底蕴也体现于此。" 在汤瓶八诊的诊疗中，汤瓶中置入温度适合的水，根据它的温度刺激人的经脉窍穴，加之通过八诊所用的器具与内病外治的颤、推、点、按等手法， 直接调节人的精神状态，激发调动人体的自身潜能，达到自我修复的目的。在此，又不能不提到汤瓶 八诊的诊疗器具——骨诊棒、耳诊棒、刮痧板、经窍 仪、推经锤、搠罐、震骨板、水牛角等。制作这些工具的材料都是农牧民家养水牛的牛角，成牛只食用天然牧草，绝不用现代化养牛场的成品。牛龄在 3 岁、 身高在 130cm 左右，雄性，取其根部位往上向尖部 的 7cm~30cm 处为上品。牛角根部透明、血脉清晰 者为刮痧板，尖部成骨齐长、质地坚硬者为骨诊棒，全部产品均为纯手工制作，由汤瓶八诊传承人亲自挑选。

Wash Body, Wash Heart
Tang Ping Curative Effect in Culture

In addition to the eight treatments, another key point is the name Tang Ping itself, which is especially unique to China: during the Tang Dynasty, when Muslims in Persia and the Middle East contributed to the prosperity of China's economy, the Emperor, Li Shimin, in order to commend it, practiced the Muslim "Abu Dys" custom. A bottle-shaped "washing pot" was created, named "Tang hu" (Tang-style pot), for use by Muslims for the greater and lesser cleansing. Since the pot contained hot water, which was in ancient times called "tang" (now meaning soup), so the vessel was renamed "tang ping" (hot-water bottle, or soup bottle). The Tang Ping is a characteristic special utensil for Muslims. Yang Huaxiang said: "The 'Abu Dys' cleansing is an Islamic religious ritual. To washing the face is to face people with a new look; to wash the ears is not to listen to bad things; to wash the mouth is not to speak bad words; to wash the feet is to take the right path... This ritual contains the meaning of

purifying the soul. The cultural heritage of Tang Ping Eight Treatments is also reflected in this." In the application of Tang Ping Eight Treatments, the soup bottle is filled with water at a suitable temperature, and the patient's meridian or acupuncture points are stimulated according to its temperature. Such techniques directly adjust the human mental state, stimulate and mobilize the human body's own potential, and achieve the goal of self-healing. Here, we should mention the particular diagnosis and treatment tools of the Tang Ping Eight Treatments – bone treatment stick, ear treatment stick, scraping board, meridian opening instrument, meridian pushing hammer, cupping pot, bone vibrating board, water-buffalo horn and so on. These tools are made from the horns of water-buffalo raised by farmers and herdsmen on natural pastures without the use of artificial materials used on modern cattle farms. Top grade horn is taken from male water buffalo at 3 years old with a height of about 130cm, when the horn is 7cm~30cm in length from root to tip. Horns with transparent roots and clear blood vessels are made into scraping plates, and those with long bones at the tip and hard texture are made into bone treatment sticks. All products are handmade and selected by the inheritors of the Tang Ping Eight Treatments.

海外扬名 马来西亚大放异彩

1991 年，受马来西亚海鸥集团董事长的邀请，杨华祥赴马来西亚为其爱子治病。其间，马来西亚雪隆精武体育会邀请他去讲授中医、回医传统疗 法和回族武术。这次出访在马来西亚引起巨大反响，为杨华祥后来在马来西亚传播汤瓶八诊开了个好头。

名度逐渐扩大。在此期间，以汤瓶八诊为纽带，他与马来西亚首富郭鹤年等知名人士结下深厚友谊。前不久，马来西亚卫生部副部长拉迪夫先生和 自治区政府达成共识，将汤瓶八诊列为马来西亚

东 方医疗保健中心保健项目之一。

Famous Overseas Malaysia Shines

In 1991, at the invitation of the chairman of the Malaysia Seagull Group, Yang Huaxiang went to Malaysia for treatment for his beloved son. At the same time, Malaysia Selangor Jingwu Sports Association invited him to teach Chinese medicine, traditional Hui medical treatment and Hui martial arts. This visit prompted a huge response in Malaysia, and presented a good opportunity for Yang Huaxiang to spread Tang Ping Eight Treatments in Malaysia.

Its reputation slowly grew. During this period, with Tang Ping Eight Clinics as a bridge, he forged a deep friendship with Malaysia's richest man, Kuok Hocknien (Guo Henian), and other celebrities. Not long ago, Mr. Abdul Latiff Ahmad, Deputy Minister of Health of Malaysia, and the autonomous regional government, agreed to list Tang Ping Eight Treatments as one of the health care projects of the Eastern Health Care Center in Malaysia.

加大培训 文化瑰宝造福众人

鉴于杨华祥在马来西亚为推动马来西亚与中 国宁夏在经济文化交流中所做的一些工作，马来西亚电视台、《南洋商报》等众多媒体将他称之为中马“民间外交大使”，自治区政府则聘请他担任自治区 驻马来西亚经济贸易联络处主任。近几年，杨华祥 奔波于马来西亚和中国之间，以汤瓶八诊为桥梁， 传播回族医学文化。汤瓶八诊是中阿医学文化交流的结晶,历经杨氏家族八代人的承传与坚守，成为宁夏回医药重点 项目之一，该疗法经过无数病例的临床检验，将成 为现代治未病预防医学领域重要的干预方法。杨华祥说他接下来要做的，就是建立回族汤瓶八诊亚健康培训学校，将回族汤瓶八

诊传统医学与现代中医经络学有机结合，加大培训力度，更好地传承与弘 扬回族汤瓶八诊疗法，使这一民族医学文化瑰宝代代相传，造福更多人群。

Increase Training

Cultural Treasures Benefit Everyone

In view of Yang Huaxiang's work in Malaysia to promote economic and cultural exchanges between Malaysia and China's Ningxia Province, many media outlets such as Malaysia TV and Nanyang Commercial Daily called him China-Malaysia's "civil diplomatic ambassador", and the autonomous regional government hired him to serve as Director of the Economic and Trade Liaison Office of the Autonomous Region in Malaysia. In recent years, Yang Huaxiang has travelled between Malaysia and China, spreading the Hui nation's medical culture, using Tang Ping Eight Treatments as a bridge. Tang Ping Eight Treatments is the crystallization of the medical-cultural exchanges between China and Arab States. With eight generations of the Yang family's cumulative heritage and perseverance, it has become one of the key projects of Ningxia Hui Medicine. The treatment has been clinically tested in countless cases and will become a modern curative and preventative treatment – an important intervention option in medicine. Yang Huaxiang has said he will next establish the Hui Tang Ping Eight Treatments Health Training School, organically integrate the Hui Tang Ping Eight Treatments traditional medicine with modern Chinese medicine meridian study, increase training intensity, and better promote the Hui Tang Ping Eight Treatments so as to enable this treasure of national medical culture to be passed on from generation to generation, benefiting more people.

西域天山派传承人物

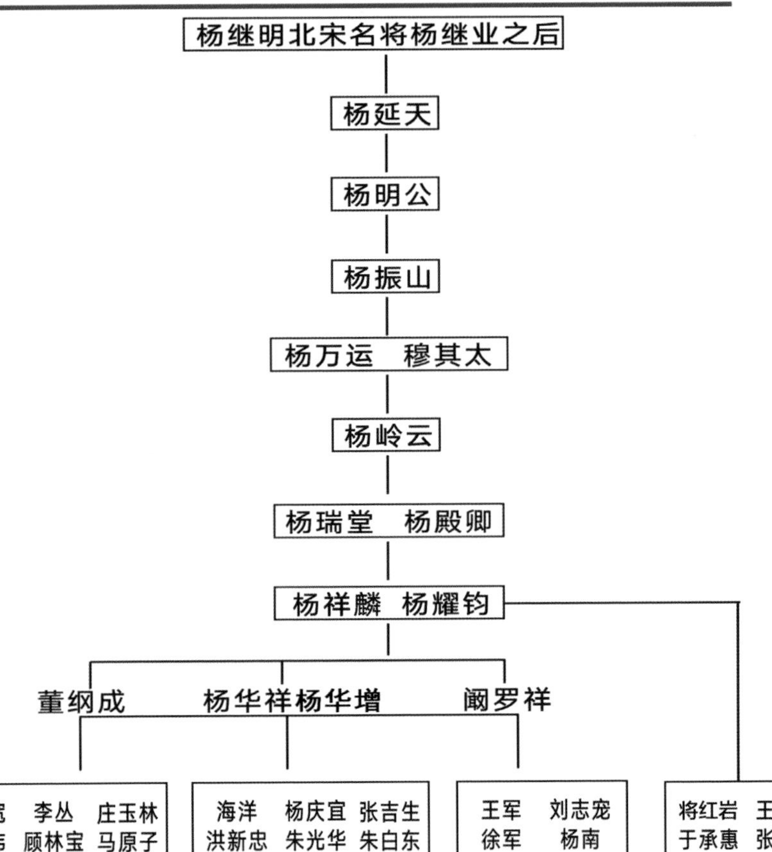
杨继明北宋名将杨继业之后
杨延天
杨明公
杨振山
杨万运　穆其太
杨岭云
杨瑞堂　杨殿卿
杨祥麟　杨耀钧
董纲成
杨华祥杨华增
阚罗祥
董玉宽　李丛　庄玉林
黄大伟　顾林宝　马原子
李勇　王红军　郭嘉
王雪锋　周昆山　徐兔林
孔爱毅　刘虎成　王艮良
翁季纯　刘宝鼎　张玉虎
马泰鑫　童嘉昊　王新中
田欢欢　魏从成　王庆科
徐露萍　徐龙生　张青路
海洋　杨庆宜　张吉生
洪新忠　朱光华　朱白东
盛友春　袁小建　古小辉
刘胜利　刘旭晨　王学军
杨庭亮　马原子　马泰鑫
童嘉昊　张青路　杨文舜
王军　刘志宠
徐军　杨南
王义志　尹向东
黄金虎　苏荣茂
范厚斌　苏荣
雷震
将红岩　王新武
于承惠　张全乐
袁济生　张新乐
吴尚文　杨金柱
白恒祥　杨俊峰
郭惠生　李亮

国家级非物质文化遗产
回族医药·回族汤瓶八诊疗法
中华人民共和国国务院公布
中华人民共和国文化部颁发
2008年6月
微信号:tangpingbzhen

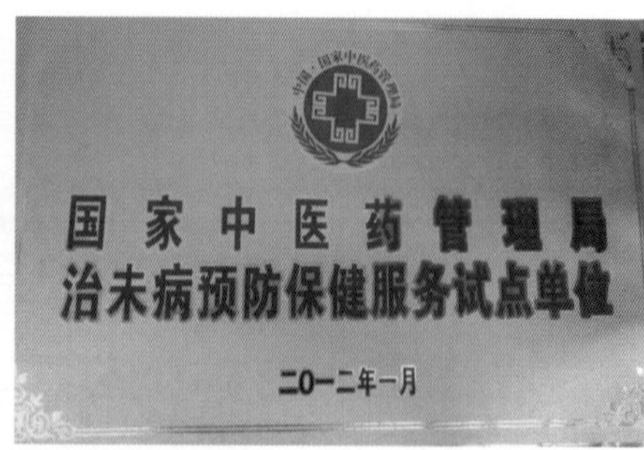
国家中医药管理局
治未病预防保健服务试点单位
二〇一二年一月

世界唯一 中国独一
《汤瓶八诊传承谱系》
杨华祥教授简介

汤瓶八诊
奇效療法
微信号:tangpingbzhen

兵团第十二师非物质文化遗产
西域天山武学
兵团第十二师公布
兵团第十二师文体广电和旅游局颁发
2019年12月
华人头条

作品登记证书
作品名称：西域天山派
作品类别：美术作品
创作完成日期：2019年09月18日
登记日期：2019年11月26日
登记机构签章
中华人民共和国国家版权局统一监制

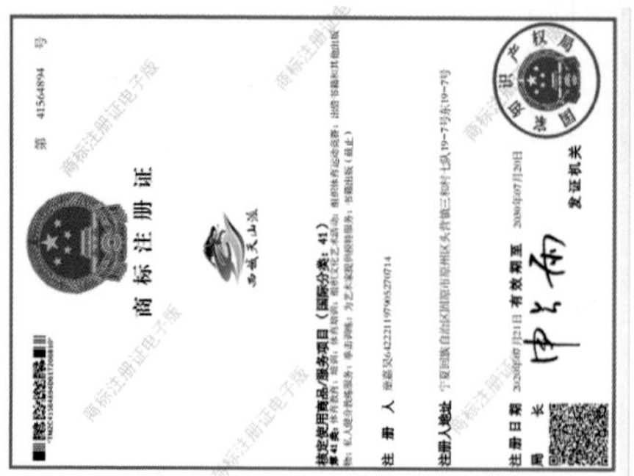
商标注册证
西域天山派

西域天山派

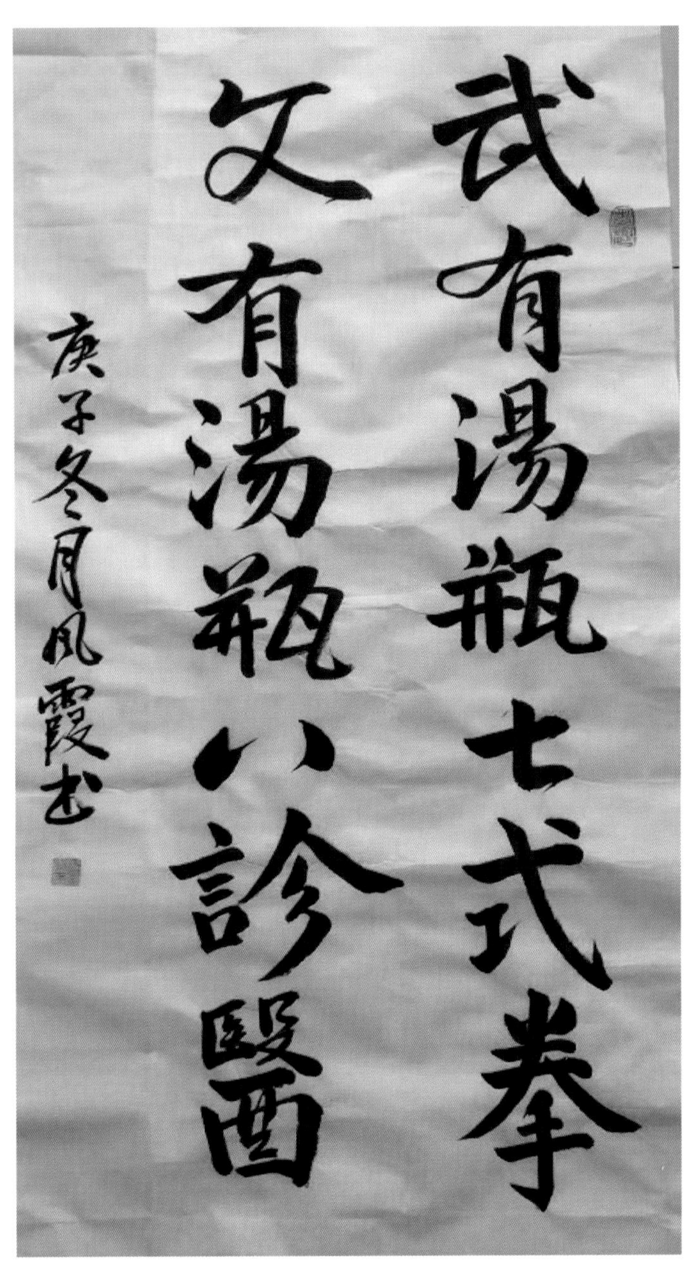
武有湯瓶七式拳
文有湯瓶八診醫
庚子冬月鳳霞書

心意六合起源

心意六合拳首创于明末初姬龙峰，时值名家辈出，高手如云，威震武林，俗称“黑拳”，是独立发展的拳种。既不属于少林派也不属于武当派，是少林僧人从姬氏学了心意十二势，作为寺内秘传的拳术珍品。它是我国著名的内家名拳，内功精微，妙法神力，素以技击著称于世。

姬龙峰（又作“风”，名际可），龙峰乃其字，系明末总兵师承道士董秉乾所创的董氏六合枪法，人称为“神枪”。明万历三十年（1602）生于山西蒲州诸冯里北义平村，清康熙二十二年（1683）谢世。享年 82 岁，在中华武术长河中，贡献卓越。

北义平村乃明时之称，至清初易家宗村，清中叶改为蕁村，此村在蒲州府（辖六县）西端之黄河东岸上同陕西隔河相望，相传为古圣君舜帝的故里舜帝村（原称诸冯村），皆属诸冯里（昔之“里”相当于今之“镇”）。据蕁村《姬氏族谱》所载，此村姬氏一世祖姬从礼（字恒信）是明初自山西洪洞县大槐村迁至蒲州的。传至姬龙峰之父姬训，已是第八世。姬训（字学古）有两子两女，长子名际时（字龙峰），在蕁村并无任何武事记载或传说，而姬龙峰则有非凡的武功造诣。谱言：“技勇绝技”，即是对其的武技之定论。

蒲州地区农产丰富，素为三晋之粮仓。姬龙峰家小康，地两顷，院十座，陕西数处有营业。龙峰自幼村中苦读，文成秀才，鹤立鸡群。然蕁村地处闭塞，时有强人出没，尤为河西流寇所掠，村民如坠深渊。姬龙峰，少负壮志，河滨练功，南观中山习虎踞，西望黄河仿龙腾，酷暑严寒，未曾中断一日。正在村西偶遇一叟，相指点并试手，追其形，退其影，纵横往来，目不及瞬，结果姬败北。遂恳切求教，叟言：后生，法力尚佳，唯眼神不及，去河边洗之即可。姬从之。

走进河边水中洗眼，顿觉清亮，回首欲谢，叟已经全无踪影。姬大悟，及后练功，首重二目“观察之精”技遂大进。后来并在其技击理论《三性调养》中将眼应“常循”列为第一性。

世乱御敌，刀枪当先，姬龙峰率众挥戈退群寇，搏杀在最前，为精御敌本领，素日苦练大枪不辍，巧认檐椽为群靶，精习“飞马点椽”功。尊村街巷宽正，房舍高大，每间前后檐下搭椽十五根。龙峰在巷道上练点椽功时，握大枪，乘战马，打之飞奔。从檐旁疾驰而过瞬间，妄刺何椽必是举枪即得，枪枪点中椽头中心。龙峰家多座院落的房椽经过无数次点练，炸得根根见深痕，练就他神枪技艺。为访天下豪杰，龙峰二十余岁于明末天启五年（1625）始奔少林寺，出潴冯经虞乡，过解州（关羽故里）翻中条到平陆，由茅津过黄河，达河南嵩山少林寺，与寺僧及武师切磋技艺，并从那由武技高强的僧众把守的古刹山门初三出三进，安然无恙，一时晋、豫震惊，昔日绝技，蓴村至今仍传颂。龙峰曾经多次往返少林寺与蓴村间。一次在翻越中条山时，突然马失前蹄直坠深涧，险些丧生，只凭一身绝艺，臂挂悬挠枝，徒壁攀登，才得以至少林寺，其精神赤胆，无不令人惊叹。尔后，龙峰以其绝艺神勇被聘为少林寺武技高师。精传其技，直至清军入关，派亲信入寺住持方归蓴村。龙峰在寺内累计达十余年，但龙峰所授拳却在该寺秘传下来。

龙峰德高艺绝。一年隆冬，前往陕西赤水，筹款过年，南行九十五里，达风陵渡时，已近傍晚，忽闻船上老幼呼唤妇婴泣啼，他疾步上前，只见船上后生无理欺人，但此时船已离岸丈余，急呼停船，船工不从，反而辱骂。此时已过天命之年的姬龙峰，怒火中烧不顾船离岸已三丈余也不管黄河激流之险，飞身一纵，疾落船舷，神功天降，众人愕然，船客中有人辨出是姬龙峰，惊呼这不是县北龙峰公嘛言罢，艄公跪地赔罪，欺人者叩头求饶。龙峰命其赔礼。众人皆称快，共奔陕西。后龙峰在少林寺读书见雄鸡相争悟出道理，于是枪法变拳法。在创拳造谱时讲到三要，即为：有服尊长者可要，

有德年高者可要，有笑顽童者可要。

天启四年（1624）创就举世闻名的心意拳。此以神枪所创之拳，神妙莫测，盖从末有之龙峰是个聪智超凡智勇双全的先师。他所创“心意六合拳”绝不是简单的枪法改拳法，而是他那出神入化的枪法为主，认天地之道的大理性（天人合一），并认阴阳相生的宇宙规律来诠释。“智”“仁”“勇”“六合”“五行”“动静”“进退”“起落”至变化无穷的境界。“孝悌忠信”是其仁也。英锐之气过人是其勇也。将此理贯注散招之中创世多势短拳绝艺。其势貌似鸡腿、龙腰、熊膀、鹰、，虎抱头，妙合诸多生灵之绝，成功地创造出内涵十大形功法。心意拳其前后六势，前六势坚硬如饿虎扑羊、野马奔槽、熊出洞，真形实相等，后六势其柔软，燕子取、，鹞子钻林、蛇分草等。它和陕西曹继武、山西戴龙邦、河北李洛能所传形意拳同出一源。龙峰八十岁那年，河南洛阳北窑马学礼慕名到蕈村求艺，龙峰言：吾年逾八十，不能授之，我有一弟子郑某，曾在南山居住遂指示马氏扮作雇工于郑家窥习其艺。两年后艺成，马氏复至蕈村拜见。姬公感其心诚“孝悌忠信者可交”，而将拳艺概而言之，曰“文武之道，古今之盛传，且国家之大典，上有益于江山社稷，下能趋吉避祸，此生不可阙也”。龙峰论及时之流行拳法曰“今之武者，专论架势封闭闹法，不知日间瞭然在目，还可少用，若黑夜之中，伸手不见，如何用之，必致误自身，悔何及哉”。言及六合拳威，曰“惟刚大之气，养之于素，而忽然发于一旦，依本心本性，直捕商丘，随高打高，随左打左，随右打右，不怕身大力勇者五行顺一气放胆进成功”。马学礼得其真传后，二百年一直在河南省西部地域回教中秘密流传，为当地看家拳术。后由武林大侠买壮图尽得心意拳艺之奥秘，而继承发展了这门拳术。

明末，大将洪承畴与清兵在松山战败被俘。清人极力劝其投降，但洪承畴誓死不降，骂不绝口，表示只求早死，别无他求。皇太极无可奈何，只得再烦劳范文程前往劝降，后经范文程巧妙而耐心地

劝说，一向信誓旦旦表示要以死报国的洪承畴终于乖乖就范，俯首帖耳地投降了皇太极。而先公年老，国已破，犹念先朝，不失民族气节，存绝技不为官，挥戈而保国家，身沦清国数十载，至死不着清朝衣冠，清康熙二十二年（1683）先公谢世，终年八十二岁，葬于老尊村西之姬氏祖墓中。后人念其德高艺绝，绘其巨幅老年坐像。敬尊村姬氏家庙中。庙内供敬七位姬氏先祖之像，龙峰在东墙，但见面瘦白髯，身修长，二目炯炯神光，每年正月初一至初五挂出，全村拜之。然后卷起仍珍藏如此持续，直至 1959 年迁村庙方休。少林寺僧闻公故后，诵经悼念，立碑刻像载其身世。

而今，龙峰遗艺业已传及神州内外，其绝伦技勇，造就了无数举世闻名的拳家，其深妙的功理，更引起天下有志者不断探求。

歌曰：心（形）意初祖姬龙峰，神枪创拳绝艺成，少林内外得此术，九州四海皆豪雄。

Origin of Xinyi Liuhe Quan (Fist of Mind-Intent and Six Harmonies)

Xinyi Liuhe Quan was first created by Ji Longfeng in the late Ming Dynasty. It was a time when famous masters appeared in large numbers. Though neither Shaolin Sect nor Wudang Sect, it was the Shaolin monk who learned the Xinyi twelve forms from the Ji family as a treasure of martial arts secretly passed down in the temple. It is a famous Chinese internal system of boxing, in which the inner strength is subtle, the magical powers are superb, well-known as a martial art.

It is the Liuhe spear technique of the Dong clan created by the Taoist priest Dong Bingqian in the late Ming Dynasty, known as "Divine Spear". Ji Longfeng was born in North Yiping Village, Zhufengli, Puzhou, Shanxi in the 30th year of Wanli in Ming Dynasty (1602), and died in the 22nd year of Kangxi in Qing Dynasty (1683), at the age of 82, having made an outstanding contribution in the long river of Chinese martial arts.

North Yiping Village was first named in the Ming Dynasty; it was later called Yijiazong Village in the early Qing Dynasty, and Li Village in the middle of Qing Dynasty. This village is across the river from Shaanxi on the east bank of the Yellow River at the western end of Puzhou Prefecture (with six counties under its jurisdiction). According to legend, Shundi Village (formerly known as Zhufeng Village), the hometown of the ancient sage Emperor Shun, belonged to Zhufengli (the former "li" is equivalent to the current "town"). According to the "Genealogy of the Ji Clan" of Li Village, Ji Congli (Hengxin), the first ancestor of the Ji Clan, moved to Puzhou from Dahuai Village, Hongdong County, Shanxi in the

early Ming Dynasty. Ji Xun, the father of Ji Longfeng, was the eighth generation to live there. Ji Xun had two sons and two daughters, of whom the eldest son was named Longfeng. At that there were no martial arts records or legends in Li Village, whereas Ji Longfeng achieved extraordinary martial arts accomplishments. It is said "consummate skill" is the conclusion of his martial arts.

Puzhou was rich in agricultural and known as the granary of the Three Jin Dynasty. Ji Longfeng's family was well-off, with two hectares of land, ten residences, and several places of business in Shaanxi. Longfeng studied hard from childhood in the village. However, the village was ever besieged and plundered from time to time by bandits from the west of the river; and the villagers fall as if into the abyss. Ji Longfeng, with little lofty ambitions, practiced by the riverside, Zhongshan to the south like a crouching tiger, the Yellow River to the west like a coiling dragon, in the sweltering heat and cold, throughout the day. He encountered an old man to the west of the village, challenged him and tried his hand, but chasing his form, retreating from his shadow, unable to focus as he moved unhindered, Ji was defeated. So he earnestly asked for advice, and the old man said: The younger generation, have great power, but vision is lacking, just go to the river to wash. Ji went there and, going into the water to wash his eyes, he felt refreshed, but looking back to thank him, the old man was nowhere to be seen. Ji achieved awareness and, after practicing the exercises, made great advances in the skills of "Essence of Observation". Later in his martial arts theory “Three natural nourishments”, he specified that the eyes should always follow.

Fighting the enemy in chaos, taking the lead with swords and spears, Ji Longfeng led the crowd to retreat from the bandits, fighting in the forefront, in order to defend against the enemy, working hard with his

large spear, he cleverly recognized the eaves as the target of the group, and practiced the "galloping strike". The streets of Zuncun were wide and straight, and the houses large and tall, with fifteen beams under each pitch of the roof. As Longfeng was fighting in the roadway, he carried a large spear, rode a war horse, and galloped. The moment he galloped past the eaves, he stabbed at the center of the head with his spear. The residences of Longfeng's vilage were defended many times, and the roof-beams were scarred, and they used their spear skills. In order to seek out the heroes of the world, at the age of 20 in the fifth year of the Apocalypse at the end of the Ming Dynasty (1625), Longfeng went to the Songshan Shaolin Temple in Henan Province to exchange skills with monks and martial masters. Longfeng travelled back and forth between Shaolin Temple and Li Village many times. Once when climbing over Zhongtiao Mountain, his horse suddenly stumbled and fell into a deep stream, and he almost lost his life: only with a superb skill, pulling himself up branches to climb the cliff, was he able to at reach Lin Temple – his spirit was bold and amazing. Afterwards, Longfeng was hired as the Shaolin Temple Martial Skills Teacher for his skill and bravery. He passed on his skills until the Qing army approached and sent its cronies to the monastery and the abbot Fang sent him back to Li village. Longfeng had been in the temple for more than ten years, but his boxing technique has been secretly passed down in the temple ever since.

Longfeng's skill and virtue are absolute. One year in the middle of winter, he went to Chishui, Shaanxi to raise funds for the Chinese New Year. He traveled 95 miles south and reached Fengling Crossing. It was almost evening. Suddenly he heard women and children sobbing on the boat. He quickly stepped forwards, only to see that a young man was cheating them. The boat was a little way off shore and he anxiously called

out to the boatman to stop, but the boatman refused, and insulted him. At this, Ji Longfeng, whose year of destiny had arrived, burning with anger and irregardless of the boat being 10 metres off shore and the danger of the Yellow River rapids, with a single bound he leapt aboard the ship as with a divine power – everyone was stunned. Some of the passengers recognised him and said, “Isn't that Longfeng from the north?” The boatman knelt and kowtowed to beg for mercy.

In the fourth year of the Apocalypse (1624), he created the world-famous Xinyiquan. This spear fighting system was unpredictable, and Longfeng was a clever, extraordinary, wise and courageous master. His Xinyi Liuhe Quan is by no means a simple spearmanship, but his supernatural spearmanship, the great rationality of recognizing the way of heaven and earth (heaven and man are one), and the cosmic law of yin and yang coexistent. Wisdom, Benevolence, Courage, Six Harmonies, Five Elements, Dynamics, Advances and Retreats, and Rising and Falling in a state of endless change. "Filialty, loyalty, and faithfulness" is its benevolence. The heroic spirit is his courage. He put this theory into the creation of a close boxing system of loose movements. It combines a chicken's leg, a dragon's loin, a bear's limb, an eagle, and a tiger's headhead. It combines the uniqueness of many creatures and in the ten major forms. Xinyiquan has six forward and backward positions. The first six positions are as tough as a hungry tiger rushing toward a sheep, a wild horse running through a valley, and a bear coming out of a cave. It has the same origin as the Xingyiquan passed by Cao Jiwu in Shaanxi, Dai Longbang in Shanxi, and Li Luoneng in Hebei. When Longfeng was 80 years old, Ma Xueli from Beiyao in Luoyang, Henan came to Li village to seek art. Long Feng said: I am over 80 years old and cannot teach you. I have a disciple named Zheng who once lived in Nanshan, go

as a servant Zheng's house to see his art. Two years later, Yicheng, Ma returned to Li Village to pay a visit.

In a spirit of sincerity, "filial piety and loyalty can make friends", and summarizing the art of boxing, he said, "The way of civil and martial arts, ancient and modern, and the grand ceremony of the country, the upper level is beneficial to the country and the community, the lower level can seek good luck and avoid misfortune, and this life cannot be missed." Longfeng said of contemporary popular boxing, "Today's martial artist specializes in a closed posture, which should be used sparingly. How wonderful". Whereas speaking of the prestige of Liuhe boxing, he said, "Only the strong spirit, the nourishment of its quality, and its sudden occurrence, according to the nature of the heart, directly capture Shangqiu, follow the heights, follow the left to the left, follow the right to the right, and not be afraid of the body. The five elements of the vigorous and brave go smoothly and boldly to succeed." After Ma Xueli found his calling, he has been secretly circulating in Islam in the western part of Henan Province for two hundred years, as a guardian of the local martial arts. Later, the martial arts heroes learned the mystery of Xinyi Quan, and inherited and developed this martial art.

At the end of the Ming Dynasty, general Hong Chengchou and Qing Bing were defeated and captured in Songshan. The Qing people tried their best to persuade him to surrender, but Hong Chengchou vowed not to surrender. Huang Taiji had no choice but to press Fan Wencheng to surrender. After Fan Wencheng persuaded him ingeniously and patiently, Hong Chengchou, who had always pledged to serve the country with death, finally obediently surrendered to Huang Taiji. Yet Longfeng was old, the country broken, he missed the first dynasty, yet he did not lose his national integrity, kept his unique skills and did not become an official,

and protected the country. In 1683, the father died, he was eighty-two years old, and he was buried in the tomb of the Ji family in the west of Zuncun Village. Later generations remembered his virtues and exquisite art, and painted him a banner of his seven ancestors, which they hung out from the first day to the fifth day of the first month every year for the whole village to worship. Then it was rolled up and kept in the collection until it moved to the village and temple in 1959. After the monk of Shaolin Temple heard about his death, he chanted sutras to mourn and erected a stele to convey his life experience.

Nowadays, Longfeng's heritage art has spread to the inside and outside of China. His extraordinary skills and bravery have created countless world-famous boxers, and his profound techniques have aroused the constant exploration of aspiring people all over the world.

The song says: Ji Longfeng, the first ancestor of Xinyi, was a master of the Divine Spear.

心意门西域古法气功大师传略

买壮图为河南省鲁山县西关里虎桥回族人，原为武秀才，得心意拳真传，遂无心功名，潜心拳道，艺臻化境，对拳师做了较多改进，创编了四把捶，为南阳派心意拳的一代宗师。并以皮货生意为业，往来于鲁山、周口之间，授徒颇多，他生于道光初年，活动于咸丰、同治时期，卒于光绪三年，享年八十余岁。这时期中华武术登峰造极之年，他与“半边崩拳打遍天下”的郭云深大师齐名。黄河南北，同车毅斋大师并为“意拳三绝”。

买师祖，入室弟子有丁兆祥、李海森、安大庆、陈英奎、李豪发、袁凤仪等人，诸弟子亲承师训又奖掖后人，故买壮图师祖事迹绝招在河南心意门中有口皆碑，传为美谈。

咸丰年间，舞阳县北舞渡镇，清真寺阿訇丁兆祥，某日见一老者礼拜，因面目陌生而叩问其名，始知是鲁山买壮图武术气功大师，经商路过渡口，入寺礼拜，二人促膝长谈，感情相投，买师祖于寺内试技，随手从衣袋拿出七枚铜钱，盘膝坐于地，然后，放在腹部上，往里一缩。“嗨的一声七枚铜钱像箭一样射到对面墙梁上。然后，伸出右掌一个抓握回收，那七枚铜钱，竟然被其魔力拉回到自己右掌心里。这种技艺名为布袋功与软玄功，寺中众人看了目瞪口呆，无不齐声喝彩。当时在一片赞扬邀请下，众人求买师祖再一次献技，盛情难却，只见买师祖，在寺外用手掌近按一只蝴蝶，让其任意飞翔，自己随蝶转折飞奔五里之许，其蝶仍在掌中。这种粘蝶之功，使丁兆祥赞叹不已，当即拜师祖为师，留其在寺教习心意拳法。

郏县心意拳师李海森，去鲁山探望其表兄买壮图一日，那天雨后复晴，骄阳似火，表兄弟在屋内品茶乘凉，恣谈拳法。其表弟听到高兴之处，不禁手舞足蹈。适门外，石榴树上麻雀喳喳乱叫，惹

起心烦，欲拔掉此树，却被表兄制止，买师祖从座椅上突然跃起，左手指在空中挑起竹帘，飞跃上树，右手指早已夹住一雀，这种飞手擒雀之功实属罕见，使表弟十分折服。

咸丰年间某日，袁凤仪在盆河口高台茶馆，当众试技，单掌劈断生铁碾槽腿，适遇买师祖，被买师祖只用了一招“熊形单把”一掌制服，即地拜买师祖为师，弃效子拳而改学心意拳。

光绪十年(1884)买师祖在南阳结识了石桥寨的武林高手唐万义，唐万义热情邀请买师祖到家做客切磋武艺。席间，唐武师命儿子唐九洲演习家传绝技唐家枪。九洲见有机会露一身手，便拈枪在手，把丈八长枪舞得犹如出水游龙。数名家丁头上各顶一枚铜钱，唐九州持枪跃起，只见铜钱被一一扎飞。唐武师面有得意之色，请买老表赐教，买师祖谦逊地答道，凭着对真主起誓，枪法我可是不行。唐万义怫然作色，道，买老表既然不肯赐教枪法，那么我倒要领教拳法。说罢，便忽地亮出了猴拳的架势。交手中，唐武师有意争先。使出了抓、、，打，咬、踢、蹬、踹、跺等狠毒招数，躲、闪之法，步步防守。数个回合下来，唐万义心内诧异，心意拳以勇猛进攻见长，怎么不见他有进攻之势？这时买师祖有意露一破绽，唐武师见有机可乘，立刻双勾手化掌，就势抓住对方双肘，接着脚下使出勾挂连环脚，只见买师祖缩身后坐，双臂猛地内旋，一下子裹住对方双手，猛抖丹田之气大喝一声“出去”，这一招是四把捶中的一式叫“出手横拳势难招唐万义被甩围外。买壮图师祖眼疾手快，飞步扶住并连声道歉：多有冒犯，得罪，得罪！看到父亲败北，唐九洲冲上前来：买老伯小侄还要请教！唐万义呵斥道，放肆：当下化干戈为玉帛，结为莫逆。

A Brief introduction to the Qigong Masters of the Western Regions Ancient Method Xinyi School

Mai Zhuangtu was a Hui from Huqiao, Xiguanli, Lushan County, Henan Province. Formerly a military official, after getting to the truth of Xiniquan, he cast aside his rank, concentrated on boxing, and refined his art. He made many improvements, created the “four hammers”, and became the master of Nanyang School of Xinyiquan. He also had a leather goods business, traveling between Lushan and Zhoukou, and taught many apprentices. He was born in the early years of the reign of Qing Emperor Daoguang, and he was active in Xianfeng and Tongzhi periods. He died in the third year of Guangxu aged over eighty. In this period, when Chinese martial arts reached its peak, he was as famous as Guo Yunshen, whose "half-step crushing fist defeated the world". Along wth Master Che Yizhai, he known as one of the “Three Essentials of Yiquan”.

The disciples of ancient master Mai, including Ding Zhaoxiang, Li Haisen, An Daqing, Chen Yingkui, Li Haofa, Yuan Fengyi and others, inherited the teacher’s instruction and rewarded future generations. Therefore, Master Mai Zhangtu's deeds are well-known and highly-regarded in the Henan school of Xinyiquan.

During the Xianfeng period, Imam Ding Zhaoxiang saw an old man praying one day in the mosque in Beiwudu Town, Wuyang County, and asked his name because of his unfamiliar face. He then became aware that this was wushu qigong Master Mai Zhuangtu of Lushan. They passed through the commercial district and entered the temple, where they talked for a long time, and they had similar feelings. The master showed his

skills in the temple – he took out seven coins from his pocket, sat cross-legged on the ground, and then placed them on his belly and contracted it "Ha! The seven copper coins hit the beam on the opposite wall like arrows." Then, he stretched out his right palm and drew it back. The seven copper coins were pulled back into his palm as if by magic. This skill is called Laughing Buddha skill and soft mysterious skill. Everyone in the temple was dumbfounded and applauded in unison. The, full of praise, everyone begged ancient Master Mai once again to show his skills. Though their hospitality was not good, they saw ancient Master Mai cover a butterfly with the palm of the hand outside the temple, let it fly at will, and continue to cover it for a distance of five miles, the butterfly still under his palm. Ding Zhaoxiang was amazed by this skill of covering butterflies, and he immediately adopted the master as his teacher, remaining in the temple to learn Xinyiquan.

Xinyiquan Master Li Haisen of Jia County in Pingdingshan went to visit his cousin Mai Zhuangtu. After rain, the sun was blazing, and the cousins sipped tea in the house to enjoy the coolness and talk about boxing. His cousin was please with what he head – he could not help but dance! Outside, sparrows were chattering on the pomegranate tree, causing a disturbance. Li wanted to fell the tree, but was stopped by his cousin. Master Mai suddenly jumped his seat, his left finger lifted the bamboo curtain in the air, and he flew up into the tree – his right hand had already clamped a bird. This kind of "flying hand catching a bird" is very rare, and his cousin was very impressed.

One day in the Xianfeng period, Yuan Fengyi tried his skills in public at the Gaotai Teahouse at the mouth of the Penhe River. He chopped off a pig-iron trough leg with a single strike of his palm. However ancient Master Mai simply used "bear single grip" with one hand to subdue him. He immediately worshipped the master as his teacher, and followed Xinyiquan instead of Xiaoziquan.

In the tenth year of Guangxu (1884), Master Mai met Tang Wanyi, a martial arts master of Shiqiaozhai, Nanyang. Tang Wanyi warmly invited ancient Master Mai to come home so he could learn about martial arts. During the banquet, Master Tang ordered his second son Tang Jiuzhou to demonstrate the Tang family spear technique. Jiuzhou, seeing that he had the opportunity to show his skills, held his spear in his hand and danced like a dragon in the water. Several prominent people each put a copper coin on their head, and Tang Jiuzhou leapt forward with his spear and sent the copper coins flying one by one. Tang was proud to have so enlightened ancient Master Mai, who responded humbly, by swearing to Allah, I can't match such marksmanship. Tang Wanyi was stunned, saying, since cousin Venerable Mai refused to teach marksmanship, then he would like to learn martial arts from him. Then he revealed the monkey stance. In the hands, the Tang Wushi deliberately competed for the first place. Martial arts Master Tang fought hard to overcome him. He resorted to bitting, hitting, kicking, stamping – ducking and diving, step by step to defend himself. After several rounds, Tang Wanyi was astonished. Xinyiquan is known for its brave attacks. Why didn't he see that his opponent was attacking? Then, Master Mai deliberately revealed a flaw. Seeing that there was an opportunity, Master Tang immediately double-hooked his palms and grabbed his opponent's elbows. But his opponent's arms swung inward suddenly, wrapped his own arms, shook his dantian and winded him, shouting "Out". This move is one of the four hammers called "Tang Wanyi is thrown by a horizontal strike." Master Mai Zhuangtu had quick eyes and quick hands, he stepped forward to hold Tang and apologized: How rude, how rude! Seeing his father's defeat, Tang Jiuzhou rushed forward: Uncle Mai, teach your nephew! Tang Wanyi scolded him, saying peremptorily: So friendly now, turning conflict into jade silk.

西域古法心意拳风格

拳外有拳，门内有派，自古皆然。夫派别者，个性风格之发展也。学者之性有别也，或好之刚猛，或乐乎阴柔，或喜乎正直，或溺于灵。巧学之者各因其性，教之者因材施教顺乎七性，故虽从一师、学一道而风格各异，特点各异盖在斯也。

西域古法心意拳雄浑博大、刚正险劲，阴柔之中多阳刚。气通劲正者，仅是登堂，未入其室。入其室者，气伟力健。其势如万钧雷霆，莫之能御。或如甘霖普泽沛然皆至，其气养之心意，蓄之于丹田，催动命门，发之于涌泉。运至于全体，达至于四梢。至阳刚多威猛，或至阴柔尚灵巧。在修炼过程中，尤其手、眼、身、法、步法、劲法都有特殊的要求，故学到心意六合拳的真谛，也不过二三。

其拳式动静分明、刚柔相兼，既轻灵而又沉实，其劲路阴阳互济，吞吐相兼，既沉实而又圆活，形式上又起落钻翻，“如水之翻浪”，内中则升降开合、起伏、鼓荡。起于进身之时，拇指翻下，水火易位，意到气满，去以钢锉之力，回以钩钎之能，发则力达，纵然强敌亦也可取。

卷谱曰：“练气而能壮，练神而能飞。”又曰，纵横者，劲之横竖，飞腾者，气之深微，进退随手之出入，动静任气之来去自然。在内练法上，要求气纳丹田，冲出命门，引督脉过尾闾，引任脉重楼，复归丹田，其劲路则通、透、穿、贴、松、捍、合、坚，伏如横弩，起如发机。

西域古法心意拳法，一般不主张先发制人，而是后发制人，贯彻把把不离鹰抓的说法。所谓把把不离鹰抓，就是对方心意已动，出手进招刚刚启动，尚未发出全劲之时，瞬间发招进身，彼来不及变化，我便能占上风抢主动权。当鹰捉四平脚下抛时，就是对方一

招攻来劲力已尽，此时旧力已过，新力未生，我及时发招，彼必然回手不及，被我所制。而对方发招之中，正当全劲之时，应避其锋芒不可妄动，对方进一招如此，就是数招连进，也是如此。

西域古法拳法起鹰捉把。拳谱曰：敌不动，我不动，敌动后，我方动。我动须抢在敌先，同太极拳：彼不动，己不动：彼微动，己先动，后发先至”本为一理。如遇对方也不主动发招，则我或采取引手，诱敌发招，或采取逼吸驱步近身，迫使对方之力变化而发招。当然任何一个拳种的技击原则都是相对的。

西域古法拳法在特殊情况下，也有主动进攻的，那就是观察到对方，内五行已动，意要伤害我时，不等对方动手，我立即发招制服敌人。买杨门氏拳法，虽然是后发制人，却是认我为主，这一点与太极八卦不同，也是外人不易理解之处。它主张敢打必胜，首先从精神上树立取胜的信心。自古以来，“两强相遇勇者胜”。拳谱曰“未较之时，不可轻敌，已较之时不可畏敌”。而且从招法也是以我为主，不管对方防守如何严密，也不管对方已经攻上来，都要充分发挥自己的技法，硬打硬进无阻挡地将对方打出去。就是说，你打你的，我打我的，以快制慢，迎门攻去。西域古法拳法也讲借力打人，以小力胜大力，但它不是死等对方，而是除接手要随对方劲力外，一旦近身都是首先掌握主动权，在运用时有自己的独特性，即抢在先。让对方顺应我，在变化中借力。当然，买氏拳法采取如此技法，是凭借着内劲之运发，能骤然间爆发明显的弹性炸力，与劲力路线的方向。它往往来去声东击西，围魏救赵之术，既攻对方又解我围。

西域古法拳法属短打之列，以贴身打为主，以短制长。在手法上有“两手不离腮”“两肘不离肋骨”之说，攻敌时尽量来去最佳路、，最短途径，即进，即闪。闪即进，不必远求。其拳法擅用肩、肘、胯、膝击人，因为只有钻进去，才能发挥自己的才能，也只有钻进去，才能利用身法动摇对方重心，进而将对方打出，可以拳谱曰“若

要打得远，还得脸又脸，若要打得美，还得嘴对嘴。打人如走路，看人如虎捉羊。又说制根不如制身”。所以西域古法拳法是以控制对方身体变化为最佳手段的。

西域古法拳法不似有些拳种讲究先防后攻,而是讲究攻防一体，即攻防合一，这一特点不仅表现为一个动作中，一手防、一手攻。它在拳法中，熊形单把，龙形大劈，而且还有攻与防合于一个动作，这种手法中，此手段是防手、又是攻手，是攻中有防、打中有破。攻守不分是西域古法拳法一个显著的特点，它既无单纯防守，又无单纯攻手。

西域古法拳法在抢位上以中为主,绝大多数动作都是脚踩中门，即“脚踏中门夺地位，就是神仙也难防”。手法上也是以中为主，攻守动作不离自己中线，攻击对方也是照着对方中线进击。中线是人体要害集中之线。只有攻击，这些部位才能速于奏效，也才能在攻敌时迫使对方撤回对我的攻击动作。

西域古法拳法充分发挥人体各部之技能，头、手、肩、肘、胯、膝、足七处，互相配合，综合应用，并利用身法，发出极大的杀伤力。使对方难承受一击。它在使用身体各部分击敌时，绝不是牵强附会和故意使用某一部分，它很注意各部分联系的合理性。在平时通过六合身法练习形成了协调配合之习惯，一旦临场应敌，则根据实际情况。手押肩出、手落膝起，往往过手一两招，胜负即见分晓。俗话说，行家一伸手，便知有没有。

练习西域古法心意拳，其拳好学难精，必须循序渐进，初练习者一定要按照三层道理、三步功、，三种练法依次而行。即炼精化气、明劲易骨为第一功夫，多是刚劲兴直劲。炼气化神、暗劲易筋为第二步功夫，即找横劲兴柔劲。化神还虚，化劲易髓为第三步功夫。可辨虚劲兴实劲。每一步功夫，必须分清要求，练法目的要一步一步地依次刻苦练习，即、既不可专求其一，也不可越级而行。若专求其明劲，虽然明劲是运用时必不可少的劲，则太刚易折。如虎扑

羊、鹰抓鸡，此均刚劲兴直劲。苟稍避其锋，则其劲无用！而且年长日久，只练明劲而不另换劲，不但无益，而且会把筋骨练僵，更容易使筋骨受损，因为明劲主刚，发力甚猛，日积月累就会积劳成疾，反受其害。如虎直扑时，稍闪而旁击之，则可借其力而扑之矣！此即横劲兴柔劲之力。若专求柔劲，又过柔不坚，不但长功缓慢，而且也容易形成软拳无力。至于化劲易髓，更为深妙，是非精于武术者难以辨别，此劲乃用于交手时，人实我虚，乘虚即实，人刚我柔。乘柔即刚，所谓“逢强智取，过弱活拿”柔中之刚，是为真刚，刚中之柔，是为真柔，此即刚柔济之论，无虚无实。即虚即实，而随机应变者为化劲也。所以初练习者，必须循序渐进，在练好第一步功夫之后，再练第二步功夫，继而进入第三步功夫，古拳法云，“三年一小成，十年乃大成”，就是说每层功夫，少则也须苦练三年，方能体会和领悟其中之奥妙。当第一步功夫练至功深圆满，劲已入骨之后，则应转换为第二步，不同劲节“暗劲”的练法，不可固执

专求其刚。当第三步功夫练至功深圆满，筋已入槽之后，就需要转入第三步“化劲”功夫，以入其化境。

初练习者，不可贪多求快，急于求成。一招一、，一起一落、一开一合、一转一换，都必须循规蹈矩，顺其自然。不可自以为是，不听师训，若专求其重，则必形成沉而不灵，若是专求其轻浮，又必神意涣散，急于求成，像墙头的芦苇——头重脚轻根底浅，似萍草无根之弊。所谓“孤阴不生，孤阳不长”，就是说不可求其一，一定要有刚有柔、有阴有阳、有内有外、有开有合、有升有降。因此在练习西域古法心意拳时，必须求得张而不疏、放而不肆，其次求得敛而不拘、约而不迫，最后求得含而不露、含而不僵，身灵而不偏于飘浮，沉静而不偏于迟钝，方符合买氏心意拳的要求。因此，学者必须持之以恒勤练习，细心体会悟其奥，正是“书不熟，多读则熟，艺不精，熟悉则精”。望习练者，学必至熟，熟而加思，由思生巧，则个中玄奥，久而久之方能达到“拳无拳，意无意”，无意之中藏真意的高级艺术境界。

Western Regions Ancient Method Xinyiquan

There are always fists upon fists without, and factions within, each with their own personality and style, scholars have their own nature, fierce or gentle, straightforward or yielding. The skilled each have their own characteristics, those who teach according to their own aptitude conform to the seven natures, so that though they each learn from the highest masters, they each have their own characteristics.

The Western Regions ancient method Xinyiquan is powerful and extensive, truly dangerous, and hides strength in weakness. Those who practice are filled with qi (energy). It's potential is like rolling thunder and there are none who can resist. Or, like rain filling a pond, qi is stored in the dantian (energy centre) and then released like a gushing spring. Delivered throughout the body, it reaches the very tips. Masculine in its power, feminine in its dexterity. While in cultivating the method the hands, eyes, body, feet, and deliering force each have special requirements, yet the true meaning of Xinyi Liuhe Quan (Mind-intent Six Harmonies Boxing) has no more than two or three elements.

Its movements are distinct, both hard and soft, quick and solid, yin and yang in balance, absorbing and projecting - in form, it rises and falls again, "turning waves like water". Water and fire exchange places, full of energy, advancing like a blade of steel, withdrawing with a hook and gimlet, releasing power, however strong the enemy.

The chart of boxing says , “Practice qi to become strong, practice the spirit to be able to fly.” He also said, One moves unhindered, whatever his strength, he flies and soars, his qi deep and profound, he advances and

retreats without effort as he moves to and fro, in movement and stillness he releases qi naturally as he coms and goes. In the internal training method, it is required to draw the breath into the dantian, through the migngmen (gate of life), down the du meridian and up the ren meridian to return to the dantian. Its strength is open, penetrating, piercing, fitting snugly, warding off, closing in, standing firm, a hidden cross-bow, a cannon firing.

Western Regions ancient method Xinyiquan generally does not advocate preemptive strikes, but following strikes, according to the saying "hold fast to catch an eagle". The meaning of this saying is that once the opponent's xinyi (mind-intent) is committed, his strike has begun, but before its force is delivered, one instantaneously counter-strikes, and with no time for one's opponent to change, one gains the upper hand and seizes the initiative. The opponent's attack is exhausted, the old force has passed and the new force has not yet come into existence. If one makes a move in time, he will inevitably fail to respond and will be under one's control. When the opponent makes a move, when he is at full strength, one should avoid the point of force and not move rashly – this is the same whether he makes one move or a series of moves.

Western Regions ancient method Xinyiquan catches the eagle. The cart of boxing says: When the enemy is still, I am still, when the enemy moves, then do I move. I have to get ahead of the enemy when I move. It is the same as taijiquan: when he is still, I am still, when he moves slightly, I move first, last to start, first to arrive." If the opponent does not take the initiative to make a move, I will either draw my hands to lure him into making a move, or step into his body forcing him to change his stance and make a move. Of course, the principles of martial arts for any style of boxing are relative.

Under special circumstances, the Western Regions ancient method Xinyiquan also proactively attacks, that is, observing the opponent, the inner five elements having already moved, with the intention of hurting me, without waiting for the opponent to act, I immediately subdue him. Mai Yangmen's boxing method, although it is a late-comer, yet it recognizes me as a master. This is distinct from taiji bagua, and it is also not easy for outsiders to understand. It advocates that if you dare to fight, you must win. First of all, you should build up the confidence to win in spirit. Since ancient times it has been said, "when two strong men meet, the brave wins." The chart of boxing says, "When you are not in dispute, you must not underestimate the enemy, and when you are already in dispute, you must not be afraid of the enemy." Moreover, the trick is based on oneself. No matter how tight the opponent's defense is, or whether the opponent has already attacked, one must give full play to his skills and hit the opponent without blocking. That is to say, if you strike, I strike even faster at your opening move. Western Regions ancient method boxing also speaks of using force to strike, where a small force defeats a strong force, but it does not wait for the opponent, but in addition to exploiting the opponent's strength, once up close, takes the initiative and in its own unique way takes the lead. Of course, Mai family boxing method adopts such a technique, relying on internal movements suddenly to explode with elastic force in the direction of the strike. It often comes and goes, "threatening the east to attack the west" (creating a diversion), relieving the siege by attacking the besiegers, attacking the opponent and yet extracting oneself.

Western Regions ancient method boxing is one of the short strike methods, focussed on up-close fighting as a means of control. In terms of tactics, it is said "the two hands should never leave the cheeks" and

"the two elbows should never leave the ribs". When attacking the enemy, the best way to move is by the shortest route, advancing in a flash. He strikes with his shoulders, elbows, hips and knees because only when you get in close can you give full play to your talents and use your body skills to unbalance your opponent and then overcome him. Thus the chart of boxing says, “If you want to strike far, you must be face to face; if you want to strike beautifully, you must be mouth to mouth. Striking people is like walking, watching people like a tiger catching a sheep. Root control is not as good as body control." Therefore, Western Regions ancient method boxing is the best method to control the opponent's body movements.

Western Regions ancient method boxing is not like those styles of boxing that emphasize first defense and then offense, but emphasizes the integration of offense and defense, that is, the combination of offense and defense. This feature is not manifest simply in one action, one hand in defense and one hand in attack. Rather, it has a bear-like grip, a dragon-like slice, and a combination of offense and defense: thus in this method all is both defense and offense attack – attack in defense and defeat in attack.

Western Regions ancient method boxing gives full play to the skills of various parts of the human body – the head, hands, shoulders, elbows, hips, knees, and feet are coordinated with each other and applied comprehensively, using the body's stance to produce great lethality. Non-discrimination of offense and defense is a notable feature of Western Regions ancient method boxing. It has neither a simple defense nor a simple attack.

Western Regions ancient method boxing swings around the central position – most of the movements involve stepping around the

centre, thus, "step to the centre to gain status, even the immortals may be defeated." The tactics are also centered, offensive and defensive movements do not depart from the center line of the opponent, attacking the opponent means attacking opponent's center line. The centre line is where the vital organs of the human body are concentrated. Only attack these parts for effect, and so force the opponent to withdraw his attack.

Western Regions ancient method boxing gives full play to the techniques of various parts of the human body, the head, hands, shoulders, elbows, hips, knees, and feet are coordinated with each other and applied comprehensively, and they use whole-of-body techniques to produce great lethality. This makes it difficult for the opponent to withstand a blow. This is by no means far fetched, and in making a deliberate choice to use a certain part, it pays rational attention to the connection between the various parts of the body. In peacetime the habit of or-ordination and co-operation is achieved by practicing the six stances. Hands hold and shoulder out, drop hands and raise knee, it often takes only one or two tricks, and the outcome is determined immediately. As the saying goes, when an expert reaches out his hand, he will know if there is anything there.

In practicing Western Regions ancient method Xinyiquan, the technique is easy to learn but hard to master. It must be done step by step. The beginner must follow the three principles, three steps, and three training methods in sequence. That is, the first step is to refine energy into qi, and strengthen the bones, vigorous and straightforward. The second step is to refine qi into spirit, and release the hidden energy of the tendons. The third step is to transform spirit into emptiness, and transform strength into essence. The strength of emptiness can be contrasted with actual strength. At each stage, the requirements must be

distinguished, and the purpose of the practice method understood and practiced step by step in sequence, that is, neither specialize in one of them nor skip over a level. If you focus only on strength, although it is indispensable when you use it, it is too rigid and easy to break. Like a tiger catching a sheep, or an eagle catching a chicken, this is vigorous and direct use of strength. But if one avoids its blade only a little, its strength is useless! Moreover, if you only practice strength without variation for a long time, it will be useless, and your muscles and bones will stiffen, and you will likely suffer injury. When the tiger pounces straight ahead, leap to the side, and you can take advantage of its strength to pounce! This is the power of supple strength versus direct strength. Again, if you focus only on suppleness, and if you are too soft but not firm, not only will progress be slow, but you are liable to form soft punches lacking in strength. As for transforming strength into essence, this is more profound, and it is difficult for martial artists to distinguish right from wrong. This power is used in actual fighting, when he is substantial I am empty, and so taking advantage of weakness I become substantial, he is firm and I am supple. Use softness against firmness, as it is said "to outsmart the strong, become weak and live to catch them out." Firmness in softness is firmness, and softness in firmness is true softness. This is the theory of firmness and softness. That is, the empty is the substantial, and the one who adapts to changes transforms the energy. Therefore, beginners must proceed step by step. After completing the first step, practice the second step, and then go on to the third step. The ancient boxing method says, "Three years is a small success, ten years is a great success", that is to say, at every level of skill, only after at least three years of hard work, can one experience and comprehend its mystery. When the first stage skill is deep and complete, after strengthening the bones, then move on to the

second stage, the practice of “hidden strength” is different, so do not be stubborn or insistent. When the second stage skill is deep and complete, and the tendons are in the groove, then move on to the third step of "refining energy" to enter its state of transformation.

Beginners should not be greedy for more speed nor eager for success. Move by move, rise and fall, open and close, turn and change, all must follow the rules and let nature take its course. Don't be self-righteous and ignore the master's instructions. If you are too serious it will become heavy and ineffective, if too frivolous you will become distracted and eager for success, like a reed on top of a wall, top-heavy with shallow roots – with all the disadvantages of rootlessness. The saying "lonely yin does not grow, lonely yang does not grow" means something that cannot be asked for. There must be firmness and softness, yin and yang, internal and external, opening and closing, rising and falling. Therefore, when practicing Western Regions ancient method Xinyiquan, one must seek to be open but not sloppy, indulgent or unrestrained, secondly seek to be controlled but unconfined, lastly seek to keep up the practice without being exposed, continue without becoming rigid, body quick and light, calm but not inclined to dullness, and so meet the requirements of Mai family Xinyiquan. Therefore, students must persevere in practice and carefully understand its mystery. It is precisely "if you are not familiar with the book, you will become familiar with more reading, the art is not perfected, but the familiar is perfected." Those who wish to practice must become familiar through learning, thinking through familiarity, perfect through thinking – it is mysterious, and will take time to reach the highest realm of art of "fist without fist, intention without intention", unintentionally hiding the true meaning.

西域古法心意六合拳习技体练习秘要

六合式

首先要身成六式；鸡腿、龙腰、熊膀、鹰爪、虎抱、，雷声。

六合者，鸡、龙、熊、鹰、虎、雷。

心意拳之身法六形合为一体也。俗称预备式，又叫侵扑站，也叫扑来式，或三体式。所谓六合是内外三合，内三合即心与意合、意与气合、气与力合。外三合，手与足合，肘与膝合，肩与胯合，共为六合。

七捶，斩、截、裹、挎、挑、领、去步步不离鸡行，势势如虎扑，把把不离鹰捉，这是心意拳的功法和技击高度要求。也就是说在心意拳中每一式每招中，都必须在全身总体中具有“鸡腿、龙腰、熊膀、鹰爪、虎抱头、雷声”，这六合之心意，也是心意六合拳的总体锻炼的主要法则。

“鸡腿”，它在心意六合拳中的用法，就是一身而言，腿为根节。它在站立时有独立之功，在动作时又有提低踏远变化敏捷之特点，心意拳中十分重视鸡腿之步法，以它来指导锻炼出扎实的下盘功夫。习武者均知道下盘功的重要意义和实际作用，拳谱曰：“下节不明，多练七十跌朴”。

脚是我们世人的立身之根本，千里之行，始于足下，俗话说，

“人老先由脚上见”。脚上的力量之源是基于腿部的，要练出扎实的下盘功夫，“雄鸡起斗腿当先”，鸡腿是最理想的锻炼方法，也是一种很有效的健身方式。也可以说就是不断行走的一种桩功。以鸡步统贯每一动作，总是前弓后蹬，似鸡行路状。《谱论》中清楚地说明，“肩要摧肘，肘要催手，胯要催腿，腿要催足，一身之法，如此作用无不取胜，如不胜者，是无恒久之功也”。

何为鸡腿呢？在心意拳中鸡腿的体现并非一种，诸如前足虚、后足实时为鸡腿；前足成实、后足成虚时也为鸡腿，一脚独立，另一脚提起时呈寒鸡蹲架还为鸡腿，当站立六合式势时，从前之后还是为鸡腿，当后足变成前足向前进步时，在正落而未落之间，后足蹬劲，促使前足再进，还未鸡腿，所以讲鸡腿。并不是单纯的某一个动作的定势后体现，而是要在每一个动作的过程中都体现出来。

以上，很明确地指示练习者，在练鸡腿（鸡步桩）调身之时，必须两足站在一条面对正前方的笔者中心线上，不可开裆散势，三弯要对，三尖要照，三新要实，三意要连，三节要明，五指要分。全身节节放松，内开外合，用沉身功夫，把全身散之力急于腰尾，贯于后膝与足顺其势，由上而下，肩催胯（腰尾），胯催膝，膝催足。后膝往前往下沉，让重心下降，前移，在行鸡步时前腿不可主动迈进，全凭后足蹬进。蹬进时，前离地少许，脚尖上钩，让胯劲到膝、膝劲到足，后足把全身蹬进时，前腿应为挤劲，遇空则虚，受阻则实，前腿落地时，脚跟应先着地，落地无声，顺势脚掌落地要下踩，接住向前的惯性力。前膝顺势挺，使全身合为一体，这时人体的重心，就自然落在前脚之后，速由蹬进的后腿接住，迎其锋，顺其势，不顶不抗，完成鸡步过程，双脚磨胫前进，前足变后足之，先要向前进一足，后足变成前足磨胫直进，脚尖正对前方。《谱曰》：“虽然两脚有前后，不胜两脚并一脚……前脚领后脚，后脚伸腿弯，后脚催前脚，前脚实正踩。前脚未落，后脚追，后脚未落前脚踩。起如箭，落如风，追赶日月不放松”。

鸡腿是心意六合拳中首要法则。还必须很好地配合心意六合拳的重要法则“龙腰”，“龙腰”是此拳中全身总体法则的精髓。

龙腰，龙是古代神话传说中派生而成的一种神奇的动物，神出鬼没，其动作既轻灵奇巧，又能纵高跃远，体态绵软而用之则刚，且能变化无穷，世有神龙见首不见尾之说，是吉祥和威力的象征，在功法中第一位肝属木，色青为青龙。肾属水色黑，为黑虎。龙为

阳，是元神的代表。虎为阴是元精的代表。龙腰从功法的角度要求，就是要在心意六合拳的锻炼过程中，通过脾土的真意沟通，使龙虎交合为达到龙虎自伏而结成的内丹。

龙脊虎胯功

腰，是人体最大活动关节，也是人体生命和力量的发源地，人体的生命源泉，肾脏就位于腰间。肾脏是人体五脏之首，是脏腑之根、精气之本，故人有病时须养肾气，使真精长存不妄泄，则疾患自除。肾在人体五脏之中又属于水宫，为水脏，主润五脏、六腑、九窍、百骸，所以肾为天一水源。从这里我们可以知道腰在人体中的极大作用和主要位置。

龙在心意六合拳种得实在取意为“龙形搜骨之法”，传说中龙的运行使身体左右不断地两边拧转前进，犹如搜骨。心意六合拳取意“龙腰”，就是指在通过身体左右不断地拧转锻炼，脾土之真意，沟通龙虎之性情合一而结丹。脾脏也在人体的腰部，因为腰是人体最大的活动关节，所以它是人体全身力量之源。人体只有通过腰部的运动来带动四肢百骸，协调整齐的作用才会产生巨大的力量。谱论中所曰：一枝动来百枝摇，四稍无不齐，内劲无不出矣。这均是龙腰在心意六合拳中的内涵。

龙腰的调身法则是要求心意六合拳，练习者必须鼻尖、膀尖、脚尖。这三尖相照在一条垂直于地面的直线上。这就是要讲练习者在鸡腿的基础上，要以头部和臀部为轴承，以身躯为转轴，这样不断地左右拧转运动，来达到三尖相照、三弯相对。三尖能相照在一条垂直线上，才可能功法和技击双管齐下地并练，得到理想的效果。

龙腰在技击法则中是以“先打顾法后打空”为指导方针的三尖相照，三弯曲相对法，非常有效地缩小了练习心意拳的受打体积和面积，利用“龙有搜骨之法”的法则，极大限度地自我保护，同时又以龙腰拧转全身最大力量打击敌方。这力量的发挥是通过“风吹

大树百枝摇”而来的。

心意拳的身法就在龙腰中体现，身法是要求以头、臀两部为轴承，以身躯为转轴，达到鼻尖、膀尖、足尖，三尖相照，心意拳大部分行拳练功动作，均要求身躯垂直地面。谱曰：论身法，不可前俯，不可后仰，不可左歪，不可右斜。往前三直而起，往后三直而落。大抵以中本为宜，以征治为妙。这就要求练习此艺者，在练习之时，身体要垂直地面，并要平胸直背，左右拧转运动，这样既可舒畅调和人体气血，又可很巧妙地化解对方击来的劲力。但值得提示的是练习者在练定势桩功时，身法必须三尖相照、三弯相对，身体垂直于地面与鸡腿相和，这种基本功练扎实以后，才可练寸步、垫步、快步、剪步、倒撤步、测风步等。

买氏心意六合拳要求，身正胸平背直，练习者，必须垂肩坠肘。练习者不可含胸拔背，含胸拔背不易使两肩松垂，不利于前后阴阳的调和、全身气血的舒畅。

“熊膀”：身体中正，平胸直背为自然象。垂肩坠肘，劲攒两膀为练体之意。

熊，是一种形体笨拙和行动迟缓的动物，然而它的笨力却是十分大的，尤其是熊的膀力。膀是人体稍节之根节部位。谱曰：十大真形篇有“熊有站斗之精”之说。熊是人们普遍熟悉的动物，熊膀发劲于掌，其掌能打出势不可挡。谱又曰：两肘不离肋、两手不离腮，出洞入洞紧随身，察其无备而功之，由其无意无出之，就是熊膀在心意六合拳中，上三节的功法和技击之法具体取意。通过“熊膀之取意，两肘不离肋，坠裹紧固，不断锻炼，才可达到《谱曰》中五行篇脾动肋加功的作用，脾脏是人体五行之首，练好脏腑，则人体气是神全。两肩相重，两肋坠裹，与腿法中“不胜两腿并一腿，吞脚踩腿弯”是统一的腿法要求，都是经过极力地夹裹紧固，再由丹田气动而以“龙腰”带动鸡腿、熊膀，这四肢百骸的整齐作用发出撬劲。只有夹裹得理想，发出撬劲，才会像山洪暴发一样，犹如

水坝间的突开，急流奔腾，威不可挡，根据这些我们就能明白，《拳谱》中束长二字一命亡的真实含意了，上肢之根节“熊膀”之意明了，梢节鹰爪的内涵也就很清楚了。

“鹰爪”，鹰是非常凶猛的禽鸟。鹰盘旋高空，一旦发现目标，便俯冲而下，喙爪并用，一举擒获猎物，使物不能逃，心意六合拳手法取此意。临场对阵，也必须利用对方一些弱点进行攻击，因此，分散发挥各部威力攻击对方要效法鹰。谱曰，十大真形篇中有“鹰有捉拿之精”之说。何为“鹰捉”人们是比较陌生的。但是拳经云，“出势虎扑”，起手“鹰捉”的说教并有“鹰捉四平”，足下存的技击要求，说明它是独具技法，早已存在的，吾人具有四体百骸伸之而为阳（鹰势也）。

“鹰爪”的技击法则，主要通过全身整体运动把丹田之气运用双手十指上，起到鹰爪的捉拿使用，“梢起中节随根节追之”，特别它是追求“六阳纯全”，刚至柔生，沾身纵力，起落翻钻，最主要基本功夫，被人称为摩擦劲和划劲，这些叫法都是象形的，它的技法实名人多不知，实叫翻浪劲，指用手掌在人身上从上往下一划，就可以把人打倒或放出很远，如水之翻浪。“鹰捉”就是锻炼这种特殊劲的方法和手段。因而它用的这个掌就成为心意六合拳中具有代表性的特长。

虎抱头，虎在动物中是最凶猛的，故被称为“山中之王”。

关于虎抱头的含义及定义，在心意拳界中也曾存在着认识上的分歧。有的认为虎抱头是形容老虎在扑食之前的头伏、目聚、爪潜的形状，有的则认为虎抱头之“抱”字，应为“豹”解。对于这两种说法，我觉得都有一定的道理，因为鼻祖传留下这个拳种之时，并没有什么文字记载，而后来的拳经也好，拳谱也好，都是根据自己的老师的口传整理的，出现音同、字不同之误在所难免。众所周知，头是我们人体的首脑，是极为重要的部分。拳谱曰：含于尾闾、发于项梗是为正劲，识见不使随时变，无事不到头不可轻用。这可见

心意六合拳中取意虎抱头的作用。虎是不会抱头的，“虎抱头”之“虎”是内意，“抱”是外表。虎是百兽之王，虎威在头，但虎的气血是首尾贯通的。谱曰：四梢循环，血梢，发脚掌心倒天门，也就是说头（后脑骨）向上顶，有冲天之雄，头为周身之主，上顶则后三关易通。肾气因之上达泥丸，以养性。

练习心意六合者必须下骸内收，竖项顶劲这样才具有“虎抱头”之意，才可使气血灌顶，脑是人体之髓海，人身之真精元神聚于头脑，练习者时时有“虎”头之意，头之意，则可气足精满。

虎抱头的“抱”，是对技击法的直接指向，如单虎抱头、以头凿壁、乌牛摆头，运用手的拨转之能，破开对方防御，并保护头部技击对方。“虎抱头”是功法和技击法的统一称谓，也是这两法的统一之意，“虎”是内在的功法，“抱”则是外表技击之势，它防中有攻、攻中有防，攻防兼顾。练习心意六合拳只有真正领会“虎抱头”之真意，刻苦锻炼，才会血梢发起不知凶、牙骨内梢不知情，才知灵山大光明。

“雷声”是心意六合拳中全身总体法则的高度集中统一的概念。雷声从何而来，谱曰，五行一发响雷声，拳去雷动风声响。

“雷声”是心意六合拳每练动作后，趁鹰捉下落之势，丹田后吸，横膈膜上升，压缩肺气去全部外呼，发喝“噫”声，源出于此。是专练人体丹田内气外发，肋加吐声一种功法，属内功法，主要是练内壮阳气。此功来源甚久，古时人们往往在抵御野兽，和对手较技时，出其不意大喝出声以慑服敌方。历史上楚霸王有气吞山河之势，借助其粗犷声威，战国孟贲喝声使水倒流，三国张飞喝断长坂桥。正如拳谱曰：奇人千古仗先声，声里威风退万兵，就是痴情神不怕，速雷震荡亦应惊。随年月的推移，被纳入心意六合拳进行吐纳，导引、遂发展成独门攻心法。

练习时，可择树林或山崖上，先呼吸三十余次把气理顺。然后，行拳当收势练鹰捉，俯身而下。同时微微吸气，下流到丹田。随即，突发身起，吐声疾出，声出手落。如此反复锻炼，日久天长，便发

出之声与晴天霹雷相仿，足以刺耳膜，射达人之神经。

“雷声”练成后，内劲十足，遇弱者，应势发声，使立卧。遇敌力相等或更强者，其妙用之可显威，相搏关键时，突发雷声，闻者顿感毛骨悚然，浑身酥软无力，一刹那我即拳脚交加，敌无不应手而倒。俯首就擒，制敌之妙法。

人体三节法

手、肘、肩为梢节，胸腹为中节，腿、膝、足为根节。然分而言之，则“三节”之中，亦各有“三节”也，如手为梢节、肘为中节、肩为根节，此梢节中之“三节”。胸为梢节，心为中节，丹田为根节，此中节之“三节”。足为梢节，膝为中节，胯为根节，此为根节中之“三节”。练功中对三节，都要求梢节灵活，中节要柔，根节要稳。其中之要，不外乎起、随、追而已。盖梢节起，中节随，根节追之。而且自然松静，熟知此法，庶不致有长短、曲直、参差、俯仰之病，此“三节”之则，所以贵明也。

人体九窍法

人体各部都有三节，而每节又各有三窍，以手臂而言，劳宫是稍节。“窍”，曲池是中节“窍”。肩井是根节“窍”。以腿而言“涌泉”是梢节“窍”，阳陵泉是中节窍，环跳是根节窍，以身而言，上丹印堂（有人说百会）为梢节窍，中丹（膻中）为中节窍。下丹田（气海）为根节窍。人体九窍与五脏六腑相生相通也。练习者重点是练习怎样使九窍受意念控制，就梢节窍而言，“劳宫”窍最代表。就根节窍而言，下丹（丹田）则是气之库，人体之气最终汇集于此，“肩井和环跳”实际上是连接梢节窍与体之间气通道的重要关口。而中节窍则是运气上通达的中继站。各部三节运动，九窍也随着运动。那一窍运动，意念那一窍，意守某一窍。就是为了把“气”集中引导到那里，疏通经脉，最后

使窍窍相通、脉脉相连，从而促进气血调节内脏功能，阴平阳秘，达到内以养生、外以祛病技击作用。

齐四梢法

人之血，内筋骨之末，谱曰：梢盖发为血梢，舌为内梢，牙为骨梢，甲为筋梢，四梢齐到内劲出。有谓两手两足为四梢，或致于齐知之法，其发欲冲冠，甲欲透骨，舌欲催齿。牙欲断金，心战而动，气自丹田生，如虎之狠，如龙之惊。气发而为声，声随手发，手随声落，故一枝动而百枝摇，四梢劲则可变其常态能使人生畏惧感。

“血梢”怒气填胸，竖发冲冠，血轮苏转，敌胆自寒。发毛虽微，催敌不难。

“内梢”舌卷气降，大山亦撼，内坚以铁，精神勇敢，一言之威，落魄丧胆。

“骨梢”有勇在骨，切齿则发，皆裂目突，惟齿之功，令人恍惚。

“筋梢”虎威鹰猛，以爪为锋，手擢足踏，气势兼雄，爪之所到，皆可凑功。

闭五行法

五行者，金、木、水、火、土。内对人之五脏，外应人之五官。皆与五行相配合，心属火，心动火焰蒸，肺属金，肺动如闪电，肾属水，肾动快如风。肝属木，肝动如飞剑，脾属土，脾动肋加功。五行顺，一气放胆即成功。

“心”五脏之主宰，色赤属火而通舌。心为火宫，锻炼心脏，调血理气，心神安逸，身体安适，性定命固，火种不灭，故心动火焰蒸。“肝”主周身之色，色青属于木而通眼。肝为木宫，锻炼肝脏，肝气畅达，呼吸协调，耳聪目明，能生三光，明快如剑。“肺”主七元气，色白属金而通鼻，肺为金宫，锻炼肺脏，元气调和，神安息静，身爽体快，动如闪电。

"脾"为后天之本，色黄属土而通口，脾为土宫，锻炼脾脏，身体强壮，消除百病，气体充足，百谷消磨，故脾动肋加功，"肾"为先天之源，色黑属水而通耳。肾为水宫，锻炼肾脏，真精不泄，体液充沛，循环流转，故肾动快如风。此五行著于外，故曰：五行真如五道关，无人把守自遮拦。再者，"鸡腿"属土归脾足太阴，"龙腰"属水归肾足少阴，"熊膀"属金归肺手太阴。"鹰爪"属火归心手少阴，虎抱头属木归肝足厥阴。又曰，要得真法在用心，心与鼻合多一力，心与耳合多一灵，心与眼合多一明，心与眉合多一神，心与意合多一艺，心与舌合多一吻，心与口合多一响，心与气合多一攻。这是心意六合拳。内、外五行都在心的号令下，高度地集中统一协调作用，才能真正做到五行一发响雷声、拳去雷动风声响，山林不能阻隔。

罗汉七星势（七曜）练法

七体，头、肩、肘、手、胯、膝、足、合尾闾（或称背尾）相助为友。七曜者，头、肩、肘、手、胯、膝、脚七体，左右一十四个用法，合尾闾（背尾）共为十四拳。

谱曰：打法定要先上身，脚手齐到才为真。拳如炮形，龙折身，遇敌好似火烧身。头打起意站中央，浑身齐到人难当，脚踩中门夺地位，就是神仙也难防，肩打一阴返一阳，两手只在动内藏。出动入动紧随身，左右全凭蓄势取。束展二字一命去。手打起意在胸膛，其势好似虎扑羊，沾实用力须展放。胯打阴阳左右便，两足交换须自然，左右进取剑劲，得心应手敌自翻。膝打几处人不明，好像猛虎出木笼，洞内动转不停势，左右明拨任意行，眼要毒，手要奸，脚踏中门满力攒，手为箭，身如弓，前腿弓，后腿蹬，武艺全在后腿中，起势好似卷地风，打挑岭放丹田，一去天朝前，打鹰捉提裆前，一落朝前，一齐到用也，来无影，去无踪，打人如走路，看人如拔葱，嘴如甜面带笑，内中暗揣一把刀，与敌耐战，放胆竟成功。

七疾法

七疾者，眼要疾，手要疾，脚要疾，意要疾，出势要疾，进取要疾，身法要疾，具此七疾方能制胜，谓之纵横往来，目不及瞬，如生龙活虎，令人不可琢磨。

七顺法

肩要催肘，而肘不逆肩，肘要催手，而手不逆肘，手要催指，而指不逆手，膝要摧胯，而胯不逆腰，胯要催膝，而膝不逆胯，膝要催足，而足不逆膝，首要催身，而身不逆首，心气稳定，阴阳相合，上下相连，内外如意，此为七顺。

两仪法

箕无极生太极，太极生两仪，两仪者，拳中动静，起落、伸缩往来之理。拳中鹰熊之势，防守进取之理。人具有四体百骸，伸之而为阳（鹰），缩之而为阴（熊）。故曰：阴阳暗合。昔人见有鹰熊竞志，因取法为拳，防守象熊，越此二势，其拳失真。名为心意者，象其形而思其意也。

四象法

四象在古代时指朱雀、玄武、青龙、白虎，后被道教所信奉。朱雀也称朱鸟，是由南方、七宿（井、鬼、柳、星、轸、张、翼）所组成的鸟象。在方位属正南，在八卦中为离，在五行之中为火，在天干之中为丙丁，故谓丙丁火，在地支为午，在色为赤，在四季中为夏。

玄武是由北方七宿（斗、牛、女、虚、危、室、壁）所组成的龟蛇相缠之象，在方位中玄武属正北，在八卦之中为坎，在五行之中为水，在天干之中为壬癸，故言北方壬癸水，在地支中为子，在

色为黑，在四季为冬。

青龙是由东方七宿（角、亢、氐、房、心、尾、箕）所组成的龙象，在方位中为木，在天干之中为甲乙，故言东方甲乙木，在地支中为卯，在色为青（绿），在四季之中为春。

白虎是由西方七宿（奎、娄、胃、昴、毕、觜、参）所组成的虎象，在方位中白虎属正西，在八卦之中为兑，在五行之中为金，在天干之中为庚辛，故言西方庚辛金，在地支之中为酉，在色为白，在四季之中为秋。

在心意六合拳中所讲的“四象”是指十大真形中的鸡、龙、熊、虎四种动物形象。

鸡形，主取其腿有独立之功。龙形，主取其身有三曲之才，熊形，主取其膀有竖项之力，（项不竖则膀无力）。虎形，主取其扑食时之抱头凶相。所以在心意拳中很强调鸡腿、龙腰、熊膀、虎抱头此四象。

四拳势论

出手横拳世间稀，翻身挑岭最难习，鹰捉好似猫扑鼠，回首摇涮急上急。

出手横拳师势难招，展开中本前后梢，转身挑岭阴阳势，鹰捉四平足下抛。

前打青龙出水，后打白虎收山，左打乌牛摆头。右打鹞子入林。去了真宝换假宝，一天三宴吃不好，真正良言，见字存心。

身法

身法有八要，起、落、进、退、反、侧、收、纵。起落者，起为横，落为顺，进退者进步低，退步高。反则者，反身顾后，侧身顾左右。收纵者，收如伏猫，纵如放虎。大抵以中平为宜，以正直为妙，与三节相关，此不可不知。

步法

步法者，寸、垫、过、快、溅。如与人交手时，相离二三尺远，则用寸步，寸步一步可到，若四五尺远，则用垫步，垫步者，即用后腿店一步，仍上前步。即进前腿，急过后腿，所谓“步起在人前，步落过于人”。若有一丈八尺远，则可用快步。快步者，起前脚而带后脚，平飞而去，并非跳跃而往。此为马奔虎践之意，非艺成者，不可轻用。唯远不发腿，如遇人多，或有器械，即连带脚并箭而上，即取侧脚，如鹞子入林、燕子取水，此所谓踩脚飞身而起之说。善学者随便用之，习之纯熟，用之无心，方为其妙。

手足之法

手法者，出手、起手、领手、截手。当胸直出者，谓之出手，劲力稍发，有气有落，曲而非曲，直而非直，为了起手，劲力稍发，起而未落者，为之领手。顺起顺落，参以领搓之意为截手。但起前手如鹞子入林，须束身束翅而起。催后手，如燕子取水，往上一翻，长身而落，此单手之法。两手交互，并起并落，起如（锉）抽落如钩，此双手之法。总之，肘发护心，手起撩阴，起之如猛虎扑人，落入鹰之捉物。

足法者，起翻落钻，忌踢，宜踩脚为佳。盖起足望膝，起膝望怀，足打七分而出，而其形上翻，如手之撩阴而翻起。至于落则如以石拈物，如手落之拂眉。忌踢者，脚踢浑身是空。宜踩脚，如鹰捉物，置物于足下。此足之用法，手足之法，本自相同，而足的用法如虎行之无声，龙飞之莫测。

上法与进法

盖上法者，以手为妙，进法者，以足为奇，而总以身法为要。起手如丹凤朝阳之势，其进步，如前步抢上抢下，进步后脚踩打。

必须明三节、四梢齐、五行闭、身法活、手足相连，而视其运近，随其老嫩，一动而即至。然其方法有六：攻、顺、勇、疾、恨、真。攻者，巧妙也；顺者，自然也；勇者，果断；疾者，尽快也；恨者，愤怒也；动不容情，心一颤内劲出；真者，发必得中，贝之真，而彼难以变化。六方具要明，则上法，进法得矣。

顾法、开法、截法、追法

顾法者，单顾、双顾、上顾、下顾、前顾后顾、左顾、右顾也。单顾则用截摇，双顾则用横拳。顾上用冲天炮，顾下则用握地炮，顾前后则用括边炮或括身炮。此亦随机而用，非若他人之钩连捧驾。

开法者，开左、开右、硬开、软开。硬开者，如前六势之硬劲。软开者，如后六势之软劲是也。左开力括，右开用外扩。

截法者，截手，截身，截言，截面，截心。截手者，彼先动，而我后截。截身者，彼身未动，而我先截之。截言者，言露其意，而即截之。截面者，彼露其色，而即截之。截心者，彼喜眉面笑，言甘貌恭，而我察其有心，而迎机以截之，是知其截法岂可少哉！

顾法，截法，追法，一气贯注。即所谓随身紧起，追风赶月而不放松。彼虽欲走而不能，又何患其有邪术！

三性调养法

眼为见性，眼见则明：耳为灵性，耳听则聪，心为勇性，心到则力生。此三性者，艺中之妙用。因此，眼要不时常循环，耳要不时常报应，心要不时常惊醒。其法如脊背后物一动一静，必入于耳、眼、视之而心动。故曰：三性者乃艺中妙用也。

劲法

劲寓于无形之中，接于有形之表，而难以言传，而其理亦可参焉。盖志气之帅，七体之充也。心动而气即随之，气动而力即赴，

此为必到之理也。今以功与艺者言之，以为撞劲者非也，功劲者非也。即谓之怎蹭劲，崩劲者亦非也。殆颤劲是也。撞劲太直，而难起落。攻劲太死，而难变化。蹭劲，崩劲太促，而难招展。惟缠劲出没甚捷。可使日月无光，而不见其形。手到劲发，天地交合而不费力。总之，运用于三性之中，发于一颤之瞬，如虎之抖爪不见爪，而物不能逃；龙之用力不见力，而山不能阻。如果以上诸法合二为一，而克人岂有不利乎。

十大真形

鸡有争斗之情，龙有搜骨之法，虎有扑战之勇，鹰有捉物之精，熊有护身之本，猴有纵身之灵，蛇有分草之巧，燕有取水之能，鹞有侧身展翅之力，马有奔蹄之功。

抖身而起，藏身而落，起如风，落如箭，打倒敌人还嫌慢，起而箭，落如风。追赶日月不放松。论身法不可前俯，不可后仰，不可有斜，不可有歪。往前三直而起，往后三直而落。论步法，寸不可不急，践不可不快，攒不可不疾。肩要催肘，肘要催手，胯要催腿，腿要催足，为一身之法，如此用之无不取胜，如不胜者使武恒火之心也。

十六阴阳之法

一，寸之法，寸氏步，步即要快，成其步也。

二，践之法，践是腿，腿要凶猛，成其践也。

三，钻之法，钻是身，身要强壮，成其身也。

四，就之法，就是束，上下束而为一，成其就也。

五，夹之法，夹是夹也，如夹箭之夹，成其夹也。

六，六合法，手与足合，肩与胯合，肘与膝合，是外三合。心与意合，意与气合，气与力合是内三合。称其六合也。

七，齐之法，齐是疾也，内外如一，成其齐也。

八，正之法，正是直也，看正却有邪、看斜起有正，成其正直也。

九，经之法，径是手摩内五行，心意相连成其行径也。

十，胫之法，胫即驚起四梢也，四梢并发，成其胫也。

十一，起落之法，起是去也，落实打也，起如水之波浪翻，落如水之泛泡沫，成其起落也。

十二，进退之法，进是步低也，退则步高也，当进则进，当退则退，成其进退也。

十三，阴阳之法，看阴而有阳，看阳而又阴也，天地阴阳交合，能以下雨，拳术阴阳交合，才能打人，成其一块，皆又阴阳相交之气成其阴阳也。

十四，五行之法，内五行要发，外五行要随，发耳即遂，成其五行也。

十五，动静之法，静为本体，动为作用，如言其静，未露其机，若言其动，未见其迹，动静发而未发，为止动静之法也。

十六，虚实之法，虚者是精也，实者是灵，灵为玄妙之宝，成其虚实也。

内功（经）真义卷一

内功得传，脉络甚真，不知脉络，勉强用之无益有。经：前任后督，气行滚滚。（注；任脉起于承浆直下阴前高骨。督脉起于尻尾，直上右夹脊骨过泥丸下印堂至人中而止。）井池双穴，发劲循循。（注：井为肩井穴也，肩头分中，池者曲池穴也，肘头分中。）此为周身发劲所在。千变万化不离本，得其奥妙，方为无垠。（注：本者为自然之真气，用功以得之才能悟其妙也）。尻尾升起，丹田练习，注尻尾骨尽处也，用力向上翻起，真气自然即上升矣。气下于海，光聚于天心。（注：小腹正中为气海，额上正中为天心，形光于外也。脐下三寸为丹田穴也。）用功时存元气于此处也。即明脉络，后观格式。格式者入门一定之规也，不明格式，脉络亦空谈耳，头正而起，肩平而顺，胸含而闭，背平而正。（注：正头起项，项面神顺，

肩活背式平正，胸含身微有收敛，此式中真窍也。）足坚而稳，膝曲而伸裆深而藏，肋开而张。（注：出气莫令耳闻，劲必先松而后紧，缓缓以行之。）先吸后呼一出一入，先提后下，一升一伏，内有丹田，气之归宿吸入呼出勿使有声。（注：提者，吸气之时存想真气上升至顶也，下者真气落下也。）伏者，觉周身之气渐小坠入丹田也。下收谷道，上提玉楼，或立或坐，吸气入喉，以意送下，渐至于底。（注：收者防气泄，提玉楼者，提耳后之高骨也，使气往来勿阻碍。）不拘坐立，气自喉以达肺也，气虽聚于丹田，存想渐至于底方妙，即明经络，姿势，七窍再详解决。通透穿贴，松悍合坚，通筋之顺也，曰：透骨之速也。通透往来无碍也。伸筋拨力以和缓柔软之意也。穿劲之连也，贴劲之络也，穿贴横竖过络也。伸筋拨力绳之系，悍如冰之坚。曰；合劲之整体也。坚劲之旋转也。合者，合周身之劲使之整一也。坚者，横竖斜缠之谓也。按肩以练步逼臀坚膝，圆裆固胯，提胸以下腰。按肩者，将肩井穴之劲沿至涌泉，逼臀极力贴住也，圆裆者，向内外极力挣横也，提胸者，提前胸以坐腰也。提下骸以正项，贴背以转斗，松肩以出劲。(注：两背骨用力贴住，觉其劲自脐下而出)。自六腑穴向外转出，至斗骨而回，出劲之时，将肩井穴之劲，顺意松开自无碍矣。横劲，竖劲，辨之明白，横以济竖，竖济横。(注：竖者肩至足底也。横着)。两背与手也。自裆至足底，自膝至臀，是以腿而言，之竖与横也。若以身而言，竖者，自腋至二肩穴也，横者，自六腑穴转头骨也。五气朝元，周而复始。四肢元首，收纳甚妙。(注：吸气纳于丹田，升真气于头)。一运真气自裆下于足底，复上至外胯，升于丹田，复自于口降于丹田。二运真气，自背骨膊里出手，复自六腑转入丹田，一升一降，一下一起，一出一入。并行不悖，周流不息，久久用之妙处甚多，练神气还本退元。天地交泰，水升火降，头足上下，交接如神，静伸光芒，动则飞腾。(注：气胜形，形随意，意劲神，神帅气，气帅形，形随气，性调气)。凡初入门者，每日清晨静坐，盘膝闭目，钳口，细调呼吸，一出一入

皆从鼻孔，少时气定，遂吸一口纳入丹田，助以津液，则真火自降矣，但吸气时须默想真气自涌泉发出，升于两肋，自两肋升前胸，自前胸升脑后，渐升于泥丸。将气时须默想真气由泥丸自印堂，由印堂至鼻，由鼻至喉，由喉至夹脊，由夹脊透于前心。由前心沉于丹田。丹田气足吗，自然能从尾闾升夹脊，二上于泥丸，周而复始遵循天地循环之理也。

纳卦（经）真义卷

乾坤：头项效法乾，取刚健纯粹。足膝效法坤，取其镇静厚载。(注：凡出一手先试虎口穴，前骸用力，平正提起，直达提气穴，着力提住，由百会穴转过昆仑，下明堂，贯两肋)。其气由鼻孔泄时，即便吸入丹田，两耳各三寸六分，谓之象眼穴，用力向下截住，合周身全局。用之久，自知其妙也。凡一用步，两外虎眼，极力内向，两内虎眼，极力向外，委中大筋竭力要直，两盖骨竭力曲，四面相交，合周身之力向外一扭，涌泉之气自然能从中透出。

巽兑：肩背宜于松活，时乃巽顺之意，裆胯宜于紧靠，须玩兑泽之情。(注：塌肩井穴，须将肩顶骨正真落下，与比肩骨相后)。曲池穴必肩顶骨略低半寸，手腕与肩井，背骨遂竭力贴住，此是竖劲不是扑劲。以竖则实，以横则虚。下肩井穴，向背骶骨直至足底，故谓自竖。右背则将左肩子劲，自骨底以意送于后背，直送两肩门，故谓横劲。两劲并用而不乱，元气方能升降如意，而异顺之意得矣？裆胯要圆而紧，气正直上下，不可前曲，不可后仰。两胯分前后，前胯用力向前，后胯用力向下涌泉，来时向上顶，两胯极力按之阴阳两窍，用力收位，总以逢口相兑，外阴内阳互吞并为生。

艮震：胸要立束起，艮山相似，肋有呼吸，震动莫疑。艮象曰：时行则行，时止则止，其义深哉。肋者，肋也。鱼鳃也，胸虽出而不高，肋虽闭而不束，虽张而不开。此中玄妙。呈以口援，用力须以意出，以气胜，以神足，则为合式。非出骨劲也，用肋之纵横为开闭。高

步劲在手足，中步在肋，下步劲在手背，自然之理也。

坎离：坎离之卦，乃身内之义也，可以意会，不可以言传。心身为水之象，水宜升，火宜降，两象即济，水火相交，真气乃萃，精神渐长，聪明且开，岂但劲乎。是以善于拳者，讲劲养气，调水火，在此一定不易之理也。用功之时，塌肩井穴，提胸肋，反龟尾欲神气上交于心也，须以意导之，下气聚劲练步，皆欲心气下达于肾也，亦须以意导之。

神运（经）真义卷三总决四章

神运之法，练形而能坚，练精而能实。练气而能壮，练神而能飞。(注：因形势以为纵横之本，萃精神以为飞腾之基)。故气胜能纵横，精神敛能飞腾。

神运之用：击敌有用形，用气，用神之退速。被击者有仆也，怯也，索也之深浅。(注：以形击形，自倒后乃胜，以气击气，手方动而生畏。以神击神，身未动而得入)。形受形攻，形伤而仆于地，气受气攻，气伤而怯。于心神受神攻，神伤而索于胆。

神运之意：纵横者肋中开合之式，丹田呼吸之间。(注：气欲漏而神欲敛，身直稳，而步宜坚，即不失于轻，复不失于重，来如雁往之飞腾，疾若虎豹之强悍)。

地龙（经）真义卷四

地龙真经，利在底功，(注：用腿足擦人，胫部下节)。全身练得强固精明。气血精神练成一团随用，伸可成曲，住亦能行。伸屈自由，行住任我，何为不可。曲如伏虎，升比腾龙。(注：缩四肢，头伏，手腕上挺，起立如常)。行往无迹，伸屈浅踪。上下伸缩变化莫测。身坚似铁，法密如龙。不坚则乱不密则失。翻猛虎扑，搏疾鹰捉。虎猛而鹰疾，倒分前后，左右分明。闪展腾挪使敌固不能顾。门有变化，法无空形。反侧仰伏，手足攻击奥妙无穷。前攻用手，二三而同。

攻前掌当先，肩肘济之。后攻用足，踵膝通攻。下步用攻以足当先。远则劲击，近则迎接。凭裆要迅速。大胯着地，侧身而成。侧倒在地，用手轻按活动。仰倒若坐，尻尾单凭。高低任意，远近纵横。暗屈一足地即起。

经简论

一、阴阳养修，动静并练

静功，心（形）意拳，练气循行得道和方法。内功经开首就提出了前任后督起行滚滚，以静功循环道路。以及先呼后吸，一出一入，气调而匀，气下于海，下收谷道，上提至五楼或坐或立吸气于喉，以意送下渐至底，这些都是说明静功得法和丹田气循环途径，具体练法后述。

动功，心（形）意拳姿势要求。头项，头正而起，提骸以正项，头项效法乾，这是说明头部练功时的要求，头在人体最上，所以说象乾的意思，要求正直步斜，又必须把骸部提起向后上方。这样就能够使头向上顶劲，项有竖动的意思。

背、肩、胸、腰、肋（肩平而顺，胸含而闭，背平而直，提胸以下腰，肋开而张）要求两肩平顺，不要一高一低，前后活动须平而顺，背平而直，切忌背部弯曲成弓。胸含而闭，是要求胸要内含，不要挺胸，两肋要以肘护，但要张开而不能用肘靠紧肋部。裆胯膝足，圆裆以固胯，逼臀以坚膝，膝曲而伸，裆深而藏，足坚而稳。裆要求是要圆要深，就是用力向后下坐，两足跟站在中行线上，这样就能做到圆裆固胯，裆深而藏，臀要逼，膝要曲，臀逼是用力将臀部向上提起，这样做，膝也能坚而有力，从而两足同时也能坚而稳。

心意拳精萃

“尻尾升气，丹田练气”这两句话的意思，注意在练拳时，丹田要充实，尻尾要求上提，在拳经上尚有精养灵根气养神，元阳不

要走得其真，丹田养成前日宴，万两黄金步兴人。就是告诉我们在练拳时，经常注意道充实到丹田，这是最根本的根本（按肩以练步）。凡是练拳时，要求手与足合、肘与膝合、肩与胯合。先说在出足时要求，肩跟着足走。因为肘手是由肩力所摧的。井池双穴，发劲循循，劲送而紧，松肩以出劲，肩背宜于松活，贴背以转斗。这些都是说用劲的松紧问题，就是说在练功时，最主要的是要肩肘松开，不要用力。如此，就可以形成沉肩垂肘是也。

通是顺的意思，透是快的意思，穿贴是联络的意思。松是松开不要用力。悍是要求用力如冰之脆。合坚是由松悍形成的最硬的劲。这一条很重要，是要求练功特别的弹劲问题，不过是单以松紧来说的，（弹劲）先送而后紧。就是松韧转到悍之紧，在先松后紧过程中，须要通顺快而联络，不能有任何的障碍，而这样才能够先松后紧，合而成为硬的坚劲，在松紧区别上（膝曲而伸）曲如伏虎、伸如腾龙来练弹劲，那就全面了。

三种练法合三种步功夫

明经是初步功夫，练形而能坚，练精而能实，初步功夫主要是以外形为主的练法，就是要求身法、姿势架势的练法，凡练一式，总要合乎以上说的那样各项要求循序渐进，把身体各部的姿势固定下来，达到发劲自然。最后就能运用自如，不想而行，不思而动，即所谓“拳无拳，意无意，无意之中是真艺”也。至于说练精合练形是一种道理，因为精是人体骨骼肌肉的基础。这步功夫练之日久兑人体首先精足，而后即筋骨肌肉坚而且实。

暗劲，练法二步功夫（曰，炼气而能壮）。练暗劲功夫是在明劲的基础上而转向以练气为主的暗劲练法，以丹田为充气之本，而后灌注全身，以意领气，内外充实，练之日久，周身气足，气足全身新陈代谢旺盛，各项功能亢进，更能促进消化和呼吸，因此，精气越加充实，身体不但坚实，而且壮矣。化劲练三步功夫（练神而

能飞）。这步法是在练精练气的基础上，转向炼神的法，是以意还神，意所到之处即气到，气到即神至，练之日久，自然神气充实。神就是精神，人体精神充实，百病不生，内能促进身体百骸的功能，外而表现出精神饱满，行动轻松的姿态。运用时意到神到，既意率领精气，所以形如飞状。

三步功夫技击之概述

击敌有用形、用气、用神之迟速。被攻者有仆、有怯、有索之分，原注曰："以形击形，身倒后乃胜，以气击气，手方动而生畏，以神击神，身未动而入，形受形击，形伤而仆于地，气受气攻，气伤而怯于心，神受神攻，神伤而索于胆。"具体地说就是，明劲阶段是外形击外形的一种方法，是用以久经锻炼有功夫完整的统一的外形，所以被击者形伤而倒于地。以气击气是功夫已到暗劲，击时用气，被击者内脏被击震动，因而立即产生一种如同过电一样的难受感觉。所以说气受伤而生畏也。以神击神是说已到化劲功夫，因为用神，所以出入神速，快如疾风行如闪电，被击者身未动而神受伤，精神受伤故怯于胆。

丹田精义之说

丹田者阳元之本，气力之府也，欲精技艺必练丹田，欲练丹田尤必先练技艺，二者互为因果，吾道皆知丹田为要，买师祖有口授而少书，传后之学者，究难明其所以然，谨将授之吾师兴三十年多，所体验者略述，所谓欲精技艺，必先练丹田，一般认为丹田亏，则气不充盈，不充盈则力不足，彼因捶，十大真形空有架势，以之为顾法则如守者之城池空虚，以之为打法则如战者之兵马羸弱，故必于临敌挫阵之际。常若有一团"精气"健凝于腹之间。倏然自腰而尾，而背，而项直贯于顶，当时眼做先锋以观之，心做元帅以谋之，攒翻横竖起落随时而应用，鸡、龙、鹰、熊、虎、猴等，变化而咸

宜毫忽之间，胜负立判，此丹田充盈而技艺所以精也。何谓练丹田必先练技艺。大家认为丹田受之于先天，有自足于内无待于外，但能善自保养足矣，何待于练。我认为不然，若不溺色，欲不丧肾精，保养有方，则元气自充，这样即可延年益寿，然究不能将丹田之气发之为绝技。欲发之为绝技，必自练始练之，之法，一在于聚，一在于运，聚者，即舌顶，齿叩，谷道提三心并诸法，也有必先去其隔膜，如心、肝、脾、肺、肾之五关层层透过一无阻拦，五行要顺也。行之即久而后，气始可全，会于丹田。然聚之而不善运亦，未能发为绝技，必将会于丹田之气由背骨往上迴住于胸间，充于腹，盈于脏，凝于两肋之中于脑顶更兼，素日所练之身体异常，手足异常活动，应敌之来而架势即变，而气力随之即到，倏然之间千变万化，有非言语所能形容者，此所谓善运用也，总其所以聚之运之者，要在平日之勤练技艺与丹田内功。

西域古法心意拳丹田内功精髓，即以丹田之气发动肢体运动。练丹田内功共分，竖丹田、搂丹田、坐丹田、闸丹田、开丹田、射丹田、摩丹田、搓丹田、屈丹田、养丹田。彼此互为结合，不可截然分开。

丹田功练功方向

地磁场有南北极，磁场方向从南极出发向北极，生活在地上的人和自然界各种生物，无时不受地磁的影响。气是一种生物能场，即一种复杂的电磁场，人体经络是生物能场循环的通道，经络在人体中基本是左右对称分布，气在经络中运行，地磁场就要对它发挥作用。当人体迎着地磁场方向时，可使生物能场得到加强从而调整和加强了人体器官的机能，起到良好的锻炼作用。由南背北的练丹田功方向，能使人体内达到“水火相济境界”，祖国医学叫作心肾相交。

丹田功练功注意事项

一，行功地点宜选择在空气清新、明亮清洁的室外，切不可当

风行功。

二，遇疾风、暴风及雷电等恶劣气候停止行功。

三，每日早、午、晚，三个时辰行功三次不可间断。如因有事耽误，就于早5时至7时空腹行功。中间一次午功则何时习之皆可，晚日后行功。切记，本功应空腹行之，气才得以在腹臓流通，否则，易因气滞而致伤。

四，回行功时，不可用拙力，总要出于自然。

坚丹田

预备式：六合式盘法：左足向前迈一步成弓步，右足向前迈步落于左足心，成莲枝步。屈膝，右掌从右胯上抄到左肘旁，顺左臂向前，以意导气至上丹田，两手随之升起，五指分开，手背向前，双掌相叠，左掌在外，右掌在里（图1），至不能再升时翻掌，随意气由上丹田下降中丹田，用抓劲下抓（图2），同时，右足也随之往后退一步成弓步成虎扑把，先练左式，后练右式，反复练习，次数不限。

要领：动作时眼平视，身体端正，将口张大深吸入一口气，然后，如吞咽食物般将吸入之气咽下，吞气后须略定片刻，长短约为常人三次呼吸。手臂随着身体慢慢向上升起伸直，下抓时，勿前俯后仰，腿保持弓步，重心要平稳，脚跟不抬起。

搂丹田

六合式盘法：右足向右斜方迈一步成骑马式，两脚与肩同宽平行站立，重心在两腿之间（图3）。两手掌心朝上置于肋侧，但不可靠得过紧。同时，手用搂劲，腰随势转动，或往下搂，或从左右直搂，或两臂外伸转圈回搂（图4），或从左右面部呈圆形轮番转动均可。或从前往回搂，身皆取骑马式。交替反复多练。（图5）

要领：动作时注意，头、颈、脊柱中正，平视前方，但脚不能移动，自然呼吸，手上下、左右，搂时动作要协调。

坐丹田

六合式盘法：身体慢慢先正身站立，心神定全身放松，两手自然下垂。同时，双掌从左右两旁提到胸前，左掌在前五指分开，右掌与左掌呈一条线（图 6）。意气经下丹田顺右腿下涌泉，两手随之由正前随身体下蹲，右腿缓缓弯曲，右腿大腿外方与小腿紧靠，左腿前弯，脚跟落地，脚尖上翘。然后，双掌往下翻，掌心朝下（图 7）。意气与身、手即起。意气升至中丹田，两掌抓力提起，身体站立。一上一下以意导气带劲，左右反复多练。

要领：下蹲时，右腿缓缓弯曲，身体随之下坐，上提时双手随体上升不可左斜、右歪，要气贯五指。

闸丹田、开丹田

盘法：闸丹田，开丹田为内含大力功，运气完毕，意气回收下丹田，只收不放，如关水闸，再将闸伏之气，意向四肢百骸散发。这样以意运气充满全身，即会产生爆发出天塌劲与抖决劲。

摩丹田

直立，两脚分开与肩同宽，平行站立，重心在两腿之间，转腰屈膝下蹲，身体向左转体 90 度，右肩在前下沉，右臂自然下垂于两膝之间，五指松直，拇指朝内，掌心内转朝右，左手置于左腰胯后外侧，掌心朝外，左肩高于右肩，头颈正直，平视前方（图 8）。

然后，右肩带劲，肘和手直线朝上拎起，屈肘过顶提到最大限度，顺势向右转腰带动胯、膝，踝关节向右转动，右手手背经腋下沿右背部下行至右腰胯后外侧处，掌心朝外，同时，左肩下沉，向右转体 90 度，左手手背沿左腿后侧下行，前移到两膝之间，五指松直，拇指朝内，掌心内转朝左，右臂自然下垂于两膝之间（图 9）。再以右臂那样上提，并顺势向左转腰带动胯、膝、踝关节向左转动，

反复练习。

要领：动作时注意保持头、颈、脊柱中正，平视前方，肩、肘、腕、胯、膝、踝各关节同时转动，呼吸自然，手上提、下行时动作要协调。

搓丹田

六合式;左脚向前方迈进一大步，成左弓步，左手掌心朝上置于膝上，右手合于左手上，手指松直，头颈、腰、背均自然放松（图 10）。

然后，右手用内劲沿左臂内侧收腹提气，朝上提经左胯前至右肩上，同时用鼻吸气（图 11）。接着右手再沿原路线下搓复原，同时用口呼气。上提下搓各一次为一遍。做完 10 遍后换右脚在前，再做 10 遍。

要领：上提时上体随肩向侧后转动，挺胸，手尽量上提至肩上，前脚保持弓步，后腿可以略屈，下搓时后腿仍蹬直，上下搓动时两脚均不得移动，一提一搓走内劲，气贯五指，逆腹式呼吸，且要“细、匀、深、长”。

屈丹田

六合式：左脚向左侧跨一大步，重心在两腿之间，平视前方，右手背贴近右腮，左臂在身前伸直。掌心朝下护裆（图 12）。

然后，屈右膝，左腿蹬直，重心右移，同时上体向右下侧倾倒至最大限度（图 13）。同时右手经胸前换成护裆掌，左手经右胸前向膝部画弧，随势手贴近左腮，重心左移，上体向左下侧倾至最大限度，屈左膝，右腿蹬直（图 14）。左右交替各做 10 次。

要领：上体侧屈时，不要前俯后仰，头颈、躯干与腿呈拱形曲线，平视前方，立直身体时用鼻吸气，屈时用口呼气。

射丹田（逞）

射丹田（逞）练上述功夫后，丹田气越足，周身气力也越大，

体力日增体魄自健。内功发动起来如虎之狠、如龙之惊，拳上一气，无不取胜。

养丹田

养丹田，又称静气功。与武功有密切关系，且却疾延年极裨益于身体。人赖气以生，犹鱼赖水以活，气充足则康强，气微弱则衰惫，气耗尽则身亡矣。故道家以为气为至宝而有运气法。然非得明师传授，强行之，则不惟无益而反有损。守心以养气，不仅可行而有益无损。孟子曰：志为气帅，故气常随乎心，心驰于外则气亦散而不收矣。心动于中则气亦犹而不宁矣。故养气之法，莫如守心，而心又易驰易动，极难把握，欲求守心之法，莫如两目回光返照。古人曰，目之所至心亦至焉，心定所至，气亦至焉。目定而心自定，心定而气自定。故或以目视三田，泥丸为上丹田，心为中丹田，脐为下丹田。上视山根（鼻为山，鼻之上为山根）或视鼻端白，（朱子调息箴内尝言之），此皆以目定心，以心定气之法，道家所言若要长生，先须久视，意正如此，以之修仙则不足，以之养生，却亦有余，也顾与高明。

练习者，能另有静坐房室。自练更佳，每日可于早晚，略坐片时，不在乎久，缓缓从事，勿管相，勿管呼吸，取其自然之理，牙合闭，舌则轻抵牙关间，脊椎须正，先可行预坐式，两手按膝头，身躯可稍前左右晃之，再始坐正，则腰椎自直，臀部自正，两手轻握置丹田下（脐下三寸），或呈太极图，或三昧印式（太极图乃左大拇指轻掐中指，以有大指插入左虎口内，而以右大指食指轻捏左手之无名指根也。三昧印乃两掌皆仰，以右大指交叉左大指上后）（后图，此式）。坐拥单盘、双盘，均无不可，早间坐时（大便后再坐为宜）先将窗户推开，换一换空气，冬日闭窗为好，凝神趺坐，自口中吐出浊气一口，再自鼻中缓缓吸入新气咽下，以补丹田呼出之气。呼时稍快，吸则须慢，呼须呼尽，吸须吸尽，如此续续之呼之吸，将

腹中浊气吐完，再行次序。

养丹田又叫炼内丹，它和中医大夫炼丹的原理一样。吾师常说，炼丹要用炉，炉上要用鼎，鼎中要装药，炉中药烧火。初时以武火烹炼，继后以文火温养，这样药物才能升华为丹。武术气功家炼内丹也是一样，要有炉、有鼎、有药、有火候，才能炼就内丹。人身的炉在哪里？会阴穴就是炉。此穴又名会阴，居于前后阴之间，女子阴户之后、肛门之前。男子阴囊之后、肛门之前。无论男女此场有动脉隐约跳动。李濒湖云，“此脉一开，百脉俱开”，这就是指炼功者，真火即此穴升起，上烹于鼎，其形好像半边锅形，故丹象之说“半边锅内煮乾坤”。这就是练气功家练内时用以盛药之鼎。什么叫药呢？药就是精气神三宝（玉皇心印经），说上药三品神与气精，历代丹经多譬况借喻之语，时而龙虎，时而水火，时而铅汞，时而坎离，时而朱砂水银、雄黄白银，弄得学者望洋兴叹，不得其门而入，畏难而退。什么是火呢？火就是意念。单以意念注于丹田，呼吸任其自然，就叫文火。因为文火需要以气助之，自然呼吸，就是鼻孔中出入之气任其自然，不疾不迟，不粗不滞，一心注视丹田，心静呼吸自然细长，元气自然藏于腹中，老子说“虚其心，实其腹”。这就是炼内丹关键，也是九还、七返、八归、六居的必不可少的条件，心息相依，即心随呼吸一上一下，每呼一口气都用意念缓缓地将气吸入丹田，这样的呼吸法就叫武火，武火对于上药三品——精、气、神起着烹炼的作用。

贯（采）气法

泥丸灌注法（上丹田），此法，行、站、坐、卧都可以用，但以站和坐两法最为适宜。

采气方法，先静心息虑，意守会阴穴片刻，然后以意念观其呼吸之升降。当鼻中吸气时，意想虚空中的元气，从自己的头部正中（泥丸穴即百会穴）灌入顶内，从后脑玉枕关处，分为左右两路，沿着

背脊两旁一直走道尾闾骨处，绕过肛门，入于会阴穴内，暂停一瞬间。

然后，随鼻中出气时，意思来入之气从胸腹正中任脉两旁的冲脉而上行于面部，再上额内，注于祖窍之中，如此采气7~21遍，然后，意守会阴穴，任其自然呼吸，不拘时间长短，收功时将两手搓热，擦头、项和面部，然后睁开眼睛，以两手摩一摩胸、腹、腰、腿及肘臂和两膝、足等处，就可以自由行动了。

脐轮灌注法

此法行、站、坐、卧都可以炼，但以卧法最为适宜，无论平卧、侧卧都可以。

采气方法，仍然是先静心息虑，意守阴穴片刻，然后，以意念观其呼吸之升降，当鼻中进气时，意想虚空中的元气，从自己的肚脐眼灌入整个小腹和会阴穴之内，暂停一瞬间，然后随着鼻中出气时，意想从脐轮采入之气，旧说谓之“久视长生活”，停练时可做气息归元法收功，即以丹田为中心从左到右，从小到大，划三十六圈，又从大到小，从右到左划二十四圈，领气归于丹田。

气透骨髓法

宁神固气于脐下丹田，将内气引至尾骨，沿脊柱提气至头顶百会穴，略停片刻，内视全身解剖骨骼，以意领气（配合呼吸）从头顶由上至下沿原路线返回头顶，如此上下往返，使呼吸逐步加深加长，久练后气息深透骨髓，打通全身关窍，上下内外畅通无阻，可以消除隐患，大有益于健康。停功时，用平园立柱收功法，即从头顶以意领气至脐下丹田中心，沿腰围部位，以丹田为中心点画圈为轴，上顶喉头，下达会阴，呈园柱体，由左向右转五十次，反向也转五十次，转时似圆柱在中宫转动，转完后意将此柱上下两端，同时向中间挤压，化为一点，潜入脐下丹田，固守三息，即行停功。这两次功法能增长元气。

环抱明珠法

行放松清净诱导法后，凝神静气于脐下丹田，使气息交融呼吸极其微细。设想自身周围环抱一大蔚蓝色的大圆球的中心，蓝关四周环抱。此时百脉充积一片光明，除有心音搏动及极其轻微呼吸外，别无他物，进入高度宁静境界。此时意想呼气时，圆球上端的清气沿顶门直透中宫而达下端,吸气时圆球左右两边的清气向中宫挤合，一透一合，上下左右，通透无阻，轻灵飘逸，神虚体静，霎时眼前一片白光，与自身合而为一，片刻一个金光灿烂的火球，在眼前上下闪耀浮动，古人谓之“觉明”，这种现象一般出现不长，有时忽隐忽现。有时出现较长，取决于练功境界的深度，但不应有意追求。如停练即以平圆式收功法（如前述）收功即可。

宝瓶住气法

姿势及松静诱导法同上述。练功时设想一轮皎洁的明月，高悬于头顶之上，照耀着自身清凉明净，顷刻化为五色光彩，凝成晶莹的甘露，从顶门灌入，直透自身中宫而达会阴，再分两股通道左右足心涌泉穴，想甘露所到之处，将一切疾病、痛苦、烦恼、忧郁彻底干净地从全身毛孔中排洗出去，全身干净明彻、纯洁，一尘不染。此时，复想此甘露上从头顶下降，下从足尖回开，同时归至脐下丹田会合停住，将气吸入后，封住上下二口，使内气不外泄、外气不内透，停闭口鼻呼吸，能停就更好。至不能再忍耐时，只以鼻微微以意呼气，不可出净。此时设想脊柱中有一导管，将余气慢慢地渗入管中，渐渐消失，不得外散。此功法要求较高，全凭丹田内呼吸，极为绵细，久之能达神清气静、虚灵无身、经久不息的高度境界。停闭呼吸的锻炼法，必须循序渐进，初练时间不宜过长，练后如出现头昏感，应及时以贯气法纠正，久勤而行之，则气功之道，日渐领略殊深。

六合大撞护体功

易筋经义（一）易筋总论

欲学上乘内功之人，筑基之功分两步，一步是“消虚”，一步叫“勇往”。如果不懂这层道理，那么进道则无根基。

这里的“清虚”，指的就是“洗髓”，“勇往”指的就是易筋。所谓“易筋”就是改变人体劲力的方法。人的身体骨髓之外皮肉之内，四肢百骸之中，无处没有筋的存在，没有筋就没有力，“筋弛则靡，筋缩则挛，筋靡则痿，筋弱则懈，筋绝则折，筋壮则强，筋舒则长，筋颈则刚，筋和则康”。以上所举的各种情况，都说明筋在人体中所占的重要地位。如果想变弱为强，变挛为长，变柔为刚，“变衰为强”，就得借助于“易筋”之力。此功即是强身健体、祛病延年的法宝，又可作为继续修进高深内功的基石。

修习本功不但要树立坚定的信心，还须有顽强的恒心。行动要由先后、先易后难、由简入繁。只要依法行持，进修不懈，定可获得成功。

膜论

髓骨之外，皮肉之内。以及五脏六腑到处都有筋，也到处都有膜。膜与筋比较，膜比筋略软，膜与肉比较，膜比肉稍硬。筋分缕，半附于骨肉之间。而膜则全部附着皮肉，与筋不同，故此，两者的锻炼方式也不尽相同。

练功时，筋膜都须练到，练筋比较容易，练膜则比较难，其原因在于，筋体半附于骨之间，较膜体虚灵。行动气至时，筋体易起，而膜体比较呆滞，除非内气备至，否则难以腾起。所以，练到筋起之后，必须倍加功力。务必等周身膜体尽皆腾起，与筋气俱坚，外应于皮，内坚其肉，至此方为成功。否则，筋没膜的辅助，那么就如同植物

没有种在土壤之中一样，无从吸取养分，枝干必然枯朽，生命就危险了。这样又怎能算得上是全功呢？

内壮篇

内与外相对应，壮与衰相对应。壮与衰比较，壮更令人羡慕。内与外相比较，外就要放在较次要的位置上。

内壮侧重于练道，外壮侧重于练勇。练道可以步入超凡入圣之高深境地。而练勇则难脱俗套。

如此看来，内壮与外壮真可谓天壤之别。

练习内壮的要领有三条。第一条，此功的要点在于积气。揉法乃积气之妙法。行揉法时，手掌推揉的胸腹中间，就叫“中”。中处乃是积气之地。行揉法时必须守之。方法是，双目神光内敛，耳不旁闻，调匀鼻息，闭口不语，四肢不动，一意冥心存想中处，先存想至后来渐渐达到坐忘的程度。如此修习，则人体内之精、气、神都贯注，积累，久久自成无量功力。如果在行揉法守中时杂念纷纭，精神不能内守而驰情外情，那么神、气将散而不凝，行动就收不到效果。

第二条，人体内的精血、神气都为意念所驱使，意行则行，意止则止。行揉法守中之时，全部意念都集中于推揉的手掌之下。如果意念散布于身体其他部位，那么精气也将随之注入各肢体，即成外壮之功，也不能收到预期之效果。

第三条，真气积累的过程中，应当将真气蕴藏于中处而不使其旁溢，精神专注而不外驰。直至日月已足、效验已显之时，方可将真气自然引达，使各部节之坚壮，如果中处还未充盈，就将真气散于四肢，那么就会导致内壮不固、外勇亦不全的后果。

揉法

谱曰：“筋”力磨砺而后壮。本揉法就是磨砺之意。揉法于春

月起行动最为适宜。内为本功在推揉之时须裸露身体。二月起手行动，之后天气渐暖，于行动“功”较为方便。推揉之时，须按照由右至左的顺序行之。因为腹脏之中，肺脏于右而肝脏于右下。右肺主气，右下肝主血。由右向左，然后往右下推揉，乃是推气入血，令其相融之意。

行揉法时，推揉之手用力宜轻、宜浅。应徐徐推荡，切不可骤然用力太重、太深。如果用力太重则伤皮肤，用力太深则损伤肌肉筋膜。

阴阳配合论

如行功之人，因阳衰而患有痿弱之症，则助功推揉宜选择童女或少妇。因为女子外阴而内阳，借其阳而助其衰，如果行功之人是因阴盛阳衰而患热疾，则宜选择童子或少男推揉。因为男子外阳而内阴，借其阴而制其盛，无病之人行功，则男女推揉均可。如能用童男童女相间推揉，令其阴和阳畅，则可收到更好的效果。

行功轻重

初行揉法时，推揉的力量以轻为主，最好选择小孩推揉。因为小孩力气小而平和。到一个月后，自身真气渐凝，则应当换有力者推揉，并且力量渐渐加重。但切不可骤然用力，以免导致火动，推揉之手也不可游移，以免损伤皮肤。

两肋分内外说

行功超过百日，前胸的筋膜即已腾起，真气也已盈满充寒。这就有如拍击堤岸的河水一般，稍加决导即奔涌流泻，不能控制。当此之时，千万不可用意念将真气引入四肢。如一引导，则新生之真气便走注于外，而成为外勇。此时真气散漫不凝，无法练之入骨，就不成为内壮。

导气入内的方法是，用石袋从心至两肋，骨肉腑脏交会之处密集地敲打，并用揉法推揉。如此行之日久，则腑气于脏器会合，新入的真气与先前所积的真气循循入骨。真气入骨不外溢，髓骨日益坚壮，方才成为内壮。

内壮服药法

锻炼内壮之时，外部靠揉捣，内部则须依靠药力。每日于早起行功之时，先服药一丸。大约药丸在胃里将要化开时，就可行功了。如果药未入胃就开始行功，或者药丸消化多时方行功，都与行动“功”无益。

通灵丸方

选螯足俱全，壳硬健壮，每只四两以上的深秋蟹，雌雄各八只，同荞麦面二升四合捣烂，加黄酒制成饼，文火焙干研末，当归身酒净。用蜜和成丸每次服用 60 丸，用黄酒送下。

行功的时候要经常用药水烫洗身体，这样可使血滋润，肌肤舒畅。方法是，用适量的地骨皮及食盐煎汤趁热擦身。每天洗一次或两天洗一次，至功成就可停止。

下部洗药

行下部功时，烫洗不能间断。因为行下部功须依靠药力，和气血、坚皮肤，并且药水可解热退火。只有坚持烫洗，方不致出现偏差。方法是：用适量的蛇床子、生甘草、地骨皮煎汤。先用温汤洗，然后用热汤洗，最后用烫汤洗。每次行下部功内功，完毕就用药水洗，每日共三次。

如意散

将大象皮切成片，再将鲮鱼甲，酒炒，半夏、川乌、头草再加

姜汁制成，全当成妇瓦松皮，硝蜀椒侧、柏叶、透骨草、紫花、地丁，再加食盐，以上 13 味各 3 两，加鹰爪一对敲碎共倒入砂锅内，用陈醋 7 斤河水 8 斤浸好，临时用量取冲滚汤内烫洗。

木槌杵式

木杵、木槌都用坚木为原料，如降真香更好，紫檀、白檀、花梨钱力也行，制作时用杵宜头尖，最好微圆，槌头圆而微长，中间升高，取其高处着肉，两头尚虚。

杵捣深陷，槌打周身，初做时轻，逐渐加重，用手劲必须均匀，不快不慢最为合适。

石袋式

木槌和木杵只能用于大面积皮肉的捣打，而骨缝之间则只能依靠石袋。石袋的制袋方法是，选水中光滑圆润而无棱角的石子，大如葡萄，小如梧桐子，用细帆布缝制成略像木杵形状的石袋，要两头尖中间细。这样的石袋要制作大小各四个至五个，大的长约八寸，其次是五寸，小的是三寸，石袋的粗细随大小而增减。石袋内石子要塞得坚实，要做到摆动时不能发出任何声音，用石袋捣打日久，骨缝之内的筋膜也就健壮了。

易筋经义

日精月华，清阴清阳之气，其使人愚浊潜消、清灵畅达、疾病不染、神智日增的威力，行此功如能自始至终，那么好处真是无法估量。

行功采咽法

取每月朔日（初一）和望日（十五）行动。如果是阴雨天，那么延后一二日也可，其他时候则不适宜。

朔日法（初一）

要早起，登上高处，面向东方坐定，调匀鼻息，先用火笔在上颚书写“煜”字。然后，用鼻子细细地吸气，意想将光华吸入，充盈满口，然后闭息凝神，意想将光华细细咽下，并用意想送之注入丹田。以上为一咽，如此共行七咽，最后静坐片刻，方可离去。

望日法（十五）

应择中午时行动。登高处坐定，用火笔在上颚书写“煜”字。其余也与朔日相同，也以七咽为准。

注：火笔指的是舌尖。

观心返本

行功之人，如果不是童体，就必须先行观心返本与洗心退二法。目的是要将散于五官及百骸之中的元气，再返还于上丹田之中。只有这样，以后的行动才能“积气有所附，守中有所主”，入手行动才有根基。

虚耳观心法

在六时之中，不论行、止、坐、卧，都必须正身远虑。要做到耳不旁听、目不旁瞩，双眼垂帘出现内视，自观自心。用鼻子吸入天地之清气，用口吐出肠胃之浊气。将清气以意念引导，使其遍布周身。吐纳呼吸之时，必须使纳多吐少。练习时间久了，吐纳就会勉强变得自如，由短促变得深长。

洗心退芷

此方法是：调匀鼻息，静坐。存想山根，意想上六时所吸之清气聚于根，然后随微微呼吸，由脑后渐下夹背，至两肾之间，再翻

转上透至泥丸，由天庭下前面，行至咽关，趁势咽下，存贮于上丹田之中，此功不论咽数，有空即可做。如此练之百日后，自会积气生液，积液生精，子母会合，破镜重圆。

法轮自转（功法练习）

静坐片刻，调匀鼻息。返聪内视。青龙潜于右，白虎伏于左。存想龙潜虎伏。用右手握拳，在心下脐上左转 36 圈，圆圈由小到大。再右转 36 圈。圆圈由大到小，要均圆转。

初月行功

初月行功时，需四个小童轮流推揉。是因小童力气小，推揉不重，另一个是因为小童年少气血充盛。凡行功之人，应在每日黎明分，行归根复命一遍，然后起身。内服壮药丸至药丸将要开化之时，方可行法。

行功每次大约一小时。每日分早、午、晚行功三次。如果行功太急，易出偏差。开始每功。就要制定作息时间表，以后应严格遵守，饮食也要定量，这对行功大有好处。

二月行功

行功初以后一个月，内气已逐渐聚集起来。自己可以感觉到气海宽大，腹部两旁的筋已腾起，各有过余宽。气运到此处时，可硬如木片。这时，在以前所揉一掌的两旁各开一掌，仍如前法揉之。两肋之间由心到腹部，各处下陷的地方，是因为膜的原因。膜与筋不同，深藏于皮肉之下，推揉不到，必须用木杵捣之，日久则膜体腾起，浮至皮下。与筋气同坚，没有丝毫软陷。才为得法。

三月行功

功满两个月时，腹部陷处渐起，就用木槌轻轻敲打，而两旁各

开一掌处则用木杵轻轻捣之。再于其两旁至两肋处各开一掌。如法揉之。

四月行功

行功至三个月，中间所揉的三掌都用槌打，外边的两掌先用杵捣，后用槌打。行功过百日，则腹部已气满筋坚，膜皆腾起。

五月至八月行功

行功满一百二十日，心下两旁至肋梢，应掌揉捶打，杵捣，膜皆腾起。

此时乃是内壮与外壮的分界之处，必须谨慎。应从心口上至颈，又从右肋梢上至胸，再从左肋梢上部至于肩。周而复始，不可倒行。如此再行百日，则气满前胸任脉充盈了。

九月至十二月行功

行功过二百日，前胸气充，任脉已足。则应将真气运入脊背以充督脉。行功的顺序：先前之气已上肩头，现在自右肩开始，从颈侧上至玉枕，又从左肩由颈侧上至玉枕，再从玉枕向下至尾闾，行功方法如前。

凝神气穴

行揉法满二百六十五日之后，任督之脉皆已充盈。将要行下部功。自此以后，应当将早晨所行之内功“归根复命”，改为“凝神气穴”。其原因是归根复命乃是顺其气而使之充盈，积攒起来为内壮之源。而凝神气穴则是逆运其气而为内壮之用。顺行则气满，逆行则神充。一举一逆有体有用。如此习之，气才能达到真正坚固。为什么现在方行此功呢？因为此功须任督二脉将通之时方可行之。

此法可使命府之心火降至气穴，称为“水火相见”，经中曰“久

视下丹田则命长生”，说的就是这个。

下部行功

行功至三百余日，任督二脉积气已充盈。此时须行下部功法。

下部功法的部位有两处：一处时睾丸，一处是玉茎。睾丸处行功之法，共有攒、挣、搓、拍、抚、咽、洗七法。玉茎处有握、束、咽、洗、摔五法。不计遍数，以一时为准。每日之次行功。行此功百日可通任督，功足气坚时，下部可不畏拳棒重击。

动静入四肢论

下部功足后，任督二脉已通，气充周身，可随意顺逆运行。然而手足未坚，还不能算作健壮。还须持续修习静功十段及动功十八势等诸势。

第二章

静功十段（功法练习）

动功十八势（功法练习）

神勇六合功

静功十段（功法练习）

早服通灵丸六十四丸，大约药丸入胃部将化之时，开始行功。用鼻吸气灌注于行功之处，以意运气从骨髓中行去。千万不可使拙力，如果一使拙力，就与动功没有什么区别了。每段数字渐渐增加，焚香为记直至二寸香为止。每日行功三遍，功毕则行打洗神通。有空暇时间仍行观心，洗心诸法，至十月功成之后，空暇时间也应当经常习之，丸药每日至早晨服一次，以下分十功分别介绍。

第一功　韦陀捧杵

注想尾闾上第二节，气从背上起，直通到手指梢。

第二功　独立金刚

注想项后一寸三分，气从足心起，到两肘时尖通头顶及上一拳。

第三功　降龙

注想顶后风府穴，气从腹部起至上单手。

第四功　伏虎

注想风府，气从后背到前肩再由臂到两拳。

第五功　天地泰

注想尾闾之前、肾囊之中，气从涌泉穴起直通周身直到头顶百会穴。

第六功　虎坐

注想脐前任脉穴，气从周身自上而下。

第七功　龙吞

注想天灵盖，气从足跟起直上头顶。

第八功　御风渡江

注想脐后，气从背上起直涌头顶。

第九功　回回指路

注想命门腰间，气从背下归至脚底。

第十功　观空

注想指圈空处，气通周身。

打洗神通

每次行静功完毕都要行打洗神通。起初用木槌、木杵，五十日后用石袋。先从右肩上均匀打下，至中指背，双从肩前打至大指背，又打至食指背，又从肩后打至无名指背，又至小指背，然后，从后肩内打至掌内大指尖，又打至食指尖。打完后用如意散汤洗行功之处，然后再用手揉搓。拍打时必须按顺序，每个手指都是从肩向下打。切不可倒打，每日行功三次，每次一个时辰，行功满百日后，方可再行左手打洗，与右手行功之法相同，行功日期也是百日功满。

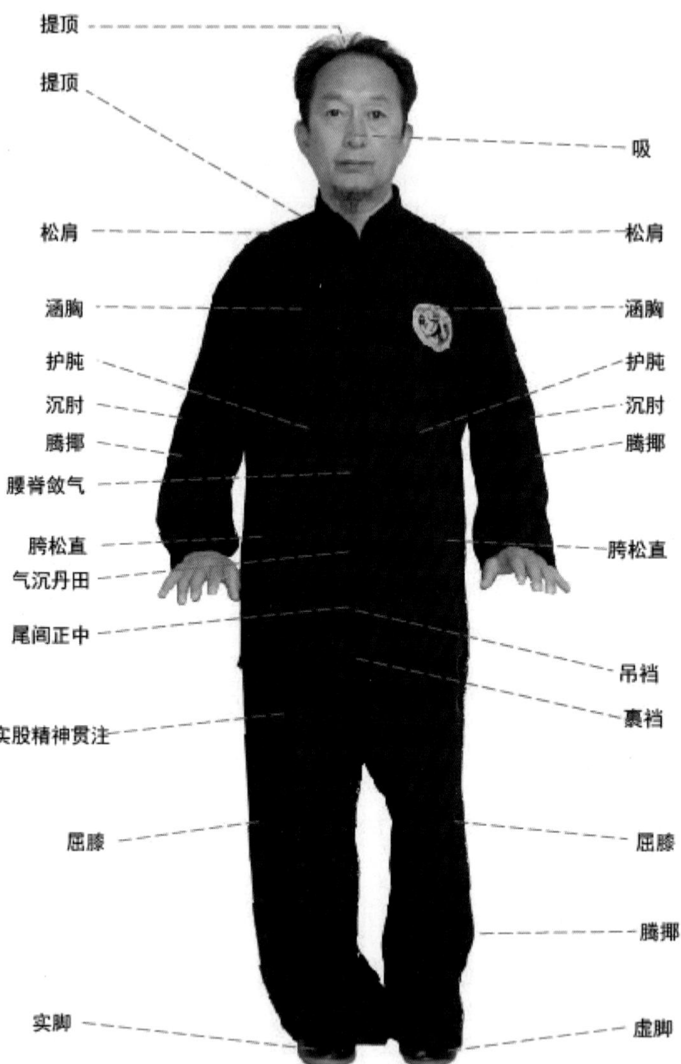
提顶
提顶
吸
松肩
松肩
涵胸
涵胸
护肫
护肫
沉肘
沉肘
腾挪
腾挪
腰脊敛气
胯松直
胯松直
气沉丹田
尾闾正中
吊裆
裹裆
实股精神贯注
屈膝
屈膝
腾挪
实脚
虚脚

动功十八势（功法练习）

静功完毕后，手足骨髓之力已充足，再行动功。真气就可以达到皮肉，内外相合了。行动功时，早晨仍服通灵丸。功毕仍行打洗神通，每日行功三次，十月功成。此功有许多人在练，大都不得法。也有的动作没有内功为基础，这样练习是有害身体健康的，下面介绍十八式。

第一　鹤舞势

面朝东南方向站立，两足距离二尺左右，足跟微向外，成坐马势。将气提至胸间，双手握固上抬平肩，双臂屈肘掌心向前，十指相对向前托开，双臂推直后，意想往后拉十下，然后双臂收回，十指张开，下按。下按时意想非常用力。如此上下各三次。

第二　龙舞势

站立如前，两手托开，然后双臂向后外展至背后，顺势收至肋间，转腕缓缓向前推直。如此共六次，三次推出时掌心朝前，十指向上。三次掌心朝前十指相对，推出时都要掌根着力。

第三　推托势

站立如前，左手阳面向上托出，然后右手托开。左右两臂伸直，两臂用力一伸后，十指握拳抓紧，缓缓收回来再用右手托出，左手托开。如此各三次。

第四　凤凰舞势

站立如前，双手握固置于胸前。双手一转，一只手张开五指托

上，一只手握固贴于乳旁。左右各行三次。收回手后两手握固，曲肘上拳，然后双手分开转下，双手合托后，张开手指，向上直推。如此三转三推。

第五　虎吟势

两足尖斜向两侧站立。两手握固，在胸前一转，一只手朝前伸出，手臂微曲，拳也向内微曲。另一只手向后伸出，要点与前手相同。如此左右各换三次。

第六　转身势

紧接第五势，手臂收回后即转身，将左手一扭，两拳伸出，双臂微曲，如抱物之状。如此左右各换三次。

第七　转环势

站立如第一势，先用左手手指张开，从内下侧转腕向后环转，手臂向上时腕向内，三转一豁，九转三豁，右手亦如此。

第八　进退势

身体正立，两手握固一扭，左足跨出一步。左手击出，伸直，右手抱于胸前，左手一扭收回。右手击出，伸直，右足跨出。如此前进后退各三扭三拳。

第九　开工势

站立如第一势，气归小腹，双脚不可移动。右手在前伸直，左手向后曲臂，做开弓的姿势，目视右手。第六开始，双手收回换左手在前。每六开一换，左右各行三十六开。

第十 童子拜观音势

双足并拢，身体直立。两手下叉平脐。反手上托至头顶，神注泥丸，用意念将手伸十下，然后渐渐向前按下至地，神注涌泉。以意念将手伸十下，至极点后，徐徐立起。如此十次。

第十一　美女观莲势

前足横，外足直，双足如丁字站立。两手握固做凭栏之状。转身，心口对左足踝，左膝微曲。身体转向右亦如此。左右各行三次。

第十二　熊顾势

并足而立，双手握固，拳前伸，臂前垂，身前俯左右摇荡，头左右转看尾闾足跟三十六次。

第十三　稳举势

一足站稳，一足钩转按膝上。两手抱之坐下立起。左右各三次，行之日久，骨节灵通，经脉舒张，可以一足钩于颈上起坐，方为全功。

第十四　仙人反背势

两足一顺一斜站立。将身体扭转左右转换，前进三步，后退三步。行之日久，胸可旋转至正对背后方为全功。

第十五　接宾势

一足用力站稳，另一足屈膝，两手板足胫，徐徐下蹲。以屈膝盖拄地，膝搓地着声，然后努力立起。如此左右各三次。

第十六　象立势

两足用力将身体左右摆荡。两手扳直，随着身体摆荡趁势在面前旋转，如转达轮之状。左右旋转三十次。

第十七　锦雉舞势

双足合并蹲下，如坐莲花之势。两手握固，从胯间打下趁势挣起，起坐共六次。再以两手握固，贴于乳下。两足平立，将足跟上举十四次。开始轻后来重，再将左手略举，将右足钩转向内，往斜后方蹬出，蹬出时足跟着力。左足亦相同，如此左右各七次。

第十八　鹤立势

两手握固，一足立定，以一足洒，左右各三次每次各十四洒。注：洒同洗。

练手余功

静功百日后加入动功。二功兼练又过二百日之时，静功火候已足，气已透至指梢。可以加入练手余功与动功兼行。

练手余功的方法

行打洗神通时，所用的如意散汤，应由温热渐至大热，洗完手后，不可擦拭，趁热摆动手使其自干。手摆动的时候，须努气于各指尖。并徐徐伸缩手指三十六次。这次做“黄龙探爪法”用黑豆与绿豆搅拌倒入斗中，用手抓豆，力量由轻至重。早、午、晚，三次或者加子时共计四次，每次三百次，两手交替相抓共两千次至二千五百次。行功日久，则从前所积之气都通行至手指皮肉与筋膜骨髓之中。不用时与常人无异。

神勇六合功

肉壮即成，骨力坚凝，引达于外。行练手余功过百日时，十八动功已完成。动静俱成，内壮完全。

外部加此八法使力充周身。八法是：提、举、推、拉、抓、按、荡、坠。八法在树旁依次行之，周而复始，不计遍数。有时间则习之，越久越神。八法中如专精一法也可以，练提举之法，所用石地由轻而重，推，用树身即可，拉、抓、按，用树的大枝练习，练习荡法，攀住树木的横枝，悬身而荡。坠法，攀住树枝，放手，仰面坠落，运气于背，着地即起。

神勇余功

内外两全，方可称为神勇，自此以后，应当经常演练以前各功，不可荒废，日精月华朔望二日不错过。凝神气穴仍须照常行持。观心、洗心以及法轮自转诸法也应经常练习。有时间就练习动静二功。

还须择树木粗大茂盛的园林任意演练八段锦，兼练两足踢、踏、钩、扫，诸势。如遇有苍松古柏高山大壑之处、大风大雨海奔浪涌之时，即行练习。这样可吸取物之精英与天地奔溢之气以助我精气。则身体更加坚固而不可动摇，成金刚之躯。

神勇六合大撞踢（铁）趾功

足蹠功又叫单风朝阳，是鸡形中专门训练腿部梢节的一种功夫，属硬功功法。

练功时，应择一棵大树进行，练习者在树前一尺半处以六合式站定，随即，右脚朝前刮地而起，以脚前掌往距树尺许高处击踢（切不可用脚趾踢树，以免骨折或伤了脚趾）。与此同时，右掌从右胯

翻上，变拳与头同高，左掌随之伸出护在右肘下，虎口抵住尺骨鹰嘴，脚踢和出掌要同时，不可分前后，右脚收回原处，再做双掌下抓动作，继而脚踢掌出，踢击时，身体正直，着力于左脚，左脚应以五趾扣地，脚跟站稳，使身体不可前俯，不可后仰，不可有斜，不可有歪。往前三直而起，往后三直而落，双掌下抓用内含劲，双手合于胸前略有停顿，掌下抓时吸气，踢脚时呼气，发雷声，均以鼻孔呼吸，抿唇闭齿，舌抵上腭，以龙腰之力助脚，初练时不可用力过猛，力量由小而大，每次练习不计遍数，略感劳累时休息。踢树练习即久，可改为埋桩练习，用三寸粗坚硬木桩数根，将其埋入土中一尺，周围以土埋实，桩露出地面二尺，如能依次将十根桩一脚踢倒，或踢断，其功大成。

单风朝阳功夫练就后二腿之力极大，临阵对敌，以此功夫加上变化多端之腿法，虽有几十人围攻弹腿挥掌间便能化险为夷。

神勇六合大撞铁膝功

六合铁膝功又叫夜马奔槽，是属于马形中专练腿部中节的一种功夫，属进攻打击与防御力的硬功功法。膝盖击人，爆发力大，隐蔽性强，尤其在贴身近战中，往往使用膝击，使敌方防不胜防。再者，膝盖外部无肌肉与脂肪保护，易被击伤。因此，铁膝功练成后，既可增加进攻力，又可进行有效的防御，在心意拳中占主要地位。神勇六合大撞护体铁膝功，练法十分简单，此功夫各派拳术都有练习，而各有其不同的练法。先用粗帆布或结实的细布缝二尺长、一尺宽的布袋一个，内装细沙、锯末或者谷皮，上用布带扎紧，绑碗口粗大树上与胯同高。练习者在树前一尺左右以六合式站定，随即，右膝朝前抖身而起，以膝往距树上沙袋撞击（初练时不可用力过猛，力量应由轻而重）。与此同时双掌向上翻合，抱于胸前变为拳，拳心朝里，左手臂再向树干击打。膝撞和手臂击打要同时触树，不可分前后，右膝收回原处，再做双拳向外翻变为掌往下抓，继而膝撞手臂击打。撞击时，身体要正直，着力于左脚，左脚应以五趾扣地，后跟站稳，使身体不随动作而摇晃，双掌下抓用划劲，双掌合于胸前，变拳略有停顿，随后，手臂击打时方可用力，掌下抓时吸气，膝提撞时呼气，均以鼻孔呼吸，抿唇闭齿，舌抵上腭，以龙腰之力助膝。每次练习应按体力而定，撞树练习即久，可改为撞铁砂袋，日久天长即可成功，铁膝功

撞铁膝

练成后，两膝坚硬异常，浑如铁铸。若用双膝施以攻击，则对方无有不应膝而倒，谱曰：“膝打击处人不明，好似猛虎击木笼，洞内动转不停时，左右明拨任意打。”

神勇六合大撞铁胯功

六合铁胯功又叫虎调腚，是属于虎形中专练腿部根节一种功夫。胯部击人，隐蔽性强，胯打根节盖相连，阴阳相济得知难，外胯转身变势难，里胯好似免滚身。

练功时，应择一棵大树进行，练习者在树前一尺左右以六合式站立，随即，右足向前踏在大树根左边，身体向左转用右胯向大树滚撞，好似虎调腚，滚撞时身体正直要稳，不可东斜西歪。右腿收回原处时转身，要双掌往下抓。继而上足转身用右胯向大树滚撞，滚撞时要有停顿，节奏不可太快，也不可太慢，次数按体力而定。遇敌运用时只要贴身转胯，敌必然跌倒无疑。

铁胯

神勇六合大撞铁掌功

六合铁掌功又叫熊形单把或双把，是熊形中专练手梢节的一种功夫，属阳刚之劲。练习者应择一棵大树进行，以六合式站定距离树一尺左右，左脚向前跨一步，同时单掌或双掌，曲肘置于体前掌心向前，五指分开朝上，向前往大树击打。吸气时，蓄力至丹田，气畅周身，击打时呼气，气到掌梢或劳官，呼吸随动作快慢而快慢，逐步达到呼吸配合，掌功击打均为无意发力之式，无意发力为真意、只有动作规矩，呼吸合法，这样发出劲路才能柔中有刚、刚中有柔，刚柔相济，久练成铁掌。如在技击中击敌如发弹，手起人落，得心应手。

神勇六合大撞铁臂功

六合铁臂功又称摇把功，是专练手臂的硬功功法。这是一种武林中常见的硬气功，不只在心意派中有，其他各派之中均有其练法。铁臂功练法简单，然而欲挥手臂断石，非常力所能及。练习者以六合式站立在碗口粗树周围，以二臂轮流击打树干，敲打的部位在小臂处，初时可轻击，以后逐渐加重，次数不论，至两臂酸痛时为止，但以血肉之躯击坚硬之物，稍用力即会皮破血流，故用力不宜过大。在练习过程之中，皮肉损破是正常现象，待经过数次的破裂与结痂后，皮肤已坚硬如铁，而又柔软如革，而此时大树也因长期击打，变得又光又滑。接着可练手臂击巨石，石块可先选光滑的，再练粗糙的，这时，手臂会再度破裂、结痂，当练至挥臂间碑石立断时，铁臂膊之功就练成了。

此功练成后，手臂有千斤之力，在遇敌交手中使用价值极大。

神勇六合大撞铁肩功

六合铁肩功又称熊出洞，或叫单跌，是属练手、根节、的一种功夫。练习时以六合式站立在碗口粗大树旁，熊善用膀力，练左膀束缩势，右腿着力，脚踏实地，左腿稍向前虚立，脚尖点地，左手随肩里扣下插于裆，右臂屈肘，手护胸平，平视前方（图 ）。中丹田吸气，此为伏势，定势后即发势，随左肩之前射向大树，呼气充实，左腿前进，脚尖蹭踩，左树旁膝前弓劲，右腿在后绷直，同时右手从胸前往后收回右胯边，掌心护住胯部，发出动作时须敏捷快速，身势要定，步伐要稳，练右肩法同左肩交替多练。

神勇六合大撞铁头功

六合铁头功又称以头凿壁功，是心意拳中头功一种。主要练头部的前额、顶门，它既练内气又练外壮之力，是一种内外兼修的武功。

初练时用前额、百会、后脑分别顶墙或大树等静止练功，每次不少于 15 分钟。具体方法是，选择有几十年日晒雨淋经历的墙，或石块、大树等，首先用前额顶住墙或大树等，然后，双手外劳重叠于命门上（图 ），自然呼吸，放松入静。脚平踏地上，全身倾斜又笔直，保持悬空静止姿势不少于 15 分钟（开始为 5 分钟，用软布垫头）。因脸朝下，所以称为“俯顶”。再练“仰顶”15 分钟，其法是足平踏地，百会贴墙壁顶着仰面朝天，双劳宫覆盖脐下丹田（图 ），自然呼吸，身悬空伸直。最后再练“后顶”15 分钟，其法是，足跟

在高处，拼双足伸直腿，后脑枕在低处石头上，腰悬空伸直。双手外劳宫护住后腰（图 ），若将手放在腿边，即可同练腰功。上述俯、仰、后三顶石法均要闭目内视，意守与石接触的头部，头腰腿呈一直线，用自然呼吸法。收功简法，双手相搓热，用一掌或双掌揉摩头部，再以掌擦面，手指梳头，后周身拍打，活动各关节。特别要认真活动腰部和颈部，三月后逐渐运内气力于石接触部位。其他部分均放松，并要求入静。

百日后可增加练习撞墙或撞树、沙袋等，初练者以六合式隔半步远站立于墙、树或沙袋前。入静后特意放松头部稍许，以意运身内之气力于头部，然后闭气（也可不闭气），用头的前额、顶心往墙、树、沙袋等撞击，初用力不可过猛，后逐渐增强力度，日行数次，撞击之数也渐增，勤习百日初步功成。再继续精修运动神力猛撞坚强已无痛感，而所撞之石立时粉碎，则功达上乘。我国武术各拳派都很重视头攻，因为它的打击力较拳脚为大，而且多用于近身手脚不便使用之时，往往能出奇制胜，因此，武林中练此者颇多，然而真正练成，油锤贯顶，双风贯耳，头碎石碑者却不多见。

神勇六合大撞铁肚功

六合铁肚功又称狸猫上树，又称盘中节。它在心意拳中占重要位置，是专练身体中节的一种功夫。首先站在大树下静站鼓气，用手摩腹，左右各顺摩 36 度（图 ）。先左后右按血气二分柔之。

然后再吐气，归原状用左右两手，再逆摩 36 度，每天早、午、

晚、子四时行之练习三年，即腹软如棉一鼓气则其刚如铁（图 ）。

随后，以六合式，左足向前迈进一步，以肚腹盘撞大树，紧接右足向前与左足相并。与此同时双掌合抱于胸前，再向树身挫击，右脚收回原处。再以双掌下塌动作，继而以肚腹盘撞大树，盘撞时身体要正直向上要用提劲，不可用力过猛。力量应由小而大，功成以后不怕重物打击，敌来拳脚踢打毫不疼痛，练至精妙之时铁棒、枪刺都不能伤其胸腹。

神勇六合大撞铁肋功

六合铁肋功又名贴墙挂画，它是心意拳中的硬功外壮法，同时也具内壮软功之劲，属阳刚之劲。是专练腰肋，增强对抗能力的重要功法，在技击中双方都是拳打脚踢，腰肋是软档，时刻都有被敌方击伤的危险。如果不经靠打，易被击伤，如果是经常练习铁肋功，腰肋就经得起敌人击打，内里的五脏六腑也没有损伤，并能发挥心意拳武技的威力，从而战胜敌方。

练习者，以六合式站立在大树旁距离二尺左右，先以左足向前迈进一步。右足紧追迈至大树右旁后，同时右手从右胯部，向上呈弧线上挑掌背朝树，左掌同时从左膝往上按，置于右肋部，掌心向外，同时

右腰肋向大树贴撞，贴撞时要聚气在肋，由轻到重，慢慢地盘撞（图 ）。左右交替多练。

神勇六合鸡腿飞行法

六合鸡腿飞行法是专练行走的一种轻功，又叫夜行术，又称陆地飞行术，也称为千里独行，还称万里追风。是心意六合拳艺中软功内壮功法，是专供练习者两腿如鸡奔跑行走的功法，实用性强，是武林中常见的武功，只不过各门派练法不同。练鸡腿飞行法前，（1）先备用铁砂衫一件，最好重 10 斤最多重 80 斤，再备沙绑腿两只，每只最轻 0.5 公斤，最多重 10 公斤（图 ）。（2）备铁甲前后两片，前片最轻 5 斤最重 30 斤，后片最轻 8 斤最重 50 斤，再备铁瓦或铅瓦两只，每只最轻 0.5 公斤，最多重 10 公斤（图 ）。无论铁、铅、瓦或沙子还是铁砂，要用猪血浸渗，先以火中烧通红时，乃放在猪血内浸一夜，烧而再浸，浸而再烧。如此反复浸烧七次，再埋入土中四十九日，退尽火毒以后，才可以供练功用。（3）穿沙衫戴沙绑腿，每日早晨初时可练鸡行步，练一段站起来慢步走一段。待身体适应后，可练鸡行步的距离长一些，飞行术练的是耐力，不像蹿纵术练爆发力，因此，每日行走的距离要长，开始一次行走二三十里，以后逐步加长距离，身上的重物也应逐渐加重，每次加重不必太重，最后加重根据个人身体而定，当 10 公里路能一气行走完时，开始练垫步、快步，捷若胜兔，纵横行来，追行随影，目不及瞬，后手摧前手，前膀领着走，右腿未起左腿遂，左腿未落右腿追。虽然两腿有前后，不胜两腿并一腿，这时每天早晨，以垫步、快步行跑 10 公里，由一个半小时，逐渐加速到半小时，最快时可以身穿 40 公斤沙衫，两腿戴 24 斤到 40 斤绑腿，20 分钟可以行跑回 20 里跑，即可以成功。（4）也可身穿铁甲、腿带、铁瓦、或铅瓦，与穿沙衫和戴沙绑同样练法，路程和时间要求相同，即告成功（图 ）。鸡腿飞行术练成后，可日行数百里不觉疲劳，而且行走时身体轻盈，快疾如风。

鸡腿飞行术秘方

川乌、草乌、红花、川黄、当归、续断、羌活、杜仲、乳香、没药、朱砂、自然铜、麻仁、五加皮、刘寄奴、茜草、血竭、牛膝、陈把，软功内壮属阴柔之劲，兼阳刚之力。是专供习武者两掌与单掌和臂的推击力，是转练手臂中梢节功夫。

每天早晨无论在屋内，或者在庭院、树林、野外等地都必须面东站立，以左足在前下蹲成左弓步，同时屈肘，左手迅速上提至与脸同高，掌心朝前下方，臂弯曲向右转体 90 度，手臂用力向前伸出，掌根用力，五指分开。掌与胸同高，右手护于左手腕上，平视前方（图）

要领；单把或双把，练习在于脚手齐到，提把时，两肘要贴紧两肋，两肘要坠，两肩要沉，出手时，手指领先，要依靠腰的转动发力，通过肩关节向前催力，弓步要圆裆撑胯，要含胸拔背，气沉丹田，沉肩坠肘，做到手脚齐到。左右交替向前推击，中午面南，晚间面西，子夜时面北，来日光天罡太和之元气，练成掌功非容易，初推击每次双掌共推出一千掌，则全身是汗，心中空虚，口中发干渴，慢慢

坚持，只许增多，不许减少，日日增力，月月加多数量、直至六年，则可每次推万掌而不觉费力，慢慢可以用蜡烛点燃，每次推击之，由一尺慢慢增至十、，二十尺，仍然可以推灭，如果继续练习日久，每日四次，共推击四万掌，三十尺远应手而灭，则功力初步成就。再继续奋斗，推击物件，可用棉花珠放在二尺远的方桌上，天天推之，如推之掉下桌子，再月月加重、移远，至十尺远推动二十斤一块棉包，功夫更为显著。即可在三步以外推倒一人。渐渐至三十年功夫，即八步以内随便一掌推击倒人，此时为五雷闪电掌也，练掌功成者很少，因时间难以坚持，不过只要坚持耐心，不可急进，循序渐进无有不成之理。此功法练习简便到处都可以练习，成功的因素完全靠个人的决心。

练五雷闪电掌内壮秘方

党参 30 克，力参 30 克，熟地 50 克，黄芪 30 克，远志 20 克，羌活 15 克，虎骨 10 克，补脂骨 30 克，枸杞子 30 克，何首乌 30 克，阿胶 20 克，菟丝子 30 克，川断 15 克，川牛膝 30 克，木瓜 30 克，蟹黄 300 克（炒）。

以上诸药物，共研成细末炼蜜为丸，练功之前每服 9 克黄酒送下，喝五大口以助药力。

功效；强筋壮骨，增力补气，疏通血液，增长功夫的进展和力度。

神勇心意超距功

心意超距功又名跳跃法，专练跳高的能力。一般人并足上跳不过二 三尺，而有此功者能跳 6 尺以上，非常人能为，故名超距功。在心意六合拳艺中属软功内壮功夫，是专供练武者身蹿跃纵的重要功法。为心意六合拳传统轻身功夫之一，是习武者经常练习的功法。

此法在心意拳术中起着重要作用，功成之后，可以越过高的障碍物，如高层屋和悬崖深涧等，可以随意纵身而过。当年买壮图祖

师探手拈翔燕之爪尖，腾身可游空之蜻蜓，而蜻蜓足不损，买祖师手不畏利刃，视锋利如朽木。内功极强，双掌能应手吸抓空中飞鸟。对敌方交战时，可以相距一丈以外，以疾步，又名快步，眨眼工夫跃至敌人身体处，突然发招制胜。如，交战中不敌对方时，可以纵力跳到丈外，闪开敌方进攻。

练此功前，先在地上挖一深二尺一大圆坑，或找一口土井在内向上跳。练者双脚缚铁沙袋，并足立于坑底，然后膝盖弯曲，两手后摆，鼓气一跃而上。练者直至力尽，而且每次不得少于半小时，以后逐渐增至一小时，每隔半月，将坑挖深一寸脚上铁砂也加重一两。渐渐跃上的难度也越来越大，当坑深三尺时难度已相当大，此时不可按惯例每半月加深一寸，要视实际情况而定，每日早晚两次练习，不可中断，练习者须延长时间。逐渐由五尺、七尺而达一丈，身上的铁砂也增至最多，如仍能出入自如，则功夫大成，到坑深一丈二尺仍然出入自如，功夫告全成。此功最低需六年至八年修炼，方可成功。

练功内壮方

酒洗当归 120 克，酒洗牛膝 120 克，鱼胶 120 克，虎骨 120 克，酥灵枸杞 120 克，川断 120 克，补骨脂 120 克（盐水炒），菟丝子 120 克，炒蒺藜 30 克，蟹黄 240 克（炒），以上众药研细末炼蜜为丸，每次服 9 克，练功前用黄酒冲服。功能；强壮筋骨，增力补气。

神勇心意轻身术

心意轻身术是轻功的基本功，是心意六合拳艺中软功内壮法，是专供习武者敏捷轻飘的功夫。心意轻身术功法在武术技击散、，擒拿技击中起着重要作用。此功练习之初是从走缸开始。置一 七石巨缸，内盛清水 600 斤。练习者脚踩缸沿绕环行，开始空身行走，熟练后便在身上绑铅块或背负铁砂，身上和两腿共戴四斤，以后每

月取出清水 15 斤，身上加戴铁砂 1 斤，当缸中水取尽，身上的铁砂已加至 40 斤，也能在缸沿行走自如而缸不摇晃时，此须三年苦练（图 ）。便可接着练走箩筐边，取一直径五尺大箩筐内放满沙子 500 斤，身上共戴 5 斤铁砂，每月取去 10 斤沙子，身上加 1 斤铁砂，早、午、晚，三时练习（图 ）。直练至能在空箩筐边上稳步行走为止。身上的铁砂加到总重 60 斤为度，早、午、晚，三时继续习练，此时轻功已有一定根底。然后练习走沙，在空旷之处铺一条厚半尺余宽二尺的沙通道，长不限制，最短不少于一丈长，上边用薄桑皮纸盖一尺厚，身上的 60 斤铁砂不减，每月加半斤，在纸上行走，练习从一端走至另一端，开始练时难免留下脚印，练者每天至少两次行动，每次一 二小时。每隔 7 日将沙道翻一次，每天去掉两张桑皮纸，桑纸越薄对练者要求也越高。依此法不懈练习，直至取走最后一张桑纸，这时身负 120 斤铁砂（图 ）。人行沙上，而沙不巨扬，又不留任何蛛丝马迹，此时方算大功告成。要练成此功，非十年耐心磨炼不可，此功成后其身轻如蝶燕，可任意穿行而不留痕迹。民间传说踏雪无痕之说，实非虚言。放下全身铁砂，可以蹬萍渡水，也可踏波浪渡江河，而不下沉。如脚踏浮萍叶过江河更为顺利。名为心意六合拳艺的蹬萍渡水功（图 ）。

可以身负二十斤铁砂，在离地二尺高的木桩上行走，逐渐加高，身上每月加铁砂一斤（图 ），至全身铁砂总数加至一百斤，木桩由粗变细，由矮渐高，用细竹竿离地上露八尺为度（图 ）。至身上的铁砂增至一百二十斤为度，竹竿上梢削成尖锐锋利的尖头即成功。可以放下铁砂，空身在竹签上练拳。名为心意六合拳艺中“签上飞腾功”（图 ）。放下铁砂，空身可在枪头上行走，赤脚跑跳，在上边练拳，名为心意六合拳艺中“枪尖飞行功”（图 ）。

进一步也可在香头行走，不灭火头，单练拳术如走平地，名为心意六合拳艺中“竖香战斗功”（图 ）。

再进一步也可在灯烛上行走，练拳，烛火不灭，名为心意六合

拳艺中“灯光战斗功”（图 ）。

再进一步，可向前离地纵身，悬空走五至八步，方可落地，要进步提起中气，行走如常，此名为心意六合拳艺中八步蹬空功，又叫空中走八步，前后练成此七大功法，轻身术需要二十年之久，学连成功很难，只有正直无私之人、心平气和之人、武德高尚之人、严遵清规戒约之人，才能真正得到师法真传。

练功秘方

川乌20克，草乌20克，桑寄生20克，五加皮20克，地骨皮20克，桂皮15克，乳香15克，没药15克，牛膝20克，鸡血藤20克，青风藤20克，海风藤20克，钩藤15克，透骨草15克，铁脚威灵仙20克，红花10克，黄芪15克，续断15克，丝瓜络20克，松林皮18克，槐树皮18克，柳树皮18克，杨树皮15克，青盐100克。

以上诸药，放上清水浸泡煎药水，温洗脚部和小腿，要在练功后洗脚，每一剂用20天后，另换新药再煎再洗。

功效：舒经络，坚肌肤和皮肉，壮骨骼，顺气血，加速功夫进展。

第三章

古法心意六合拳十大形的单练法
十大形的练法

古法心意六合拳十大形的单练法

根据鸡、猴、蛇、龙、燕、鹰、虎、马、鹞、，十种动物的活动形象，自卫搏斗和捕捉猎物时所具有的特殊技能，结合武术运动的攻防规律，演化成一个个武术方面巧妙的技能，取之为拳，成为人与人搏斗中的技艺，故言：远取诸物，和人以身形物之形，物之意以人意悟之。就是把动物的某种特长变为人的技能，称为心意六合拳的单练式。谱曰，“拳打卧牛之地”，无论是一步一式地练习，还是百步多式地练习，无论是在一米见方的地上练习，还是在百米场地上练习，都是从预备势开始，然后进入各种动作的练习，最后在预备势的位置上收势。

单练时，每一招，每一式，左右前后随动 ，根据个人身体素质而定，先练高架子，使初学者掌握动作的动力定型，然后随着功夫逐步上升再练中架子与低架子，使动作正确有力，练习时先慢而要稳、正确，后快而变化。先练柔后练刚，做到内外结合、刚柔相济、要点清楚、动作形象、动力明显。

Ten Forms of Single Practice of Ancient Xinyi Liuhequan

According to the active images of ten animals: chickens, monkeys, snakes, dragons, swallows, eagles, tigers, horses, harriers and bears, the special skills of self-defense fighting and catching prey, combined with the law of offensive and defensive Wushu, have evolved into ingenious skills in different kinds of Wushu, named as Quan, and become a skill in the boxing between people. The saying is: take everything from a distance, and people just use the shape of the body, the meaning of the thing is understood by the people's will. It means turning a certain specialty of an animal into a human skill, and this skill is named as the single practice style of Xinyi Liuhequan. Pu said, "Fisting the place where the cow lies", whether it is practiced step by step, or practiced in hundreds of steps; whether it is practiced on a one-meter square ground, or practiced on a 100-meter field, it is all starting from the preparatory position, then enter the practice of various movements, and finally finish with the finishing form in the place where the preparatory position started.

In single practice, each movement, each form, moving to left or right, forward or backward, are all according to personal physical fitness, first practice high frame, so that beginners can master the dynamics and freezing time of the movement, and then practice the middle frame and low frame as the ability of practicing Wushu gradually rises, so that the movements are correct and powerful. When practicing, first be slow, steady and correct, and then quicker with changes. Practice with soft strength first, and then with rigid strength, so as to achieve the combination of internal and external, rigid and soft, with clear main points, obvious movement images and motivation.

动物图（鸡）

动物图（猴）

动物图（蛇）

动物图（龙）

动物图（虎）

动物图（燕）

动物图（鹰）

动物图（马）

动物图（鹞）

动物图（熊）

十大形的练法

一、鸡形

谱曰，鸡有争斗之情。鸡为有智谋之物，生性善斗，鸡有独立之功，抓蹬之技又有抖翎之威、欺斗之勇。取之于拳，主要是取其有独立之功和抓蹬之技、抖翎之威和欺斗之勇，在发放爆发劲力时要和鸡斗，真正领得起、顶得实、竖得坚。

鸡形步，大合式，俗称预备式。也叫侵扑站，又叫扑来式，又称三体式，或称三才式。它要求鸡腿龙腰、熊背鹰抓、虎抱头及雷声。所说的大合是内外三合。

（1）左式：左手向上提与肩平，肘弯曲，虎口向内，五指分开朝下，两肘护肋，左手虎口向外翻，五指经胸前向腹部迅速插至左膝，同时两腿弯曲，两足前虚后实，小指一侧向前，掌心护住膝关节，肩与体的夹角保持 45 度左右，同时右手上提经左肘外侧手指朝上与左肩平，然后迅速往下拉至右胯，掌心护住胯关节，松肩沉肘，含

胸拔背，塌腰松胯，尾闾中正，谷边上提，舌舔上腭，呼吸顺其自然，周身上下合而为一，两足心要悬，三弯要照，三尖要对，三心要实，五指要抓。

鸡步图 2

先提左前足，向前迈进一步，右足紧追上前一大步，成右鸡步，身体姿势不变，左脚上前一大步成左鸡步，右脚随之前一大步成右鸡步如。

（2）鸡形步回身势：以左鸡步为例，左右两足同时以掌为肘碾地向右转体 180 度，成右鸡步，右手外翻，经体右侧上提与肩平，手指朝上，迅速经胸前向腹部插至右膝，小指一侧向前，掌心贴住右膝前，肩与体的夹角保持 45 度左右，同时左手上提经右肘外侧，手指朝上与右肩平，然后迅速往下拉至左胯，掌心护住胯关节，下巴对住右肩上方，目视前方。

（3）右式：右脚上前迈进一步，成右鸡步，右掌小指一侧向前，肩与体的夹角保持 45 度左右。要领：练鸡行步时，始终要注意三尖要对、三弯要照、三心要实、步子要大而稳，上步时脚尖上翘，脚跟落地后迅速渡到脚趾抓地，脚心要扣。行步要注意身体不起伏高低，

保持平衡，鸡行步回身势的转体同手脚的动作协调一致，外要自然放松，内要气沉丹田、呼吸自然。

鹰捉把收势，右鸡步，左脚上前一大步，右脚跟上半步，脚心悬空，五指抓地，成左鸡步。在左脚落地的同时，右手迅速经胸前用力插至左脚外侧，掌心贴住胯骨，左手上提到腮部，掌心朝外，两肋护肋，然后两足掌为轴，身向右转动 180 度，周身上下带突发抖劲，同时右手掌挑出，要求右掌带棚劲，高出于头，五指分开，掌心微向前，右足在前弓步，要求弓步不宜过大或过小，左掌同时从右腮边，边往左下按置于左胯根部带塌劲。

右脚退半步屈膝，右手同时从头上方往下收到咀前方，掌心向内，右肘紧贴右肋，左足向前迈步落于右足心成莲枝步，屈膝，左掌从左胯上抄到右肘傍顺右臂向前推出翻掌，右掌在前五指分开掌心微向前，左掌紧贴右手虎口，五指分开朝上，掌心微向前高出于头，左足前移成弓步，两掌同时猛力下按，左掌按至左膝内侧前，五指分开，右掌按至右胯根部护裆。同时腹部丹田贯意，以意催气，以气催声发出"咦"的一声。要求双掌下按时抓着天上的把柄，要将天扯塌。心意门中，此称为恨天无把，同时气冲天顶百会穴，舌顶上腭，口闭齿合，劲项要正直，下颚略向内收，眼睛平视前方。

鸡形摇闩把

六合式，俗称预备式。

如上图 1　　　　左式：如上例摇闪把

左脚向前上半步，脚趾抓地成右鸡步，同时左手右膝内侧前往后拉至右胯经肩，腮向前伸出，五指分开朝上，虎口向外与头同高，同时右手从右胯向前推出护在左肘下，虎口抵住尺骨咀，目视前方。然后右脚向前上一步，同时左掌向内翻，掌心向前，五指分开朝前方往下抓至右膝外侧到右胯经肩，腮向前伸出左绕环，肘弯曲，虎口向外五指分开朝上与头同高。右手在左手左绕环时一同往下抓至右胯，当左手向前伸出时，右手随之推出护在左肘下，虎口抵住尺骨鹰嘴咀，同时左脚向前迈进一大步，目视前方。

摇闩把回身势：以左式为例变右式，左右两足同时以掌为轴，同时碾地向右转体 180 度，左手由脸前向左肩侧伸出，右手随之在左小臂内侧经手背向前下方抓下，左脚上前一步，右掌由左膝外侧到右胯经肩，腮向前伸出左绕环，肘弯曲，虎口向外，五指分开朝上与头同高，左手在右手左绕环时以同往下抓至左胯，当右手向前伸出时，左手随之推出护右肘下、虎口抵住尺骨鹰嘴咀，同时右脚向前迈进一大步，目视前方。

收势：鹰捉把。

如上图 6

要领：练摇闩把时，手与脚要协调一致，手抓下时同身体的转动要一致，手臂向前绕环时小臂用意，手要贴住胯，肩，腮向前伸出，发劲时要呼吸自然，气沉丹田，外要沉肩坠肘，肩关节外顶，含胸拔背，身体正直。

鸡抖翎

六合式，俗称预备式。

熊出洞

左式：左脚向前迈进半步，右脚随之向前迈进一大步，右脚向前落地，脚趾抓地，左脚随之垫上半步，重心当在右足上成右鸡步。同时右手由左胯经右大腿内侧向前弹出，五指分开朝下，手背向后，两手心相对与胯平，两臂与体的夹角保持 45 度左右，两手微弯曲，目视前方。

鸡抖翎

鸡抖翎回身势：

以左式为例变右式。左右两足同时以掌为轴，同时碾地向右转体 180 度成右鸡步。右足向前迈进半步，左脚随之向前迈进一大步，左脚向前落地，脚趾抓地，右足随之垫上半步，重心当在左足上成左鸡步。同时左手由右胯经左大腿内侧向前弹出，五指分开朝下，手背向前，手指贯力。右手由前经右胯向右弹出，手背向右，两手心相对与胯平，两臂与体的夹角保持 45 度左右，两手微弯曲，目视前方。

收势：鹰捉把 （如上图）

要领：练鸡抖翎时，周身上下带突发抖弹劲，手臂发劲要顺，手指弹出要贯力，但又不能僵硬不用拙力，上步时身体重心挡在前足，步子要大而稳，要始终注意三尖照，回身势的转体动作要注意手脚的协调配合。要做到：外自然放松，内气沉丹田，百会顶，沉肩坠肘口脚心。

虎扑把

鸡啄米

六合式。俗称预备式。

熊出洞

左式：左脚向前迈出半步，右足紧追近至左脚右，同时右掌变拳由右胯从左掌内侧向前下方打出，高与脐平，掌面朝外，目视前方。然后左脚垫上半步，右足紧起向前落于左足前，左足随即迈半步在右足后，同时左掌变拳由左胯从右掌内侧向前方打出，高与脐平，掌面朝外，目视前方。如此两脚交替前进。

鸡啄米

鸡啄米：回身势，以右势为例，右脚往后退一步，两脚同时以掌为轴碾地向右转体 180 度变为左式。

收势：鹰捉把

要领：向前行步，两跨要向下催劲，身体不可过于前俯，要平稳不要忽高忽低，进步速度要快，向前打拳两肩极力催劲，使劲气贯于拳面。

虎扑把

寒鸡蹲架

六合式，俗称预备式

熊出洞

左脚先向前近击半步，右足紧追近至左脚内侧，稍内下屈，右脚提起，膝与胯平，紧靠于左腿内侧，脚尖向下，左足要实，右足要虚，含胸拔背。同时，右掌从右胯向上提至右脸外侧，五指朝上，小指外侧往下劈置于内侧小腹下,左掌由左膝内侧从下向脑前上伸。护于右脸外侧，掌心向外，且视前方。

然后，右脚向前垫上半步，左足紧追向前进一步，

寒鸡蹲架 2

右脚提起膝与胯平，紧靠于左腿内侧，脚交向下踮地。同时右掌从左膝内侧往后拉至于右胯向上提至右脸外侧，五指朝上，小指外侧往下劈置于右膝内侧小腹下,左掌由左膝内侧从下向胸前上伸，护于右脸外侧，掌心向外，目视前方。

寒鸡蹲架回身势

以左式为例变为右式。以左式右脚往后退一步，然后以两足掌为轴碾地向右转体 180 度，下巴内收对住右肩上方，同时右足向前垫半步，左足紧近至左足内侧脚尖踮地，同时，左掌从左胯向上提至左脸外侧，五指朝上，小指外侧往下劈置于左膝内侧小腹下，右掌由右膝内侧从下向胸前上伸，护于左脸外侧，掌心向外，目视前方。

收势：鹰捉把

要领：左掌上穿与右掌下劈动作要协调一致，劈掌要力贯掌指，周身紧而不僵，行步身体中正稳定，精神贯注。

虎扑把

金鸡报晓

六合式，俗称预备式。

熊出洞

左足向前迈进半步，右足随之向前进一打同时左手向前上方挑出，曲肘在前成坚掌，五指并拢掌指向上小指外侧向外，掌与额平随之手腕向下按之手指朝前。右手置于左肘下方掌心向下，目视前方。

金鸡报晓

随之左足向前迈出一步，落至右足前，同时左掌心朝里翻贴住右手臂外侧向上提到右手背，右手腕随之向上挑，掌指朝上掌心往里翻。然后，右后足再朝前迈出一步，落在左足前。同时右手掌手指朝里与手臂内侧成呈 90 度往左旋转掌指向前，左掌心按在右手背腕上。

金鸡报晓转身势：

两足掌为轴，身向左后方转体 180 度，同时，左手向前上方扫出掌指朝前与额平，右手置于左肘下方掌心向下。目视前方如图 23，

然后，右后足再朝前迈出一步，落至左足前。同时右掌心朝里翻贴住左手臂外侧向上提到左手背，左手腕随之向上挑掌，掌指朝上掌心往里翻。左足随即再朝前近击一步，落至右足前。同时左手掌手指朝里按与手臂内侧呈 90 度往右旋转掌指向前，右掌心按在左手背腕上。

收势：鹰捉把

要领：不论左（右）掌手指向上挑，往左（右）旋转朝前动作

要与步法协调一致。劲力贯指，周身柔而不僵身体中正稳定。内气沉丹田。

虎扑把

雄鸡闯群

六合式，俗称预备式

熊出洞

左足向前垫半步,右足紧追朝前迈出一大步,左足随之跟进半步,同时右手由右胯部经胸前向上钻出向前劈打，掌外缘向前，左手随之上提护在右手肘关节内侧，掌心抵住尺骨鹰嘴，目视前方。

雄鸡闯群

上势不停，左足继上一大步，右足随之跟进半步，同时左手向前方劈打右手按置于腹前,目视前方,三尖要照,三弯要对,三心要实。

雄鸡闯群转身势：

两足掌为轴，身向右后方转体 180 度，右足向前垫半步，左足紧追朝前迈出一大步，右足随之跟进半步，同时左手由左胯部胸前向上钻击向前劈打,掌外缘向前,右手随之上提护在左手肘关节内侧,掌心抵住尺骨鹰嘴。右足继上一大步，左足按置于腹前，三心要实，三尖要照，三弯要对。目视前方。

收势，鹰捉把

要领：练雄鸡闯群时，右（左）掌拳内旋，由胸前上钻于右（左）垫步，左（右）掌前劈与左（右）脚前进动作要协调一致，劈掌要含拱撞之劲，劲气贯注于掌。

虎扑把

雄鸡扑翅

六合式，俗称预备式

熊出洞

左足向左斜方垫上一步，右足紧追向前落于左足内侧，足尖抵地，同时右掌从右胯向上往下劈切，置于右膝外侧掌心护住膝关节。左掌由下向胸前上伸护于右腮边掌心向外。目视前方（如图 28）。随之右足尖外撇垫半步，左足紧追向前落于右足后，左掌下落置于右膝前，右掌随即收回置右胯，掌心护住胯骨。

雄鸡扑翅

然后，左足弧形上一步，右足紧起向前落于左内侧，同时右掌从右胯向上往下劈切，置于右膝外侧，掌心护住膝关节。左掌由下向胸前伸护于右腮边，掌心向外，目视前方。这样一步一式形成了圆圈。此式左右抖可以锻炼。

收势：鹰捉把

要领：练雄鸡扑翅时，手与足要协调一致，行步绕环时要依靠腰部的转动运动带动足，用意在掌梢节，掌由右胯向上往下劈切动作也要同身体转动下蹲协调。要注意身体正六合齐、呼吸自然、气沉丹田。

虎扑把

遛鸡腿

六合式，俗称预备式。

熊出洞

左足向外撇垫半步呈 45 度，右足紧追近置左足前。左掌从左膝迅速移至右胯往下插至右膝前，掌心往下。然后左后足再朝前呈弧形迈出一步，这时，右掌从右胯迅速移至左胯往下插至左膝前，掌心往下。左掌迅速收回到左胯，掌心护住左胯。目视前方（如图 31）。

遛鸡腿

遛鸡腿 2

这样一步一式形成了圆圈，此式左右都可以锻炼。

收势：鹰捉把

要领：练遛鸡腿时，手与足左右要协调一致，手掌往下插时同身体的转动要一致，手掌用意，插劲时要呼吸自然，六合要齐，气沉田。

虎扑把

二、鹰形

谱曰，鹰有提物之精。

鹰是飞禽中凶猛、狠毒之物。有晢目可察细微之物，放爪能有攫获之精。取之于拳主要在于锻炼手上指爪的功夫，即身猛合一的劲气。《拳经”中云：虎威鹰猛，以爪为锋总是以利步之威而获胜。可见在练习鹰形时功夫主要应关注在指上。

(1) 饿鹰捉食（苍鹰捕兔）

(2) 六合式，俗称预备式。

熊出洞

左足向左斜前方 45 度垫半步，同时身体向左侧，右足紧起向前落于左足后，右手随之从右胯向左上方斜线抛出，掌心向下至额前方停住，左掌置于右肘下方，掌心向下（如图 32）。

然后，右掌往下按至胸部掌心朝里向外翻，虎口向上，手背朝外高出于头，手臂弯曲。左掌置于右肘下方。右掌迅速往胸腹部撩出，五指分开，手背向前贯力。左掌回收到左胯部，掌心护住左胯。

这时右掌迅速往上抄掌心向里至于头高。左掌迅速从左胯向上抄到右肘傍顺右臂内侧向前推出双手翻掌。左掌在右掌虎口上五指分开，同时，右足迅速提膝，左足蹬地腾空跳起在空中变成鸡步落地时双掌要往下抓，左手在前，右手在后，双腿下蹲。

然后。右后足向右斜方呈 45 度垫半步，同时身体向右侧，左足挑起向前落于右足后，左手随之从左膝前向后上方斜线劈出，掌心向下至额前方停住。右掌置于左肘下方，掌心朝下，然后，左掌往下按至胸部掌心朝里向外翻,虎口向上,手背朝外高出于头手臂弯曲。右掌置于左肘下方，(如图 37)，左掌迅速往胸腹部向外撩出，五指分开。手背向前贯力。右掌回收到右胯，掌心护住右胯部。(如图 38)，这时左掌迅速往上抄掌心向里至于头高。右掌迅速从右胯向上抄到左肘旁顺左臂内侧向前推出双手翻掌朝外。右掌在左掌虎口上五指分开。同时，左足迅速提膝，右足蹬地腾空跳起在空中变成右鸡步落地时双掌往下抓，右手在前，左手在后，双腿下蹲。

饿鹰捉食转身势：

以右式为例，两足掌为轴，同时碾地向左转体 180 度。

收势：鹰捉把。

要领：练饿鹰捉食时，当左或（右）足向前左（右）斜前方迈出半步时，手与足要协调一致，两手合要快，翻掌要疾，眼光要准，起落要分明，上跳要高，用意在膝，手抓下时的劲要顺，落要缩身。并同脚步落地一致。

虎扑把

寒鹰蹲架

六合式，俗称预备式。

熊出洞

左手移至右胯，右掌同时由右胯向上提到左腮旁边，掌心朝外，手指向上。然后左足上前近进半步，右足紧起向前落于左足后，同时，两手双掌迅速经胸前向身体两侧展开，左手与右手掌心相对右手高于头平，左手与胸平。

寒鹰登架

左腿继上前迈半步，右步紧追近至足前上方提膝，足跟着地，脚尖上翘，重心当在左脚上，左腿弯曲（大小腿的夹角保持 90 度左右），向左转体 180 度。右手伸直，自上而下劈至左腿内侧，手指朝下，肘关节与大腿平，左掌同时收至右腮旁边与肩之间，掌心朝腮，肘贴住肋侧，目视前方。

寒鹰登架 2

右足落地，左脚随之向前一步，脚尖上翘，同时，右手自下向上挑起伸直，至头右侧前上方，还原至下劈前的姿势，左手掌心朝下，同时下按至裆前，向右转体 180 度左右，目视前方。

寒鹰登架 3

寒鹰蹲架四身势：

左足往右退一步，右手收到左腮旁边，掌心朝腮。同时左掌移至右胯，掌心护住胯部，然后，两脚掌为轴，身向左右方转体 180 度，右后脚紧追近至左足前。同时，两手双掌迅速经胸前向身体两侧展开，右手与左手掌心相对左手高于头平，右手与胸平，目视前方。

然后，右脚继上前近半步，左足紧近至右足前上方提膝，足跟着地，脚交上翘，重心当在右脚上，右腿弯曲（大小腿的夹角为 90 度左右）。向右转体 180 度，左手伸直，自上而下劈至右腿内侧，手指朝下，肘关节与大腿平，右掌同时收至左腮旁边与肩之间，掌心朝腮，肘贴住肋侧，目前前方。

收势：鹰捉把

要领：练寒鹰蹲架动作时，两手双掌迅速经胸前向身体两侧展开动作与步子要一致。后手的大劈要伸直，依靠身体转动，沉肩下

劈，同时与膝的上提要合，身体要正，不能前仰后俯，支撑腿要稳，要气沉丹田，三尖相照，上挑时全神贯注，起落分明。

虎扑把

老鹰磨云

六合式，俗称预备式。

熊出洞

右足向右后方退一步，随之左足紧起向后退半步脚尖抵地，身体微起，同时左手向下沿着右腿外侧经右胯往上擦过右手臂内侧右额角上方绕环至左额前掌心向上，肘微弯曲，稍低于肩，右手随之从右胯向上提拉到胸掌心向下。

老鹰磨云

左足上前迈一步，右足随之跟上半步。右手由胸外翻，掌心向上，右肘尖抵住左肋，认肘关节为轴向身体左侧扫击至右肩，右胯的直线上，同时左手随之内翻，掌心向下，回收到胸前，目视前方。

老鹰磨云回身势：以右式为例，两脚掌为轴，同时碾地向左转体 180 度，右脚随之向右后腿一步，左足紧起向后脚尖抵地，身体微起，左手向下沿着右腿外侧经右胯往上擦过右手内侧，右额角上方绕环至左额前掌心向上，肘微曲，稍低于肩，目视前方鹰抓把（收势）。

要领：练老鹰魔云动作时，动作要连贯，经由下向上，手向外分时同步一致，掌内外绕环外翻，用意在于虎口与外手臂。整个动作要呼吸自然，身体正直，劲贯手臂，气沉丹田。

虎扑把

雄鹰展翅

六合式，俗称预备式。

熊出洞

左脚上前半步，右脚随之上前一大步，向左转体 180 度，成右鸡步。两掌变拳自右胯左右两侧交叉插下，左手在前，右手在后，护在裆前，下巴对住右肩侧上方，目视前方。上势不停，右足上前半步，左侧伸直，成右弓步。两手变掌，经胸前向身体两侧展开，掌心向下，同胯齐平，臂与体的夹角保持 45 度左右，头向右转体 90 度朝前击出，下颚内收，头与胸平，目视前方。

雄鹰展翅

雄鹰展翅回身势：

以左式为例，两脚以掌为轴，同时碾地，向右转体 180 度，随之，右脚上前半步，左足随之上前一大步，同时两掌变拳自左右两侧交叉插下，左手在前，右手在后，护在裆前，下巴对住右肩侧下方，平视前方。

收势；鹰捉把

要领：练雄鹰展翅时，两掌变拳插下时意在肩。架子不宜过低，身体不要太前倾。两手向后分的动作要利用身体 的贯力与头同进去，头的用意在前额。腰要塌，肩要松，呼吸自然，虚领顶颈。

虎扑把

龙形，谱曰，龙右搜骨之法，龙传说时一种生活在水旱之间的两栖动物，它既右搜骨之法又有蛰升腾，既有三曲之方，又有飞腾之技。在买式心意拳中之所以要强调体现龙身（腰）。就是在吞身蓄气时犹如龙体之蛰伏，有储而待发之意，起身进攻时犹如龙之升腾，有冲天之雄，蛰是为了起得更迅速，合是为了开得更猛烈，吞是为了吐得更充分，没有劲气的集储就不会有劲力的发放，没有吞身之伏，就没有变化之灵，所以在心意拳的每一个过渡动作中都要体现出龙腰（身）的特点来。

三，龙形盘劈

六合式，俗称预备式。

熊出洞

左足上前左方垫一步，足尖外撇，右足紧起向前落于左足后，同时左掌由膝前经过胸前向前，经右手背向前推出虎口向外，当左手向前伸击时，右手随之伸出，护在左肘下，虎口抵住尺骨鹰嘴，然后左手翻掌往下回收到左胯掌心护住胯关节，右手从尺骨鹰嘴向前往下插劈到大腿外侧至左胯，手臂贴住大腿中部，两腿下蹲往下坐盘，右肩向左转体 180 度。

龙形大劈

右脚再朝前右方迈出一步，脚尖外撇，左足紧起向前落于右足后，同时右手从左胯大腿外侧经左胯，肩，腮向前伸击，右手掌与脸同高，虎口朝前，臂稍弯曲与右肩平，左手随之护在左肘下，虎口抵住尺骨鹰嘴，右掌往下回收到左胯，同时左手从尺骨鹰嘴上向前往下插劈到大腿外侧至右胯。手臂贴住大腿中部，两往下盘坐，左肩向右转体 180 度。

龙形盘劈回身势：

两足掌为轴，身向右后方转动 180 度。左掌顺势转至头顶右部上侧往下收至左胯，掌心护住胯骨，同时右手由右胯上举经右耳侧，用力向左侧劈下，手臂贴住左大腿外侧中部，两腿往下盘坐，右肩向左转体 180 度，平视前方。

收势：鹰捉把

要领：练龙形盘劈时，手与脚的动作要协调一致。插劈与身体同时转动，肩要顶，用意在肩，手经胸部插劈至胯部，要随步而发，三尖相对，后手护胯。呼吸自然，气沉丹田，沉肩坠肘。

虎扑把

龙形裹风

六合式，俗称预备式。

熊出洞

左脚向左斜前方 45 度上迈进一步，右脚随之紧追近至左脚前，脚尖上翘，同时身体向右侧半面转。左手移至右胯。内翻经体右侧，头前向左侧前方伸出，掌心向前，成龙爪手，肘稍弯曲，手掌与面部同高，下巴对住右肩侧上方，目视前方。

龙形裹横

左手向下收至右胯，掌心护住胯骨，右手向右上方经过头前至右肩上方，掌心向前下方成十字手。同时，左脚上前一步，脚尖上翘，重心当在后脚，平视前方，右脚上前半步。同时，从腰部发力身体向左扫转，脚掌不动。右手以肘关节为轴，外翻在腰转动的同时，向左平扫至左胯与左肩垂直线上，掌心向上，左手在右手平扫的同时，护于右肘内侧，虎口对住肘尖，下巴对住左肩侧平视前方，右脚向右斜前方 45 度上迈进一步，左脚随之紧追近至左足前。脚尖上翘，同时身体向左侧半面转，右手内翻经体左侧，头部向右倾前方伸出，掌心向前，成龙爪手，肘稍弯曲，手掌面部同高，左手内翻，掌心向下经体左侧自然上摆至与肩同高，下巴对住右肩侧上方，平视前方。

右手向下收至左胯，掌心护住胯骨，左手向左上方经头前摆至右肩上方，成十字手。同时，右脚上前一步，脚尖上翘，重心当在左脚平视前方。

右脚向前 半步，同时，从腰部发力，上身向右扭转 120 度左右，足掌不动。左手以肘关节为轴内翻，在腰转动的同时，护于右肘内侧，虎口对住肘尖，下巴对住右肩侧上方，平视前方。

龙形裹风回身势：以右式为例。

两脚以掌为轴，同时碾地，向左转体 180 度，在脚随之向左斜前方 45 度上一步，右脚上前一步，脚尖上翘，身体左侧半面转。左手内翻经经体右侧，头部向右侧前方伸出，掌心向前，成龙爪手，肘稍弯曲，手掌与面部同高，右手内翻，经体右侧自然上摆，掌心向下，与肩同高，下巴对住左肩侧上方，平视前方。

收势，鹰捉把

要领：练龙形裹风要做到手脚上下配合，手法、身法、步法协调连贯。成十字手，用意在肩。裹风时要由腰部的转动来带动手的摆动。整个动作要稳，颈要顺，在内要注意呼吸自然、六合相贯、三尖照、三心实、三弯对。

虎扑把

乌龙摆尾

六合式，俗称预备式。

熊出洞

左足向前迈进一步。右足随之紧追近至左足前，同时向左转体180度，左后。

脚再朝前迈出一步，落至右足前。右掌由右胯向上外摆经腹部收至左胯，掌心护住胯骨，左掌同时朝左前方稍后摆，腰部发力，下巴对住左肩侧上方，平视前方。

龙摆尾

然后，左脚上前垫一步，右脚紧追进至左足前。随之，左后脚再朝前迈出一步，落至右足前，右脚紧起向前落于左足后。同时向左转体 45 度，右手由左胯下经身体左侧，自胸部下达到腹部，左手同时从左侧经腹部迅速插至右胯，掌心护住胯关节上身向左扭转 120 度左右，腰部发力，脚掌不动。左右两手随之腰向外摆，左手背朝外，右手掌心向内收至左肘内侧，平视前方。

龙摆尾 2

右式与左式练法相反。

乌龙摆尾转身势：以右式为例。

两足掌为轴，同时踬地，向左转体180度，同时，左手收回到左膝，右手内翻到右胯，掌心护住胯骨，下巴对住左肩侧上方，平视前方。

收势；鹰捉把

虎扑把

游龙探爪

六合式，俗称预备式。

熊出洞

左脚上前垫半步，右足紧追近至足前，同时向左转体 180 度，右手由右胯向外摆经腹部收至左胯，掌心护住胯骨，左手同时由左膝往后摆，虎口对住胯骨，下巴对住右肩侧上方右脚上前斜放垫一步，左右紧起向前落于右足后，重心当在右足中，同时，右转体 180 度，右手由左膝外翻，经右侧头部至左肩侧上方，掌心向内，从上往下抓收至右胯，左手迅速从左胯经腹部，胸前向外谈出。平视前方。

然后，左右脚再向前迈出一步，落至右足前，同时，左掌自头部往下摆，收至右胯，掌心护住胯骨，右手同时往后摆，虎口对住胯骨，下巴对住左肩侧上方左脚上前斜方垫一步，右脚紧起向前落于左脚后，重心当在左脚中，同时左转体 180 度，左手由右胯外翻，经左侧头部至右肩侧上方，掌心向内，从上往下抓收至左胯。右手迅速从右胯经腹部，胸前外探击，平视前方。

青龙探爪

游龙探爪转身势：

以右式为例，两足掌为轴，身向右转 180 度。同时，右掌自头部往下摆，收至左胯，掌心护胯骨，左手同时往后摆，虎口对住胯骨，下巴对住右肩侧上方，平视前方。

收势：鹰捉把

虎扑把

云龙三现

六合式，俗称预备式。

熊出洞

右脚向左前方垫一步，右脚紧起向前落于左脚后，足掌抵地，身体微起，重心当在左足中，同时左转体 180 度，右手从右胯向右

上方经头前至左肩上方，手心向下。左手置于右肘内侧，随之右掌往下外翻，掌心向上。左手往上内翻。然后，右掌往胸中抽回绕环抛出。手心朝外，掌心向上。平视前方。

左掌置于右肘下方，随之，右后脚在朝向前斜方迈出一步，左脚紧起向前落于左足后，两腿同时下蹲，然后，右掌往左头部上侧经胸部。以两手腕关节为轴经胸前，右手在上，左手在下，掌心朝内绕环，左手下插到右膝外侧，右手上踢到左腮旁边。掌心向外，五指分开。

金龙盘柱

1. 右式与左式练法相反。

2. 云龙三现转身势。

以右式为例，两足掌为轴，同时踉地。身向右后方转动 180 度，左掌由右腮边自然放下经腹部前收至左胯，掌心护住胯骨。右手由左膝外侧经右大腿内侧向前击出，至右膝前停住，小手指一侧向前，五指分开。臂与体的夹角保持 45 度左右，平视前方。

收势：鹰捉把

虎扑把

要领：练云龙三现时，手脚要协调，动作连贯，升降自然，往前三直而起，往后三直而落。

大龙形

六合式，俗称预备式。

熊出洞

左脚向前垫一步，右脚随之紧追近至左足前。同时向左转体 180 度。左手由左膝前稍后摆。虎口对住胯骨后 20 厘米左右处，右手由下经体右侧，自头部、左肩擦下。收至左胯，掌心护住胯骨，下巴对住右肩侧上方，平视前方。然后，左后足再朝前迈出一步，落至右足前。同时，向右转体 180 度。左手由下经体左侧，自头前，右肩擦下收至右胯。掌心护住胯骨，右手同时经腹部后摆至右胯后 20 厘米左右处，虎口对住胯骨，下巴对住左肩侧上方，平视前方。左脚再向前迈进一步，右脚随之上前一大步。同时，向左转体 180 度，两手外翻，由体右侧向上举至额头上方，肘稍弯曲。稍高于肩。掌心相对，两手似棒球状，相距 20 厘米左右，下巴对住右肩侧上方，平视前方。

大龙形

1. 右式与左式练法相反。

2. 大龙形转身势：

以右式为利，两足掌心为轴，同时碾地，身向左后方转动 180 度，左脚随之向前垫一步，然后，右足再朝前迈出一步，落至右足前。向左转体 180 度，左手由体左侧自然放下。经腹前收至左胯后，五指分开，虎口对住胯骨，右手由上经，左肩擦下，收至左胯，掌心护住胯骨，下巴对住右肩侧上方，平视前方。

收势、鹰捉把

虎扑把

要领：练大龙形时。身法、手法、步法要协调连贯。左右擦肩时，身体要转，手的摆动也要靠腰的转动来带动。用意在肩。两手上举时肘关节发力，不要挺腹，挺胸，要含胸拔背。整个动作要呼吸自然，气沉丹田。

双龙戏珠

六合式，俗称预备式。

熊出洞

左掌收至腹下，五指分开，掌心向上。右掌由右胯上伸胸前掌心向下。同时左足向前迈进一步，成左弓步。左掌由下向上外翻，掌心向外，五指分开，高于头平，右掌同时也向前撑出。掌心向左下方置于左轴下方，平视前方。

二龙抢珠

然后，左足再朝前斜方垫一步。右脚紧起向前落于左足后，同时左掌收回到胸，掌心向下，五指分开。右掌外翻，手置于腹部下。平视前方。

随之，右脚向右斜前方 90 度迈进一步。同时，右掌由下向上外翻。掌心向外，五指分开，高与头平。左掌叶同时向前撑出。掌心向右下方置于右肘下方，平视前方。

紧接，右脚再朝前斜方垫一步，左脚紧齐向前落于右脚后。同时右掌收到胸前，掌心向下，五指分开，左掌外翻收置于腹下，平视前方。

1. 双龙戏珠转身势：

以右式为例。两足掌为轴，同时踉地。身向左后方转动 180 度，

左脚在前，右脚在后。左掌迅速用力向前经裆前，左腿内侧向前击出，至左膝停住，小指一侧向前。臂与体的夹角保持 45 度左右，右掌迅速收回至右胯，五指分开，掌心抵住胯骨，平视前方。

2. 收势；鹰抓把

虎扑把

要领：双龙戏珠练习在于手脚整齐。提掌抱珠时两肘要紧贴两肋。双掌相对成珠状。两肩要沉，两肘要坠，出掌时，手指领先，要依靠腰的转动发力，通过肩、肘关节向前催力，弓步要圆裆撑胯，要含胸拔背，气沉丹田，做到手脚齐到，才为真。

龙抢珠

六合式，俗称预备式。

熊出洞

左足向左斜前方 90 多迈进一步。成左弓步，右掌由左胯提到胸前，虎口向外，同时，左掌由左膝向上提架，掌心向外翻，身体向左转体 45 度左右，右掌在胸前变剑指向外击出。平视前方。

随之，左脚向前垫一步，右脚紧追向右斜前方 90 度迈出一步，左脚紧起向前落于右脚后。右手剑指里翻回收到右，然后，外翻提架右侧额前变成龙爪，同时，左掌由左侧额前里翻回收到左肋，经胸部变剑指向前击出，平视前方。

二龙戏珠

二龙抢珠转身式。

以右式为例，两脚掌为轴，同时蹍地，身向左后方转体 180 度，左脚在前，右脚在后，左掌迅速用力向前经裆前，左脚内侧向前击出，至左膝停住，小指一侧向前，臂与体的夹角保持 45 度左右，右掌从右额前迅速收回至右胯，五指分开，掌心抵住胯骨，成六合式，平视前方。

收势；鹰捉把

虎扑把

要领：练二龙抢珠时，手臂提架要滚，顺劲。手指击出要贯力。手指击出要贯力，上步时身体重心当在前脚，步子要大而稳。要始注意三尖照。转身时的动作要注意手脚协调配合。

虎形：谱曰，虎有拨战之勇。虎为兽中之王，虎行风生，威在蹲山。搜林为最，以虎为山林之王，山林者虎之势也失其势则威难发。然则虎之威究何威也？买式祖曰：收纵以扑，转侧以掀，贯用三绝，掉尾如歉。以三绝而伏众兽，是虎威之师在也。虎形之劲起于尾闾，而循督上升，补还于脑。云从龙，风从虎。虎形与龙形轮回相属，能够起到通任开督之促进作用。龙为真阴，虎为真阳故二形又谓之阴阳相配。

四、虎扑把

六合式，俗称预备式。

熊出洞

左足向左斜方45度迈进一步，右脚随之紧追迈至左脚前，身体下蹲，腿稍弯曲。然后，左足再朝前迈出一步，落至右脚前。提膝至于胯平，脚尖上翘。同时右掌从右胯提至胸部，左掌从左胯经，右肘内侧下插至右胯，手背沿右大腿外侧，向左大腿上方挑起，治左膝上方，五指分开，虎口向上。左肘弯曲，抵住左侧肋下，右掌也迅速收至右胯，掌心护住胯骨。平视前方。

然后，左脚上前垫一步，成左弓步。在左脚向前上步同时，两掌迅速内翻向前推出，两拇指相叠，掌心向前与胸同高，肘稍弯曲，两肘夹紧，距离保持一拳左右，平视前方。

左脚随之再迈出一步，身体下蹲，腿稍弯曲，身体向右斜方转90度。右后脚紧起向前落于左脚前。提膝至与胯平，脚尖上翘，同时左掌从胸部前收回，右掌由左肘内侧下插至左胯，手背沿左大腿外侧，向右大腿上方挑起，至右膝上方，五指分开，虎口向上，右肘弯曲，抵住右侧肋下，左掌也迅速收至右胯，掌心护住胯骨，平视前方。

然后，右脚上前垫一步，成右弓步，在右脚向前上步同时，两掌迅速内翻向前推出，两拇指相叠，掌心向前与胸同高，肘稍弯曲，两肘夹紧，距离保持一拳左右，平视前方。

虎抓把转身势：

以右式为例，两脚掌为轴，同时踬地，身向左后方转体 180 度，左脚向左斜前方迈进一步，身体下蹲，腿稍弯曲，右脚紧追迈至左脚前。提膝至与胯平，脚尖上翘，左手随身体左转，从右胯经右肘内插，手背沿右大腿外侧，向左大腿上方挑起，至左膝上方，虎口向上，左肘弯曲，抵住左侧肋部，下巴对住左肩上方，平视前方。

收势；鹰扑把

虎扑把

要领：练虎扑把时要注意两拇指相叠，虎口圆，两掌随身体下降，前后相对，当掌心向前推出，用意在掌根。两手推出要同脚上步落地同时完成，手臂要保持圆弧。在外要注意身体正，顶百会，提尾宫，沉肩坠肘，力要提到手指，呼吸自然，气沉丹田。

虎摆尾，虎蹬山

六合式，俗称预备式。

熊出洞

左脚向左斜前方 45 度迈进一步，右脚紧追迈左脚前。然后，左后脚再朝前迈出一步，落至右脚前，成左弓步，同时，向左转体 90 度。两手再体右侧下合掌，掌心相对，随之由体右侧经腹，胸向左随身体左转摆动，与左肩，左脚在一个平面上，左手与肩同高，虎口向上，右手摆至胸前时沿左臂内侧收至左肘内侧，掌心对住左手臂内侧，肘贴住右肋，平视前方。

虎摆尾

紧接，左脚向右斜前方 45 度迈进一步，身体下蹲，腿稍弯曲，右脚随之紧追迈至左脚前，提膝至胯平，脚尖上翘，向右转体 90 度。右手在左肘内侧下插至左胯，经右大腿内侧向前出击，到右膝前停住，五指分开，小指一侧向前，臂与体的夹角保持 45 度左右，左手随身体右转收至左胯，掌心护住胯骨，下巴对住右肩侧上方，平视前方。

虎驻山

然后，右脚向右斜前方迈进一步，左脚追迈至右脚前，随之右后脚再朝前迈出一步，落至左脚前，提膝至与胯平，脚尖上翘，右手在左肘内侧下插至左胯，手背沿左大腿外侧向右大腿上方挑起，至右膝上方，虎口向上，右肘弯曲，抵住右侧肋部，左手随身体步伐向前，右手上挑时随之收至左胯，掌心护住胯骨。右脚向前落步，成右弓步，同时，向右转体 90 度。两手再体左侧下合掌，掌心相对，由体左侧经腹，胸向右，随身体右转摆至右肩，右脚的平面上。右手与肩同高，虎口向上，左手摆至胸前时沿右臂内侧收至右肘内侧，掌心护住右手臂内侧，左肘贴住左肋，平视前方。

然后，右脚向 45 度前方迈进一步，身体下蹲，腿稍弯曲，左脚随之上前迈至右脚前，提膝至胯平，脚尖上翘，向左转体 90 度，左手在右肘内侧下插至右胯，经左大腿内侧向前出击，到左膝前停住，五指分开，不指一侧向前，臂与体的夹角保持 45 度左右，右手随身体左转收至右胯，掌心护住胯骨，下巴对住左肩侧上方，平视前方。

随之，左脚向左斜前方迈进一步，右脚紧追迈至左脚前，随之左后脚再朝前迈出一步，落至右脚前，提膝至与胯平，脚尖上翘，左手在右肘内侧下插自右胯，手背沿右大腿外侧向左大腿上方挑起，至左膝上方，虎口向上，左肘弯曲，抵住左侧内部，右手随身体步伐向前，左手上挑时，随之收至右胯，掌心护住胯骨。下巴对住左肩上方，平视前方。

虎蹬山，虎摆尾转身势：

以右式为例，两足掌为轴，同时踞地，身体左后方转体 180 度。两手自然放下至体左侧。左脚向左斜前方 45 度迈进一步，脚尖上翘，右脚紧追迈至左脚前。然后，左后脚再朝前迈出一步，落至右脚前，

成左弓步，同时，向右转体 90 度。两手在体左侧合掌，掌心相对，由体左侧经腹，胸随身体向左转摆至左肩，右脚平面上。左手与肩同高，虎口向上，右手摆至胸前时，沿左手臂内侧收至左肘内侧，虎口向上，右肘贴住右肋，平视前方。

手势；鹰捉把

虎扑把

要领：练虎摆尾，虎蹲山时，要注意手的摆动同身体的转动协调一致，身体要正，并且手的摆出要与脚的落地方向一致。手臂的外侧要用力，手臂要呈圆弧。摆动要连贯，做到身法、手法、步法上下连贯，上步要快，下蹲时步子要稳，身体不要前俯后仰，手的上挑动作同提膝要同时完成。呼吸自然，气沉丹田，内外相合，三尖对，三湾照，三心实，三意连。

单虎抱头

六合式，俗称预备式。

熊出洞

左脚向前垫一步，右脚紧追迈至左脚前，然后，左右脚再朝前迈出一步，落至右脚前，脚尖翘，重心由在右脚中。右手由右胯，经体右侧提起至与头同高，虎口向上，左手随之从右肘外侧伸出上提，手指按住左额，肋用力外顶与肩平，手指朝后，右手同时收至左肘下，虎口抵住肘尖，掌心向下，下巴抵住左肩侧上方，平视前方。

虎报头

然后，左脚向前垫一步，右脚随之紧追迈至左脚前，同时，左转体 90 度，右手经左肘内侧上，伸至头上方，同时翻掌，右掌在前，左掌在后，掌心向外，两掌猛力下按，右掌按至右膝内侧边，左掌按至左胯根部护裆。平视前方。

右式与左式练法相反。

单虎抱头转身势：

以右式为例，两足掌为轴，同时蹍地，身向后方转体 180 度，左足向前垫上一步，右脚随之紧追迈至左脚前，脚尖上翘，重心留在左脚，向左转体 90 度，左手由左胯，经体左侧提起至与头同高，虎口向上，右手随之从左肘外侧伸出上提，手指按住右额角，肋用力外顶，与肩平，手指朝后，左手同时收至右肘下，虎口抵住肘尖，掌心向下，下巴对住右肩侧上方。

收势；鹰捉把

虎扑把

要领：练单虎抱头时，肘要用力外顶，身体要与出手和步法协调一致。两掌猛力下按，要在劲气上分清阴阳，急速有力，动静分明，起势如崩墙倒，落地如树载根，它十分重视动作起落的均衡稳定。

双虎抱头

六合式，俗称预备式。

熊出洞

左脚上前垫一步，右脚紧追迈至左脚前，脚尖上翘，重心留在左脚，同时，向左转体 45 度，面对前方，双掌相对，两肘与肩平并间隔两拳左右，肘用力向前顶，平视前方。

双虎报头

然后，右脚向前迈进一步，左脚紧起迈至右脚前，成左弓步。同时双掌用力下方抛下，左掌按至左膝内侧边，右掌按至右胯根部护裆，平视前方。

右式与左式练法相反。

双虎抱头转身势：

以右式为例，双脚掌为轴，同时蹶地，身体起立，左转180度，右脚随之上前一步，脚尖上翘，重心留在左脚。双掌由下经腹，胸前提至额角两侧，手心相对，两肘与肩平，间隔两拳左右，肘用力向前顶，平视前方。

收势；鹰捉把

虎扑把

要领：练双虎抱头时，两手上提，两肩要扣，脊背要圆，则前胸空阔，气力到肘。外形并且要夹紧，手背向前，两脚虚实分明，双掌向前下方抛时，都必须是腕部向下屈曲踏沉，掌心向着前下方，既要有向前顶的劲。五指分开，拇指向外撑，使虎口形成半圆，掌心内涵，手背要微扣，手的各个部位都不可松软。正如吾师所说：“手背要扣”“则气力到手”“虎口要圆，手有裹抱之力”。击掌并且要同弓步的落地协调一致，注意外三合遂，内三合提，心要动。

白虎搜山

六合式，俗称预备式。

熊出洞

左脚向左斜前方 45 度垫上一步，右脚紧追迈至左脚前，然后，左脚紧起向前落于右脚前，成左弓步，同时，右掌从右胯，经腹，胸部前向外翻掌，掌心向上，左掌从左膝内侧，由下自腹经右肘内侧向外翻掌，掌心向上，掌背紧靠右肘内侧，随之，左肩向右转体 45 度，双掌内翻，掌心向下，左手掌心顺右臂外侧向左斜前方 90 度摆去。至左膝上方，肘稍弯曲，掌心向下，肘与肋相距一拳左右，右手随之护在左肘下，虎口抵住尺骨鹰嘴，下巴对住左肩，平视前方，三尖照。

白虎搜山 1

紧接，右脚向右斜前方 90 度迈进一步，成右鸡步，左脚紧追迈至右脚前。然后，右后脚再朝前迈出一步，落至左脚前，成右弓步。同时，身体稍向左转体 45 度，左掌从左胯，经腹，胸部前向外翻掌，掌心向上，右掌从右膝内侧，由下自腹经左肘内侧向外翻掌，掌心向上，手背紧靠左肘内侧，随之，双掌内翻，掌心向下，右掌心顺左臂外侧向右斜前方 90 度扑去。至右膝上方，肘稍弯曲，掌心向下，肘与肋相距一拳左右，左手随之护在右肘下，虎口抵住尺骨鹰嘴，下巴对住右肩，平视前方，三尖照

白虎搜山 2

白虎搜山转身势：

以右式为例，左脚以后跟为轴，右脚以掌为轴，同时蹍地，向左转体 180 度，左脚随之向左斜前方 45 度迈进一步，成弓鸡步。右脚紧追迈至左脚前。然后，左后脚再朝前迈出一步，落至右脚前，成左弓步。同时，右掌从右胯，经腹，胸前向外翻掌，掌心向上，左掌从左膝内侧，由下自腹经右肘内侧向外翻掌，掌心向上，掌背紧靠右肘内侧，随之，左肩向右转体 45 度，双掌内翻，掌心向下，左掌心顺右臂外侧向左斜前方 90 度摆出，至左膝上方，肘稍弯曲，掌心向下，肘与肋相距一拳左右，右手随之护在左肘下，虎口抵住尺骨鹰嘴，下巴对住左肩，平视前方。

收势；鹰捉把

虎扑把

要领：练白虎搜山时，手与脚要协调一致，所有的变招换式，左旋右转，都是着与周身的完整和协调。如果腰部松软无力，脊背歪斜不正，整个动作就会失去失掉中心，因此，身体要正，步法要活，呼吸自然，劲力顺达，摆掌要气沉丹田。

虎形盘肘

六合式，俗称预备式。

熊出洞

左脚向前迈进一步，左手由左膝内侧经体右侧向上托起至与头同高，掌心向前上方盖出成虎爪，肘稍弯曲，右掌从右胯提到右胸前曲肘，然后，右后脚紧追迈至左脚前。同时，右肘向前方由上往下砸去。左手外翻，掌心朝上，置于右肘小臂内侧上。左足紧起向前落于右脚后。三尖相照，平视前方。

然后，右脚随之再迈出一步，右手由胸经体左侧头部向前方盖出，掌心向前成虎爪，肘稍弯曲。左手由左胯提到左胸前曲肘，随之左脚再朝前迈出一步，落至右脚前。同时，左肘向前方由上往下砸去。右手外翻，掌心朝上，置于左肘小臂内侧上，右后脚紧起向前落于左足后，三尖相照，平视前方

右式与左式练法相反

虎形盘肘转身势

以右式为例，两脚掌为轴，同时踚地，身向左后方转体 180 度，成左鸡步。左脚向前方垫上一步，左手由左膝内侧经体右侧向上托起至于肩同高，掌心向前方盖出成虎爪，肘稍弯曲，右掌从右胯提到右胸前曲肘，然后，右后脚紧追迈至左脚前。同时，右肘向前方，由上往下砸去。左手外翻，掌心朝上置于右肘小臂内侧上。左足紧起向前落于右脚后，三尖相照，平视前方。

收势；鹰捉把

虎扑把

要领：练虎形盘肘，手脚要协调配合，肘分左右两拳，肘在心意语中称为二门，它不但促进了上肢的舒展，并且使上肢的关节肌肉产生了一股争衡力量。动作起来沉稳扎实有力，当掌心向前方盖出成虎爪，要注意三尖照，六合齐，呼吸自然，虚领顶颈，步子要灵活。

（五）熊形，谱曰，熊有护身之本

熊在动物中是最钝笨之物，但其膀力和臂力，掌力却是十分有力量，可以在横拳、斩捶中的裹劲和拨动，都是用的这种劲力。

取诸于拳，横格，裹拨，钻斩，均以克制对方为主，而熊膀则有打击对方的作用，如果将熊形和鹰形合练，即主求其习领和擒拿。

五、熊调膀

六合式，俗称预备式。

熊出洞

左脚上前垫一步，左手经左腿内侧膝前向体左侧摆出，掌心向下，臂与体的夹角保持60度左右，平视前方。紧接，右足向前迈进一步，左脚紧起向前落于右脚后，同时，向左转体180度，右手经体右侧，右大腿外侧、膝前向体左侧摆出，掌心向下，臂与体的夹角保持60度左右。在左脚紧起向前落于右脚后的同时，右手收至左胯，掌心护住胯骨，左手收至后腰，手背贴住腰椎骨，下巴对住右肩侧上方，三尖要照，平视前方。

龙调膀 1

然后，右脚上前垫一步，右手经左腿内侧膝前向体右侧摆出，掌心向下，臂与体的夹角保持 60 度左右，平视前方。

龙调膀 2

随之，左脚再朝前迈出一步，落至右脚前。向左转体 180 度，左手经体左侧，左大腿外侧膝前向体右侧摆出，掌心向下，臂与体的夹角保持 60 度左右，右脚紧起向前落于左足后的同时，左手收至右胯，掌心护住胯骨，下巴对住左肩侧上方，平视前方。

熊调膀转身势：

以右式为例，左脚以后跟为轴，右脚以掌为轴，同时蹍地，向左后方转体 180 度，两手同时摆出，左手至左胯前，右手在后胯，两臂的夹角成 90 度左右。左脚向前垫上一步，右脚紧起向前落左足后，左手收至右胯，掌心护住胯骨，右手收至后腰，手背贴住腰椎骨，下巴对住左肩侧上方，平视前方。

收势；鹰捉把

虎扑把

熊形单把

六合式，俗称预备式。

熊出洞

左脚向前垫上一步，右脚紧追迈至左脚前，同时，右手从右胯提到胸前，向左转体 180 度，掌心向前，肘稍弯曲，手掌与面部同高。臂与体夹角保持 60 度左右，左手从左膝内侧上提至胸前右肘内侧，在左足紧起向前落于右脚后的同时，右掌向前迅速推出，左手按在右手的手腕上，三尖要照，三弯要对，平视前方。

熊形单把

右式与左式练法相反。

熊形单把转身式

以右式为例，两脚掌为轴，同时蹍地，向右后方转体 180 度，右手从左手背往下收至右膝内侧，左手往下收到左胯，掌心护住胯骨，然后，左后脚向前迈进一步，落至右脚前。右脚紧起向前一步，落至左脚前。左后脚再朝前迈进一步，落至右脚后的同时，右掌向前迅速推出，左掌按在右手的手腕上，平视前方。

收势；鹰捉把

虎扑把

要领：练熊形单把时，走步时，全身节节放松，内开外合，用沉身功夫，把全身散乱之力集于腰尾，贯于后膝与足，顺其势由上而下，肩推胯，胯推膝，膝推足，后膝往前往下沉，让重心下降，前移，前腿不可主动迈进。全凭后腿蹬进。蹬进时，前脚离地少许，脚尖上钩，让胯劲到膝，膝劲到脚，后脚把全身蹬进时，前腿应为挤劲，前脚落地时，脚跟应先着地，落地无声，顺势脚掌落地下踩，如踩毒物，接住向前的惯性力，提掌发劲，六合齐，三尖照，气沉丹田。

熊形双把

六合式，俗称预备式。

熊出洞

左脚向前垫一步，右脚紧追迈至左脚前，同时向左转体 180 度，右手从右胯提到胸前，左手从左膝内侧上提至胸前，双掌相叠，掌心向前，肘稍弯曲，手掌与胸部同高，臂与体夹角保持 60 度左右，平视前方。

紧接，左后脚再朝前迈进一步，落至右脚后的同时，双掌迅速向前推出，平视前方。

熊形双把

右式与左式练法相反。

熊形双把转身势：

两脚掌为轴，同时蹍地。身向左后方转体180度，双掌收至小腹前，左脚向前垫一步，右脚紧追迈至右脚前，然后，左后足再朝前迈出一步，落至右足前，右脚紧起向前落于左脚后，同时向左转体180度，双掌迅速提至胸前，肘稍弯曲，手掌与嘴部同高，五指分开，向前迅速推出。平视前方。

收，鹰捉把

虎扑把

要领：练熊形双把快步时，要求上身保持两肘护肋，力由头领，丹催，足蹬，手发，身体整体猝然向前一抖撞，在抖撞之时，身体的重心稍往后移，产生惯性力量，疾步箭窜，注意呼吸自然，六合齐。

熊形连环把

六合式，俗称预备式。

熊出洞

左脚向左斜前方 45 度迈进一步，右足紧起向前落于左脚后，同时，左手从左膝内侧外翻收至左侧腰部，右手从右胯收至右侧腰部，掌心外翻，随之，双掌内翻向前迅速推出，两拇指相叠，虎口圆，三尖相照，平视前方。

紧接，右后脚再朝右前方 45 度迈出一步，落至左脚前，同时双掌收至小腹部，左脚再朝前迈出一步，左手向前提至右肩平，右脚紧追迈至左脚前，同时，右手从下往上提到脸部前，身向左转体 90 度，掌心向前，肘稍弯曲，手掌与面部同高，臂与体的夹角保持 60 度左右，左手按在右手的手腕，迅速向前推出，左脚紧起向前落于右脚后。三尖要照，平视前方。

熊形双把　　　　熊形单把

右式与左式练法相反。

熊形连环把转身势：

以右式为例，两脚掌为轴，同时踾地。身向左后方转体 180 度，成左鸡步。右后脚朝左斜前方 45 度迈进一步，落至左脚前。随之，左脚再向前迈进一步，落至右脚前，成左弓步。双掌外翻，掌心向上，紧靠腰部，然后，双掌提托在胸前，迅速向内翻掌向前推出，掌心向前，两拇指相叠，虎口圆，三尖照，平视前方。

收势；鹰捉把

虎扑把

要领：练熊形连环把时，它的练法一左一右，以左右进击为妙，起手，双掌捧气贯于周身随转体把丹田浑无气发于双手掌，发快劲推脱向前。接手，单掌提气贯于全身，随缩身展单掌，丹田叫力，突发踏天劲。

熊形大劈

六合式，俗称预备式。

熊出洞

左脚向左斜前方45度迈进一步，右足紧追迈至左脚前，同时，向左转体45度左右。左手移至右胯，经体右侧，右肩，头部上拳，内翻用力向体左侧劈下，虎口向上，右手摆至与右胯平，虎口向上，平视前方。

熊形顺劈

然后，左后足再朝前迈出一步，落至右脚前，右脚紧起向前落于左脚后。随之，向左转体 90 度，右手伸直，由体右侧上举，经右耳侧用力向体左侧劈下，手背贴住左大腿外侧，左手随之收于左胯，掌心护住胯骨，右肩对住左胯，下巴对住左肩上方，三尖相对，平视前方。

龙形

紧接，左脚内扣，向右斜前方垫上一步，同时，向右转体 45 度，右手经体左侧，左肩，头前上举，用力向体右侧劈下，虎口向上，左手摆至与左胯平，虎口向上，平视前方。

随之，右脚紧追迈至左脚前，左脚紧起向前落右脚后，向右转体 90 度。左手伸直，由体左侧上举，经左耳侧，用力向体右侧劈下，手背贴住右大腿外侧右手随之收于右胯，掌心护住胯骨，下巴对住左肩上方，平视前方。

右式与左式练法相反。

熊形大劈转身势：

以右式为例，左脚以后跟为轴，右掌为轴，同时蹍地，向左后方转体 180 度，随之，左脚向左斜前方 45 度垫上一步，右脚紧追迈至左脚前，然后，左后脚再朝前迈出一步，落至右脚前。随之向左转体 45 度，右手由体右侧上举，经右耳侧，伸直，用力向体左侧劈下，

虎口向上，手背贴住左大腿外侧，左手随之吸至左胯，掌心护住胯骨，下巴对住右肩侧上方，三尖相对，平视前方。

收势；鹰捉把

虎扑把

要领：练熊形大劈时劲力要顺，大劈的两手要分前后，手劈下时要依靠腰的转动发劲，同时，要注意手、眼、身、法、步一致，身体不可前俯，不可后仰，两肩要沉，肘要坠，呼吸自然，动作连贯，三尖相对，气沉丹田。

熊出动单跌式

1. 六合式，俗称预备式。

熊出洞

左脚向前垫一步，右脚紧追迈至左脚前，脚尖上翘，同时，向左转体 45 度。左手由体前提起，经胸部向前伸，掌心向下，右手随之收至右胯，掌心护住胯骨，平视前方。

龙形

紧接，右脚尖向前踏下，左脚紧追迈至右脚前。脚尖上翘，重心留在右脚，同时，向右转体 45 度。右手由胯部经胸前，左臂向前伸出,掌心向下,在左脚向前上步同时,左手收回至胸前,而后经胸前,有臂上方向前按出，掌心向下，手微弯曲，同胸高，右手随之收于左胸下,肘关节贴住右肋侧,下巴对肩侧上方,三尖相对,平视前方。

然后，左脚向前垫一步，右脚紧追向前落于左脚后，左脚随之再迈出一步，成左弓步，在左脚上前的同时，向右转体 90 度。双掌下落，上身迅速下跌前俯，左手贴在左膝内侧，虎口向前，右手随之收至右胯，掌心护住胯骨，平视前方。

随之，右脚紧追迈至左脚前，左右足在朝前迈出一步。落至右脚前，脚尖上翘，同时，向右转体 45 度。右手由体前提起，经胸部向前伸，掌心向下，左手随之收至左胯，掌心护住胯骨，平视前方。

紧接，左脚尖向前踏下，右脚紧追迈至左脚前。脚尖上翘，重心留在左脚，同时，向左转体 45 度。左手由胯部经胸前，右臂向前伸出,掌心向下,在右脚向前上步同时,右手收回至胸前,而后经胸前,

左臂上方向前按出，掌心向下，手微弯曲，同胸高，左手随之收右胸下，肘关节贴住右肋侧，下巴对肩侧上方，三尖要对，平视前方。

然后，右脚向前垫一步，左脚紧起向前落于右脚后，右脚随之再迈出一步，成右弓步，在右脚上前的同时，向左转体 90 度。双掌下落，上身迅速下跌前俯，右手贴在右膝内侧，虎口向前，左手随之收至左胯，掌心护住胯骨，平视前方。

胸出洞单跌式转身式：

以右式为例，左脚以后跟为轴，右脚以掌为轴，同时蹍地，向左后方转体 180 度，随之，左脚上前垫一步，右脚紧追迈至左足前，脚尖上翘向左转体 45 度。左手由体前经胸前伸出，掌心向下，手微弯曲，右手随之收至右胯，掌心护住胯骨，平视前方。

右式与左式练法相反。

收势；鹰捉把

虎扑把

要领：练熊出洞单跌式时，出手要疾，手要伸直，而后要保持圆弧状，同时，手与脚要协调一致，在沉肩坠肘下跌时，动作凶猛，含胸拔背，整个动作上下连贯一致，贯劲在于指、肩。气沉丹田。

猴形，谱曰：猴有纵身之灵

猴在动物之中，为最灵巧之物，其性有纵山跳涧飞身之灵，又有恍惚变化不测之巧，有偷桃献果之奇，有攀枝上树之技，又有蹬枝坠枝之力和辗转挪移，神机莫测之妙。故贯师祖云，不是飞仙体自轻，若闪电令人惊，看它一身无定势，纵山跳涧一片灵。在拳之运用一定不可使用拙力，拙劲。而要求其轻巧灵敏，快利旋转如风，方不失猴形之本意。

六、猴纵身

六合式，俗称预备式。

熊出洞

左脚向左斜前方 45 度迈进一步，右脚紧追迈至左脚前，同时，向左转体 45 度，右手同时由体右侧提起，内翻，掌心向内，经脸擦左肩收至左胯，下巴对准右肩上方，平视前方。

猴竖蹲

紧接，左后脚再朝前迈出一步，同时向右转体 180 度，左手由身体左侧提起，内翻，掌心向内，经脸擦右肩以至右胯，右手随之由左胯经腹部收回原处，下巴对住肩上方，平视前方。然后，左后脚再朝前垫一步，落至右脚前，右脚紧起向前落于左脚后，左手五指并拢，成猴形手，由右胯处向下，经裆前，左大腿内侧，膝关节处向上用力，左肘与肩平，肘弯曲，右手在左手上提的同时，由掌变钩，随之上提，护在左肘下，掌心向下，虎口堵住尺骨鹰嘴，下巴对住左肩上方，平视前方。随之，左脚再向右斜前方 90 度迈进一步，同时向右转体 90 度，左手同时由左侧上方变掌，外翻经脸部擦左肩上方，平视前方。紧接，右后脚再朝前迈出一步，落至左脚前，向左转体 180 度，右手同时由体右侧提起，内翻，掌心向内，经脸擦左肩收至左胯，左手随之由右胯经腹部收回原处，下巴对住右肩上方，平视前方。

然后，右脚向前垫一步，左脚紧追向前落于右脚后，右手五指并拢，成猴形手，由左胯处向下经裆前，右大腿内侧，膝关节外向上用力，迅速提至头右侧上方，掌心向下，手背用力，右肘与肩平齐，肘弯曲，在右手上提同时，左手由掌变钩，随之上提，护于右肘下，掌心朝下，虎口抵住尺骨鹰嘴，下巴对住右肩上方，平视前方。右式与左式练法相反。

猴纵身转身势：

以右式为例，左脚以后跟为轴，右脚以掌心为轴，同时蹍地，向左后方转体 180 度，随之，左脚上前一大步，身体向左侧半面转，右手由右侧上方变掌，手外翻，经脸擦左肩收至右肩，左手左肩也同时收回，下巴对住右肩上方，平视前方。

收势；鹰捉把

虎扑把

要领：练猴纵身时，手的摆动要与身体的转动协调一致，力要由腰部传递于肩、肘、手、缩身的动作要低，要蓄劲，三尖要照，起身提手要忌挺胸、腹，要气沉丹田，以气催力步法轻活。

猴观势

六合式，俗称预备式。

熊出洞

左脚向前垫一步，右腿上步提膝，重心留在左脚，右膝与右胯平，脚尖上翘，左手外翻上提，虎口至胸腹前，向左转体90度，右手在右膝上提的同时，外翻，经体前向上提至与头同高，掌心向后，肘稍弯曲，与肩同高，左手于右手肘关节内侧，手背向上，平视前方。

然后，右膝上提，左脚蹬地，腾空向前上方提膝，脚尖上翘，落地后左脚在前，在脚跳起的同时，左手沿右小臂，由上往斜下方砍出，掌心朝下，至小腿前停住，臂稍弯曲，肘关节与膝关节相距一拳左右，右手随之收至右胯，掌心护住胯骨，平视前方。右式与左式练法相反。

猴观势

猴观势转身势：

以右式为例。左脚以后跟为轴，右脚以掌为轴，同时蹍地，向左转体180度，随之，左脚上前一步，右腿上步提膝。

收势：鹰捉把

虎扑把

要领：练猴观势时，两脚跳起用意在膝关节，上挑腾空两脚交换要疾，落下时要轻，身体始终保持正直，手的砍下动作弧线要圆，缩身要小，眼神灵活，气沉丹田，上跳时要提气，做到呼吸自然，动作灵活，起落分时，手脚配合协调一致。

猴蹦

六合式，俗称预备式。

熊出洞

左脚向左斜前方垫上一步，右脚紧追迈至左脚前，脚尖上翘，同时身体左侧半面转，右膝随之上提，左手由下经体左侧，脸部擦右肩至腹部绕环，外翻，小指一侧贴住胸部，五指并拢成猴形手，肘弯曲，稍低于肩，目视前方。

猴蹦 1

然后，右膝上提，左脚蹬地腾空，在空中变步成左鸡步，后落地，同时，向右转体 90 度，左手由胸前向下，掌内翻，经裆前沿大腿内侧向上提至头左侧前上方，肘稍高于肩，右手在左手运动时掌内翻，由上经胸前，护于左肘关节内侧，手指朝下，平视前方。

猴蹦 2

紧接，左脚向右斜前方迈进一步，同时，身体向右侧半面转，脚尖上翘，随之左膝上提右手外翻，从左膝关节处由腹部，经体右侧、脸部擦左肩至腹前环绕，小指一侧贴住胸前，左手随之外翻，摆至头前，掌心向后，肘稍低于肩，臂稍弯曲，平视前方。

随之，左膝继续上提，右脚蹬地腾空，在空中变步成右鸡步后落地，同时，身体向左侧半面转。右手掌内翻，由胸前向下，经裆前，沿大腿内侧向上提至头右侧前上方，肘稍高于肩，左手随右手运动时，由上经胸前，掌心内翻护住右手肘关节内侧，手指朝下，平视前方右式与左式练法相反。

猴蹦转身势：

以右式为例，左脚以后跟为轴，右脚以掌为轴，同时踝地，身体向左转体 180 度，右脚上前一步，脚尖上翘，左膝随之上提，手与身体的动作与左式相同。

收势；鹰捉把

虎扑把

要领：练猴蹦时，手与脚要协调一致，手的环绕用力要顺，要活，

脚的跳起蹬地动作用意在膝，落地动作要轻灵，步子要活，身体要正，两脚跳起时，在内要提气，呼吸自然，提肛收臀，气沉丹田。

猴蹬枝

六合式，俗称预备式。

熊出洞

左脚向左斜前方 45 度迈进一步，右脚紧追迈至左脚前，向左转体 45 度，脚尖上翘，左手外翻，由下经体左侧上提至与头同高，掌心向后，五指并拢，成猴形手，肘稍弯曲，低于肩。左脚随之继上一步，提膝至与前胯平，脚尖上翘，右手由下经腹部，右臂前向上提气，手背向上至头左侧前上方，左手在右手上提时由上经脸前收至胸前，小指一侧贴住胸骨，下巴对住左肩上方，平视前方。

然后，左脚蹬地，同左胯平，同时，向右转体 45 度，左手向左侧平摆，手背向外，右手向右侧上方摆出，手背向外，两手心相对，平视前方。

随之，左脚蹬出后，迅速收回至原来姿势。

猴蹬枝

紧接，左脚向右斜方45度迈进一步，身向右转体180度，同时右手外翻，由上自身体左侧向下，经体右侧提至与头同高，掌心向后，肘稍弯曲，稍低于肩，左手同时收于左胯，右脚紧起向前近至左脚前。左膝提至与前胯平，脚尖上翘，左手由下经腹前，右臂前向上方提出，手背向上至头右侧上方，右手在左手上提时由上经脸收至胸前，小指一侧贴住胸骨，下巴对住左侧肩上方，平视前方。

然后，右脚迅速用力蹬出，同右膝平，同时，向左转体45度，右手向右侧平摆，手背向外，两手心相对，平视前方。随之，右脚蹬出后，迅速收回至原来姿势。右式与左式练法相反。

猴蹬枝转身势：

以右式为例，左脚以后跟为肘，同时踬地，向右转体180度。随之，右脚向左斜前方90度上一步，向左转体90度。左手外翻上自体右侧向下，经体左侧提至与头同高，掌心向后，肘稍弯曲，稍低于肩，右手同时手与右胯，左脚继上一步，提膝至与胯平，脚尖上翘，右手由下经腹前，左手背朝前向上提起，至头左侧上方，左手在右手上提时由上经脸前收至胸前，小指一侧贴住胸骨，下巴对住右肩上方，平视前方。

收势：鹰捉把

虎扑把

要领：练猴蹬枝时身法与手法要柔，步法要轻灵，蹬腿时的劲力要由身体、胯关节的扭转来完成，蹬腿时要有弹性，手的裹法要，身体要正，三尖照，在内要呼吸自然，气沉丹田，回身时步子要稳，控制平衡，蹬腿时重心当在后脚。

七、蛇行

蛇形，谱曰：蛇有分草之巧

蛇也是动作中最灵巧之物，且有击首尾应，击中首尾相应的技能，且蛇有拔草之技能，缠绕之能，行走曲折，伸曲自如之特性。练习蛇形，要全身动转灵活，发劲浑厚，进退自如，转折迅速，不可有降滞之象。

蛇行步

六合式，俗称预备式。

熊出洞

左前脚向左斜前方迈进一步，右脚紧追近至左脚前。然后，左右脚再朝前迈进一步，落至右脚前，同时，身体向左转体 90 度，左手由左膝移至右胯。随之，右臂用力向上提起，手举至左倾额前，掌心向外，与左额角的距离保持一拳左右，肘稍弯曲，稍低于肩，然后，左脚向右斜前方迈进一步，向左转体 90 度，右手由上至下经左肩，裆前，左大腿外侧摆正，小指一侧向前，臂与体的夹角保持 45 度左右，平视前方。

紧接，右后脚再朝前迈进一步，同时，向右转体 90 度，左臂用力向上提起，手举至头右侧额前，掌心向外，与右额角的距离保持一拳左右，肘稍弯曲，稍低于肩，右手收回至右胯，掌心护住胯骨，平视前方。右式与左式练法相反。

蛇形步

蛇行步转身势：

以右式为例，左脚以后跟为轴，右脚以掌为轴，同时踝地，向左后转体 180 度，左脚向左斜前方 45 度迈进一步，同时向左转体 90 度。手法与步法同行。

收势；鹰捉把

虎扑把

要领：练蛇行步时，手与脚要一致，肘部的劲要随身体的转动发力，后脚蹬地要用力，肘提至肩部时要用顶劲，身体要正，内三合要提，外三合要随。

蛇拔草

六合式

熊出洞

左脚向左斜前方迈进一步，右脚紧追近至左脚前，身体向左侧半面转，左手提至胸前，虎口向上，肘稍弯曲，平视前方。

然后，左脚再朝前迈进一步，同时，身体右侧稍向右转。右手由下自腹前经左肘向右前上方摆击至与肩同高，肘肩弯曲，掌心向下，肘与肋相距一拳左右，左手内翻朝下经右小臂收至腹下，掌根抵住丹田，肘内侧贴住肋侧，下巴对住右肩侧上方，平视前方。

蛇拔草

紧接,左脚向右斜前方90度迈进一步,向右转体90度,右手外翻,左手收至左胯,平视前方。

随之,右后脚再朝前迈进一步,落至左脚前,同时,身体左侧稍向右转。左手由下自腹前经右肘下向左前上方摆出至肩同高,肘稍弯曲,掌心向下,肘内侧贴住左肋。下巴对住左肩上方,平视前方。

右式与左式练法相反。

蛇拔草转身势:

以右式为例。左脚以后跟为轴,右脚以前掌为轴,同时蹍地,向左转体180度,右脚随之向左斜前方45度迈进一步,同时,向左转体45度。左手外翻,右手收回至右胯,平视前方。

收势:鹰捉把

虎扑把

要领:练蛇拔草时,手与脚要协调一致,第一动作出手不要太高,第二动作手摆动要沉肩坠肘,手的外侧要用劲。身体要正,步子要轻灵,肘关节要坐,前手的肘与肋的距离保持一拳左右。在内要注意呼吸自然,气沉丹田,下巴内收,三尖要照,三弯要对。

蛇吐舌（芯）

六合式，俗称预备式。

熊出洞

左脚向左斜前方 45 度迈进一步，向左转体 45 度，同时，左手提至胸前，由外翻转至内翻，掌心向下成剑指，肘稍弯曲，平视前方。

蛇吐芯

然后，左脚随即再向前迈出一步，同时，身体右侧稍向右转。左手向下收回至腹前，肘关节贴住左肋，掌心向下。右手外翻，掌心向上成剑手。同时由下自胸前经左手背向上伸击至与头同高，肘稍弯曲，下巴对住右肩上方，平视前方。

紧接，左脚向右斜前方90度迈进一步，向右转体90度，右手内翻，掌心向下，肘稍弯曲，平视前方。

随之，右脚再朝前迈进一步，同时，身体左侧稍向左转，右手向下收回至腹前，肘关节贴住右肋，掌心向下成剑指，左手外翻成剑指，掌心向上，由腹经右手背向前上方伸出，至与头同高，肘稍弯曲，下巴对左肩上方，平视前方。右式与左式练法相反。

蛇吐舌（芯）转身势：

以右式为例，左脚以后脚跟为轴，右脚以掌为轴，同时蹍地，向左转体180度，随之，右脚继向左斜前方90度迈进一步，身体向左侧半面转。左手内翻，掌心向下，肘稍弯曲，平视前方

收势：鹰捉把。

虎扑把

要领：练蛇吐舌（芯）时，手与脚的动作要协调一致，两手在手背处交换，后手向前伸出时，虎口一侧用力，要护腰伸肩，沉肩坠肘，内要提，外要随。

蛇盘

六合式，俗称预备式。

熊出洞

左脚向左斜前方 45 度迈进一步，右脚紧追近至左脚前。身体向左侧半面转，左手外翻，由体左侧上提至与头同高，内翻，掌心向下，肘稍弯曲，肘与肋相距一拳左右，右手上提至腹前，掌心向下，掌根抵住丹田，平视前方。

蛇盘

然后，左后脚再朝前迈进一步，落至右脚前。同时，向左转体 90 度。右手由下经胸前扬，然后沿左手背向下按至左膝盖前停住，

肘稍弯曲，肘与肋相距一拳左右。左手随之收回至腹前，掌根抵住丹田，平视前方。

紧接，左脚向右斜前方90度迈进一步，向右转体90度。右手外翻，经体右侧上提至与头同高内翻，掌心向下，肘稍弯曲，肘与肋相距一拳左右，平视前方。

随之，右后脚再朝前迈进一步，同时，向右转体90度。左手由下经胸前向前上扬，沿着右手背向下按至右膝盖前停住，肘稍弯曲，肘与肋相距一拳左右，右手随之收回至腹前，掌根抵住丹田，平视前方。右式与左式练法相反。

蛇盘转身势：

以右式为例，左脚以后跟为轴，右脚以掌为轴，同时蹍地，向左右转体180度，右脚随之继向左斜前方90度上一步，向左转体90度，左手外翻，经体左侧上提至与头同高，内翻，掌心向下，肘弯曲，肘与肋相距一拳左右，平视前方。

收势：鹰捉把

虎扑把

要领：练蛇盘时，手的内翻外翻要分明，向下按的动作要以跨、利用身体下降来完成，身体要正，腰要活，三尖要照，三弯要对，在内要注意气沉丹田。

八、燕形

谱曰：燕有取水之能。燕时飞禽中最灵巧，最敏捷之物，有钻天之能，妙手之巧，动转无声之奇，飞腾高翔之秒。练习燕形时，定要去掉身体中之拙力，逐渐化拙力为灵巧之劲，且燕形在人之为用，则注重其下肢的功夫和身躯的灵活，才能体现抄手时迅速，转动时敏捷的特性。

燕子单抄水

六合式，俗称预备式。

熊出洞

左脚上前垫一步，右脚紧追近至左脚前，右手从右胯，由下经腹前收至右胯，掌心护住胯骨，下巴对住左肩上方

燕子单抄水

然后，右脚全蹲，左脚向前伸出，成仆步。左手向左脚前方横扫，掌心向下，臂与体的夹角保持 45 度左右，右手由前向右后侧上方摆出，手高于头，臂与体的夹角保持 120 度左右，掌心向下，身体稍微前倾，下巴对住左肩侧上方。

紧接，左脚向前垫一步，右脚随之向前落于左脚后，同时，向左转体 90 度，左手由下经体右侧上提，外翻，户口向上，至额前，肘与肩平，稍弯曲，右手掌心护住胯骨，下巴对住右肩侧上方，平视前方。

随之，左脚全蹲，右脚向前伸出，成仆步。右手向右脚前方横扫，掌心向下，臂与体的夹角保持 45 度左右，左手由前向左后侧上方摆出，手高于头，臂与体的夹角保持 120 度左右，掌心向下，身体稍前倾，下巴对住右肩侧上方，平视前方。右式与左式练法相反。

燕子单抄水转身势：

以右式为例。左脚以后跟为轴，右脚以掌为轴，同时蹍地，向左转体 90 度，随之，左脚向前垫一步，右脚紧追近左脚前向右转体 90 度。左手由上经体右侧摆至右肩上方，外翻，户口向上，右手由上经腹部收回至左胯，掌心护住胯骨，平视前方。

收势：鹰捉把

虎扑把

要领：练燕子单抄水时，第一式手法同脚要协调一致，前手的横扫同后手的摆动要分力，用腰部的劲力来摆动，后腿的全蹲膝关节不能低于胯关节，上体不要过于前赴，三尖相照，呼吸自然。

燕子双抄水

六合式，俗称预备式。

熊出洞

左脚向前垫一步，右脚紧追迈至左脚前，右手经体前上提，虎口向上，至额前停住，肘与肩平，稍弯曲，左手随之上提护于右肘下，掌心朝右，虎口抵住尺骨鹰嘴，肘于肋侧相距一拳左右，下巴对住左肩侧上方，平视前方。

燕子双抄水

然后，右腿全蹲，左脚迅速向前伸出，成左仆步。同时，右手掌擦肘向下，左手外翻，由右肘下，经体右侧插下，沿裆下左大腿内测向前伸出，虎口向上，臂与体的夹角保持 45 度左右，右手随左手同时伸出，护在左肘内侧，虎口向上，身体稍前俯，平视前方。

紧接，左脚向前垫一步，右脚随之跟上一步，同时，向右转体 90 度。左手上提，虎口向上，至额前停住，肘与肩平，稍弯曲，右手同时上提护于左肘下，掌心朝左，虎口抵住尺骨鹰嘴，肘与肋侧相距一拳左右，下巴对住右肩上方，平视前方。

随之，左腿全蹲，右脚迅速向前伸出，成右仆步。同时，左手掌擦右肘向下，右手由左肘下经体左侧插下沿裆下，右大腿内测向前伸出上提。左手随右手同时伸出，护在肘内侧，虎口向上。向上，身体稍前俯，平视前方。右式与左式练法相反。

燕子双抄水转身势：

以右式为例。左脚以后较为轴，右脚以掌为轴，同时蹍地，向左转体 90 度。随之，左脚向前垫一步，右后脚再朝前迈出一步，落至左脚前，同时，向右转体 90 度。右手上提，虎口向上，至额前停住，肘稍弯曲，与肩平，左手同时上提，护于右肘下，掌心朝右，虎口抵住尺骨鹰嘴，肘与肋相距一拳左右，下巴对住左肩上方，平视前方。

收势；鹰捉把

虎扑把

要领：练燕子双抄水时，手脚动作要协调一致，下蹲时要低，两手不离肘，手向前伸出时，身体不能前俯超前，提起时，要身体正，在内提肛，沉气。呼吸自然，动作有力。

燕形撩掌

六合式，俗称预备式。

熊出洞

左脚向前垫一步，右脚紧追至左脚前。同时，右手从右胯经体前上提，虎口向上，至额前停住，肘稍弯曲，与肩平，左手由左膝内侧外翻，随之上提，护与右肘下，掌心朝右，虎口抵住尺骨鹰嘴，肘与肋相距一拳左右，下巴对住左肩上方，平视前方。

燕形撩掌

然后，右脚向前垫一步，左脚随即上前，提膝至与前胯平，脚尖上翘，右脚站立支撑，同时，向右转体 90 度。左手在左膝上提时，迅速由右肘下经体右侧，右大腿，左膝关节处上提，外翻，虎口向上，至与头同高，臂弯曲，臂与体的夹角保持 60 度左右，右手同时经身体右侧向后摆下，内翻，掌心朝下，臂与体的夹角保持 45 度左右，下巴对住左肩上方，平视前方。

紧接，左脚向前落地，右脚再朝前迈出一步，落至左脚前。同时，左肘稍上提，与肩平，向左转体 90 度，右手随之由体后经右胯向前伸出，护左肘下，掌心朝左，虎口抵住尺骨鹰嘴，肋与肋侧相距一拳左右，下巴对住左肩侧上方，平视前方。

随之，左脚再向前垫一步，右脚随即上前提膝至与前胯平，脚尖上翘，左脚站立支撑，腿稍弯曲，同时，向左转体 90 度，再右膝上提时，右手迅速由左肘下经体左侧，左大腿，右膝关节处上提至与头同高，掌外翻，虎口向上，臂弯曲，臂与体的夹角保持 60 度左右，左手同时经体左侧向后摆下，内翻，掌心向下，臂与体夹角保持 45 度左右，下巴对住右肩上方，平视前方。右式与左式练法相反。

燕形撩掌转身势：

以右式为例。右脚落地，左脚以后跟为轴右脚以掌为轴，同时蹍地，向左后方转体 180 度，右脚随即再迈出一步，右肘关节上提至与肩平，向右转体 90 度，左手随之由体后经左胯向前伸出，护在右肘下，掌心朝右，虎口抵住尺骨鹰嘴，肘与肋侧相距一拳左右，下巴对住左肩侧上方，平视前方。

收势；鹰捉把

虎扑把

要领：练燕形撩掌时，步法与手法要一致，手的撩掌动作要清楚，劲要顺，用意在小臂，单脚支撑要稳，提膝用意在脚尖，身体要正，动静整齐。在内要注意百会顶，脚趾抓地，坠肩沉肘，提尾肛，呼吸自然，气沉丹田，三尖相照，三弯相对。

九、鹞形

谱曰：鹞有侧身展翅之力。

鹞的特性是雄勇而灵敏，它既有翻身之巧，入林之奇，又有展翅之威和束身捉物之捷，且有钻天之勇。取之于拳，有舒身缩体，起落翻转之作用，形要顺，外要刚，内要和而柔，要体现出灵巧而雄勇的神行，雄勇并非拙力，灵巧并非漂浮，总之，要沉稳而灵活，才能体现出鹞之特性。

鹞子单展翅

六合式，俗称预备式。

熊出洞

左脚向左斜前方 45 度垫上一步，右脚紧追近至左脚前，同时，向左转体 45 度，左手向下，沿大腿前经身体的右胯，肩，右额上方绕环至左额前，掌心向后，肘弯曲，稍高于肩，平视前方。

鹞子单展翅

然后左右脚再朝前迈出一步，落至右脚前，同时，向左转体90度，左手外翻，右手由右胯经腹部前插至左胯，掌心向下，虎口抵住胯骨，下巴对住右肩上方，平视前方。

紧接，左脚再向前方垫一步，右脚紧起向前落于左脚后，左手内翻，掌心向下，右肘尖抵住左肋。以肘关节为轴，向身体左侧扫击至右肩、右胯的直线上，平视手掌前方。

随之，左脚尖内扣，向右斜前方90度迈进一步，右脚紧起向前落于左脚后，右手内翻，掌心向下，沿大腿前经左胯，肩，左额角上方绕环至右额前，掌心向后，肘弯曲，稍高于肩，左手随之收至左胯，掌心护住胯骨，身体随之右胯，平视前方。

然后，右后脚再朝前迈进一步，落至左脚前，左脚紧起向前落于右脚后。同时向右转体90度，右手外翻，左手由左胯经腹前插至右胯，掌心向下，虎口抵住胯骨，下巴对住左肩上方，平视前方。

紧接，右脚再向前垫一步，左脚紧追迈至右脚后，右手内翻，

掌心向下，左肘尖抵住右肋，以肘关节为轴，由身体右侧扫击至左肩、左胯的直线上，平视手掌前方。

右式与左式练法相反。

鹞子单展翅转身势：

以右式为例。左脚为后跟为轴，右脚以掌为轴，同时蹍地，向左转体 180 度，右脚随之向前一步，同时，身体左转，左手内翻掌心向下，沿大腿前经右胯、肩、右额角上方绕环至左额前，掌心向右，肘弯曲，稍高于肩，右手随之收至右胯，掌心向内，平视前方。

收势：鹰捉把

虎扑把

要领：练鹞子单展翅时，手与脚要协调一致，绕环时要依靠腰部的转动运行，用意在肘，翻掌扫的动作也要同身体的转动协调。注意身体正，六合要齐，呼吸自然，沉肩坠肘，气沉丹田。

鹞子入林

六合式，俗称预备式。

熊出洞

左脚向前垫一步，左手外翻，由体左侧上提，经头前、右肩、右胯，腹前绕环，在体左侧外翻，至左胯平，掌心朝前上方，臂稍弯曲，右手同时从右胯，由体右侧上提，经右额往后摆，掌心向上，高于头。平视前方。

鹞子入林

然后，右脚紧追迈至左脚前。左脚紧起向前落于右脚后，同时，向左转体 180 度。右手经体右侧向上托起至右腰胯同高，掌心朝前上方，臂稍弯曲，左手同时内翻，伸直，向身后体左侧后摆，掌心向上，高于头。平视前方。

紧接，右脚向前方垫一步，右手内翻，由右腰胯前，向身后体右侧后摆，掌心向上，高于头。同时，左右脚再朝前迈出一步，落至右脚前。身体向右转体 180 度。左手经左侧外翻，随左体向上托起至与左腰胯平，掌心向前上方，臂稍弯曲，右后脚再朝前迈进一步，落至左脚后。下巴对住左肩上方，平视前方。右式与左式练法相反。

鹞子入林转身势：

以右式为例，右脚后撤一步，以后跟为轴，左脚以掌为轴，同时蹍地，向右转体 180 度，右手内翻，由体右侧从右胯往右额绕环后摆，掌心向下。高于头。左脚紧追迈至右脚前。身体右转体 180 度，左手经体左侧向上托起与左腰胯同高，平视前方。

收势：鹰捉把。

虎扑把

要领：鹞为最敏锐之猛鸷，有束翅之法，入林之能，在练鹞子入林时，用力在两膊，须两膊一抖一展，侧身而进，并非硬打硬进。

鹞子翻身，巧在以腰为主，向左、向右、向后，中间皆不要停顿，以腰动带动两臂，要和顺自然，保全身动作的完整性，步法要活。注意身体正，百会顶、尾肛提，三尖相照，气沉丹田。

鹞子钻天

六合式，俗称预备式。

熊出洞

左脚向前垫一步，右脚紧追迈至左脚前，脚尖上翘，同时，向左转体 45 度。两手外翻，微弯曲，由下经体左侧向上提至与肩平，虎口向上，右手护于左肘内侧，下巴对主左肩侧上方，平视前方。

鹞子钻天

然后，右腿向上提膝，左腿用力蹬地跳起，腾空，在空中变步，左脚在前，右脚在后，成左鸡步，落地时步型不变。同时，两手内翻，在跳至最高点时，手经头、胸前往下插至裆部，缩身梗头向前，头的左侧贴住膝外侧，在身体落地的同时，迅速上抬，左手向前上方托起，掌心向上，与头同高，肘弯曲，臂与体的夹角保持45度左右，右手随之收于左肘内侧，虎口护住肘尖，右肘紧贴右肋侧，下巴对住左肩侧上方，平视前方。

紧接，右后脚向前迈进一步，左脚紧追迈至右脚前，脚尖上翘，同时，向右转体45度，两手自然放下，微弯曲，经体右侧向上提与肩平，虎口向上，左手护于右肘内侧，下巴对住右肩侧上方，平视前方。

随之，左腿向上提膝，右脚用力蹬地跳出，腾空，在空中变步，右脚在前，左脚在后，成右鸡步，落地时步型不变。同时，两手内翻，在跳至最高点时手经头、胸前往下插至裆部，缩身梗头向前，身体迅速上升，右手向前上方托起，掌心向上，与头同高，肘弯曲，臂与体的夹角保持45度，左手收于右肘内侧，虎口护于肘尖，左肘紧贴左肋侧，下巴对住右肩上方，平视前方。右式与左式练法相反。

鹞子钻天转身势：

以右式为例，左脚以后跟为轴，同时踵地，向左后方转体180度，两手自然放下，微弯曲，随之，左脚向前垫一步，右脚向前紧追迈至左脚前。脚尖上翘，向左转体45度，两手外翻，微弯曲，由下经体左侧向上提至与肩平，虎口向上，左手护于右肘内侧，下巴对住左肩上方，平视前方。

收势：鹰捉把

虎扑把

要领：练鹞子钻天时，手脚要协调，起落要分明，上跳要高，用意在膝，起时手要钻，落要缩身，两手要粘，用意在脚，呼吸自然，虚领顶颈，沉肩坠肘，三尖相照，三弯相对，提肛顶腭，气沉丹田。

十、马形

谱曰：马有奔蹄之功。

马是最仁义之灵兽，兽知人心，有垂缰之义，抖毛之威，有疾蹄之功，指的是马走极快时后蹄能超过前蹄。撞山跳涧之勇，马形有心空虚之妙，故在练习时，宜外刚猛而内柔和，又有丹田气足之形，故在练习时，就是要突出其疾蹄的特点。故进步时顺后腿蹬劲，前腿进步，然后，后腿再极力拥进。宜注重气沉丹田合丹田抱起的锻炼。

夜马奔槽

六合式，俗称预备式。

熊出洞

左脚向左倾前方垫一步，右脚向左斜前方提膝至与胯平，脚尖上翘，同时，向左转体 90 度，左腿下蹲，微弯曲，两手握拳外翻，由下经体前上提至头上方。然后，迅速向前下方砸下，掌心向前，收至右膝两侧，两肘与膝平，平视前方。

夜马奔槽

然后,右脚落地,左脚紧追迈至右脚前。脚尖上翘,重心当在右脚。同时,两手向前上方冲拳,至与鼻同高,两拳相距一拳左右,肘微弯曲,掌心向后，平视前方。

紧接，右脚再向前垫上一步，左脚紧追迈至右脚前，脚尖上翘。两手以肘关节为肘内翻,在胸前绕环,向前平冲拳,拳心向下,与肩平,两拳相距一拳左右，平视前方。

随之，右脚向右斜前方 45 度迈进一步，左脚向右斜前方提膝至胯平，脚尖上翘，同时向右转体 90 度，右脚下蹲，微弯曲。两手握拳外翻，由下经体前上提至头上方，然后，迅速向前下方砸下，拳心向前，收到左膝的两侧，两肘与膝平，平视前方。

然后，左脚落地，右脚向前迈进一步，落于左脚前，脚尖上翘，重心当在左脚。两手向前方冲拳至与鼻同高，两拳相距一拳左右，肘微弯曲，拳心向后，平视前方。

紧接，右脚再向前垫一步，左脚紧追迈至右脚前，脚尖上翘。两手以肘关节为轴内翻，经胸前绕环，向前平冲拳，拳与肩平，两卷相距一拳左右，平视前方。右式与左式练法相反。

夜马奔槽转身势：

以右式为例。左脚以后跟为轴，右脚以掌为轴，同时踬地，向左转体 180。随之，左脚向左斜前方 45 度垫上一步，右腿向左斜前方提膝至与胯平，脚尖上翘，同时，向左转体 90 度，左脚下蹲，微弯曲。两手握拳外翻，由下经体前上提至头上方，然后，迅速向前下方砸下，拳心向前，收至右膝的两侧，两肘与膝平，平视前方。

收势：鹰捉把

虎扑把

要领：练夜马奔槽时，可以增强后腿大筋的弹力，提高足弓之功能。并且，手与脚的动作要配合一致。两拳向下砸要与提膝同时进行，向前平冲拳要远，步要快，练时一纵一停，一起一止。以气催力，劲贯拳峰。劲要顺、身体正，呼吸自然，三尖相照，三弯要对。

马形窜拳

六合式，俗称预备式。

熊出洞

左脚向左斜前方 45 度垫上一步，右脚紧追迈至左脚前，然后，左后脚再朝前迈进一步，落至右脚前，提膝与胯平，脚尖上翘，同时，左手外翻由体左侧上提至头部。经右肩，腹前作环绕至左脚内侧，肘微弯曲，小指向前，右手收于胯部，掌心抵住胯骨，平视前方。

马形窜拳

然后，左脚向前方落地，右脚紧起向前落于左脚后。同时，右手由掌变拳，向前冲出，拳眼向上，左肘紧贴左肋，左掌由左脚内侧往后收至右胯，掌心抵住胯骨。下巴对住左肩上方，平视前方。

紧接，左脚尖内扣向右斜方 90 度迈进一步，右后脚再朝前迈进一步，落至左脚前，提膝与胯平，脚尖上翘，同时，右手外翻由体右侧上提至头部，经右肩，腹前作环绕至右脚内侧，肘微弯曲，小指向前。左手收于左胯部。掌心抵住胯骨，左腿稍下弯。平视前方。

随之，右脚向前方落地，左脚紧起向前落于右脚后。同时，左手由掌变拳，向前冲出，拳眼向上，右肘紧贴右肋，右掌由右脚内侧往后收至右胯，掌心抵住胯骨，下巴对住右肩上方，平视前方。右式与左式练法相反。

马形窜拳转身势：

以右式为例。左脚以后跟为轴，左脚以掌为轴，同时踝地，向左后方转体 180 度。左脚向左斜前方 45 度垫上一步，右脚紧追迈至左脚前，然后，左后脚再朝前迈出一步，落至右脚前，提膝与胯平，脚尖上翘，向左转体 90 度。左拳变掌内翻，由胸前上提经头部、右肩、腹部绕环至左脚内侧，肘微弯曲，小指向前，右手收于右胯，掌心抵住胯骨，右腿稍弯，下巴对住左肩上方，平视前方。

收势：鹰捉把

虎扑把

要领：练马形窜拳时，手与脚要协调一致，进步时顺，后腿蹬劲，冲拳要由身体纵动来带动，臂要伸而稍弯曲，以气催力，拳眼向上，劲贯拳峰。劲力要顺。绕环时用意在上分下撩，步伐要活，进退如意。身体要正，呼吸自然，气沉丹田。

野马蹬腿

六合式，俗称预备式。

熊出洞

左脚向左斜方45度迈进一步，右脚紧追迈至左脚前，同时向左转体45度。左手握拳，外翻由左侧向上提起至与头同高，右手握拳由右胯经裆前，体左侧、左臂外侧向上提起至头前方，拳心向后，肘高于肩关节，臂稍弯曲，左手同时收至右肘下，拳眼抵住肘尖，下巴对住左肩上方，平视前方。

野马蹬蹄

然后，左右脚再朝前迈出一步，落至右脚前，右脚经左脚面上前一步，成倒插步，同时，左手由右肘处向下经裆前，体左侧向上提至与头同高，右手由上向体右侧经裆前，体左侧、左手臂外侧上提至头前上方，平视前方。

紧接，左腿提膝，脚掌外翻，脚后跟用力，向左侧前方蹬出至与膝同高，同时，两拳向左右两侧摆出，拳眼向下，左拳与左胯平，右拳与头同高，平视前方。

随之，左脚尖内扣，向右斜方 90 度前落地，身向右转体 90 度。两手内翻，左手由左胯部经裆前，体右侧、右手臂外侧向上提起至头前上方，拳心向后，肘高于肩关节，稍微弯曲，右手同时收至左肘下，拳眼抵住左肘尖，下巴对住右肩侧上方，平视前方。

然后，右后脚再朝前迈出一步，落至左脚前。左脚随即经右脚后侧迈出一步，成倒插步。同时，右手由左肘处向下经裆前，体右侧向上提至与头同高，左手由上向体左侧经裆前，体右侧，右臂外侧上提至头前上方，拳心向后，肘高于肩关节，稍弯曲，右手同时

收至左肘下，拳眼抵住肘尖，下巴对住右肩上方，平视前方。

紧接，右腿提膝，脚掌外翻，脚后跟用力，向右侧前方蹬出至与膝平。同时，两拳向左右两侧摆出，拳眼向下，右拳与胯平，左拳与头同高，平视前方。右式与左式练法相反。

野马蹬脚转身势：

以右式为例，右脚落地，两手自然放下，左脚以后跟为轴，右脚以掌为轴，同时踝地，向左后转体 180 度，随之，左脚尖左撇向左斜前方 45 度迈进一步，右脚紧追迈至左脚前。同时向左转体 45 度，左手握拳，外翻，由左侧向上提起至于同高，右手同时由右胯经裆前，体左侧、左臂外侧向上提起至头前上方，拳心向后，肘稍弯曲，高于肩关节，左手收至右肘下，拳眼抵住肘尖，下巴对住左肩上方，平视前方。

收势：鹰捉把

虎扑把

要领：练野马蹬腿时，手与脚要互相配合，两手绕环时劲要顺，蹬腿时要先体膝，脚后跟用力，利用腰的力量与丹田之气往外蹬，

两拳外摆要同脚蹬方向一致。三尖相照，三心要实，步稳身正。要注意坠肩沉肘时，圆裆撑胯。

勒马听风

侵步站：右脚上前一小步，成十字形，右手在怀中成抱拳，拳面朝前上方与右脚成一条线。左手紧抱，右手背成拳，拳面朝后上方与右手背成拳，拳面朝后左脚向前一大步，右脚随之根一小步，双拳向上转环推牛，如骏马奔腾。右式与左式相反。

第四章

汤瓶心意四把捶
回回十八肘解释
汤瓶七式拳
穆氏汤瓶七式拳天山派汤瓶七式拳

汤瓶心意四把捶

心意六合拳是历史上的心意家门在三百三十年的艰苦锤炼中，像沙里淘金一样精筛细选出来的武术精华，成为祖国瑰宝。买壮图始祖是精炼简化心意六合拳杰出代表之一。

心意六合拳套路四把捶，在拳谱中称为心意四象，暗含鸡，龙，雄，虎等十大动物之意。四把捶和合四象之理，名为气火水土，又名四源，在传统武术中素有短拳之称。与其他内外长拳相比。它独具一格，是一个擅长爆发内劲的优秀拳种之一。基本拳式为：出手横拳，转身挑岭斩捶（称斩手）和鹰捉把及虎步把。拳式结构极其简练，每个动作几乎是直来直往。流传最早的是马三元式四把捶，其招数多达二十八式。买壮图始祖将二十八式，马氏四把捶精简到三个半拳式，把重式和侵扑站全部删掉，仅加反背作为半式，与人交手，快步逼近，贴身发劲。充分发挥心意拳在武术技击中以少胜多，以短见长的科学道理，时隔一百四十多年，从无人能将买式四把捶随意更动，增加或减少半式，买壮图始祖对心意六合拳的贡献之大，由此可见一斑。

演练内外长拳的武术行家，大概有所体会，倘若把所练的武术招数全部化解，运用到技击中去是很费劲的，在搏斗中时会出现顾此失彼，手脚无措的现象，而买式心意拳法本着少而精的原则，大胆割弃复杂拳式，着重四把捶的锻炼，不动如山岳，动则崩翻，攻中代防，柔中寓刚浑然一体，瞬息万变，既是套路，又是散手，长期练习买式心意四把捶，以后不想练也真难！因为一旦上功，不练就会浑身觉得像得了病那样难受，好像今天有一件事没有做完。这样，您就会自觉不自觉的坚持下来。因为买式心意拳是内家拳，以炼丹田气为主。丹气结成其乐无穷，无病无痛，精神抖擞，精气神旺盛，对生活充满无限的乐趣和追求，对事业有积极的进取精神。一旦你

遇到暴徒，就会运用心意门中所的决断劲，心一动站而内劲击矣，五行顺一气，放胆进成功。一式一招奏效，制服对方，其滋味实在难以形容。

买壮图师祖曾作一首发人深省的心意拳六合歌诀。练拳容易得艺难，灵劲上身天地翻，六合相聚人难躲，遇人好似弓断弦。

下面是买式四把捶的演练动作要领。

六合式

熊出洞

开始时立正，两臂左右自然下垂，目视前方，然后，左脚上前迈进一步。向右转体 90 度，侧身而立。左肩前领，右肩侧后，同时，左手向上提，虎口向内，五指分开朝上，两肘护肋左肘弯曲，左手提至与肩平，手掌外翻，手指经胸前向腹部前插至裆部，掌心护住裆前小指一侧向前，右手同时上提经左肘外侧提至于左肩同高，然后，两脚微屈，两脚前虚后实，右手迅速往下收至右胯，掌心护住胯部。五指撑开。左手由裆前经左腿内侧向前击出，至左膝前停住，小指一侧向前。臂与体的夹角保持 45 度左右，指尖撑开向下。提顶竖项。松肩沉肘，塌腰松胯，尾闾中正，内紧外松。舌舔上颚，呼吸顺其自然。周身上下合而为一，两脚心要悬，三尖相照，三弯要对。

下巴对住左肩，平视前方。

然后，双手由掌变拳护裆，拳心向外，手背相对，中距寸许，两肩微扣，谷道上提，浑身泰然，平视前方。

六合式，俗称预备式，有叫侵扑站，有叫扑来式，有称三体式，或称三才式。

要领：此系拳中起势，原名熊出洞，有眼观四处，耳听八方之意，而四肢百骸，均有备无患，亦守我之静以待敌之劲也。故熊扑击人或动物，必定先潜伏草丛或者树后。人之分散自已的威势，也是为了掩盖自己的实力。因此说人在从事这类活动时，要效法熊的潜伏。

虎扑把

承上。右腿独立，然后，悬起左脚向前迈进一大步，屈膝前弓，右脚在后蹬直，脚跟贴地外扭，定步成左步弓右箭步，双手由拳变掌顺势由小腹向前钻出，有自下向前，向上扑之意，左肘靠住左肋腰肌，手指张开前顶，掌心内涵，掌根按劲，右手在左手后垂于裆际，肘膀紧靠身躯，掌根着力，向下按劲头向前顶劲，下颚里收，两眼上翻，平视前方。注意：丹田里抱劲。谷道上提，右胯臀勿要翘起，右腿在后延伸，勿要脚跟抬起。

虎扑把要领：此式为饿虎扑食之势，锻炼丹田精灵之气，左掌

那个在左膝内侧前，右掌垂捺裆际，丹田结实抱紧，从头顶到右胯，至于右脚跟成一条直线。拳谱曰：三尖相照，三心要实。又曰：“头顶蓝天，脚抓大地”。此时手心向下捺劲，脚趾地，背心要实，谓之三心要实。左肩领前与鼻尖左脚夹成一条直线，谓之三尖相照。头有顶天之势，脚有抓地之劲，谓之头顶蓝天，脚抓大地，好似墙倒用一根杠杆把墙顶住。

过步箭窜

成虎朴之势，左手在前，右手在后，双掌先略往前引申，复微微往后一缩，两肘随着一伸一缩，两手合抱着小腹挫劲，丹田后吸，前胸含住。同时左脚向前微提，脚跟离地寸需向前垫步，右腿仍在后蹬直，不可变屈，手足须一致动作，成欲扑向前之姿势，而左脚垫步落实，右脚毫不停滞，急速越过左脚竭力向前胯一大步，屈膝下蹲，同时右手后缩至右胯傍贴住，而左手仍在前挺身，肘贴住左腰肋，手指微屈，壮如虎爪。垫步过步时，身子要稳固动作着实，脚掌须顺着地面前进，不得显示跳跃漂浮之步法，以致身躯东摇西摆，而失去过步箭窜之精神。

要领：此步谓之过步，又名快步或为马钻虎践之意，去劲发自丹田。而腿脚以竞其功，所以腿要勇敢，则成其践也，两手如同抱一圆木，以助丹田抖动，欲纵先收时谓助后腿趁势迈进也，所以收如伏猫，纵如放虎即此把之意。

猴缩蹲

承上。右腿进步之后，身子下蹲，重心放在右脚上，左脚紧追迈至右脚前，提膝与胯平，脚尖上翘，左膝置于右膝前，两膝前后裹劲，两大腿合劲，右手在后平贴胯部。手指撑开，向前顶劲，左肩领前，左手不变，左肘仍紧贴左肋，手指轻柔掌根按劲，下颚里收，目光前视，注意身体仍吃紧于右腿上，切忌低头俯身，耸肩凸臀

要领：此式蓄而待发之劲意，譬如射箭，必先引而后发，盖弓开如满月，所以蓄也，势足则发箭之力强而射程亦远，始可收射效矣，拳技亦然，胸腰丹田之劲，必先含住，四梢裹劲。然后进身如虎践，拳发如箭窜矣。故师曰：身如弓弩，拳如药箭，不然进身无势，不能令敌畏惧。发拳虽重，而敌无败伤之患，怎能谓之拳艺呢？

青龙出水

成猴来蹲之势，左腿再朝前迈出一步，右脚紧起向前落于左脚后。同时右掌变拳，从右胯提至左掌与之会合，左掌抱住右拳，由下而上，循弧向前提击高于胸平，平视前方。

要领：龙是水中最灵敏而又最凶猛的动物，龙的性格变化无常，让人无法臆测其行动，像龙一样忽隐忽现，捉摸不定。这是心理战术的奥妙所在。它再吞身蓄气时，犹如龙体之蛰伏，有储而待发之意，出水起身进攻时，犹如龙之升腾，有冲天之胸，蛰是为了取得更迅速，合为了开得更猛烈，吞是为了吐得更充分。没有劲气的集储就不会有劲力的发放，没有吞身之伏，就没有腾身之冲，没有三曲之才，就没有变化之灵。

出手横拳

承上。左掌右拳同时弧线往后收直到腹部前，悬提之左脚向前一步踏实，左膝前弓，右腿在后蹬直，脚跟外扭，成左弓右箭步，同时右拳，与左胯合劲，自右胯由下而上，略呈弧线向前猛击。高与嘴平，左掌顺右臂向前推出，置于右拳心，五指分开并微向后。平视前方。

要领：练出手横拳时，当右拳从右胯移至小腹时，拳头必须握得结实有力，如同卷紧的爆仗一样，发横拳，当左掌顺右臂向前推出时，需肩与胯合，右腿蹬劲，肩要催肘，肘要催手，两肩向里扣劲，两肘稍下垂裹劲，手臂似曲非曲，以直非直，过直则无力且易为人所制，过曲则不远而难落敌。内五行要发，外五行要随，三节明，四梢齐内劲出。

鹞子入林

承接出手横拳之势，两脚掌为轴，同时蹍地，身向右后方转体180度，右拳变掌，置于左肘间，左掌顺势转至头顶左部上侧，两臂互相交叉，两肘裹劲，左手臂朝前右前斜方，指尖上顶，右臂斜横于胸前，手背靠于左胯际，手臂伸直，不可弯曲，两肩下榻劲，两臂交相裹于胸前，若绳索捆住一样，同时，颈项右拧，双目后后顾，以眼角视人，而身腰随着右转，右肩前领，抖身而起，右脚随着身腰右转，向后自然退半步，落至左脚前。身体战定后，前胸面对。平视前方。

要领：练鹞子入林时，要有包裹之劲，蓄而待发之意，故回身后转时须着意于背劲，双目后睨而视之，猝然而起，手腰须灵活，气势如猛虎回首，又如鹞子侧翅，不可随意为之，有头鹞形之意。

丹凤朝阳

承上式。上身右拧，左肩领前，左手自脸傍下搂到胸前，则掌

心翻下以掌根出劲往下捺止于裆际，右手以前臂向上托体提劲，自左胯际提于右太阳傍，手臂略弯曲，肘向里裹劲，手背朝外，同时左脚顺地面向前擦去，迈进半步左右，脚尖上翘，脚跟点地，左脚虚，右脚实，胸腹切勿前挺出，以至失劲，平视前方。

要领：练丹凤朝阳时，此式接前式一气呵成，右掌上托同时左手下沉，双臂交互上下撕劲，胸部内含，丹田里收，谷道上提，练时柔而不刚，顺势盘旋，以收调息平气之功。

合劈

成丹田朝阳之势，左脚向前迈进半步，屈膝下蹲，身体下沉，全身重心坐于左腿，右腿屈膝提起，悬临于左膝前，脚尖上翘。同时左掌自下而上，经过胸前，上托护右腮颊，五指在撑开，肘臂屈贴左乳前，右掌自下而下，屈肘贴肋，手掌对准鼻尖前，尽力向下臂至右膝里侧，手臂垂，指尖向下，右肩前领，头上顶，腰要领直，左右两手一沉一托，和身体一起动作，不分前后，含胸，两膝里裹，扣裆，身体不可前俯后仰，左右歪斜，平视前方。

寒鹰蹬架

要领：练合臂时，左脚向前迈进半步要与身体转动，右手沉肩下劈动作一致，同时与右膝的上提要合。下劈时必须右前臂下弦出劲，指尖向前顶劲，沉肩垂肘，腰部向里收缩，动作须敏捷有势，一股劲儿劈下，左手上托护腮助右掌下劈之势，使身体保持平衡之作用。此式肩膀、肘膝、手足相会，全身系而为一，谓之外三合。

挑岭

承上合劈之势，右掌从下向上呈现上挑，手指撑开前顶，手腕要直，肘微垂而裹劲，右肩后收，左掌自右腮边，沿胸前下按置于左胯根部，左肩微微前挺，手指撑开向前，同时悬提得右腿顺势向前迈进一步，屈膝踏实，左腿在后蹬直，成右弓左箭步，头向上顶，自手到脚成一条直线，平视前方。

要领：练挑岭时，合劈连挑岭，一束一展阴阳之理也，上挑时须敏捷而有力，右臂上托过鼻尖后，则劲移肘尖，手脚必须协调一致，周身上下带突发劲，但又不能僵硬，不用拙力。

鹰捉把

承上挑岭之势，右脚向后腿半步，左脚屈膝，右掌同时从头上方下收至胸前，掌心向后，右肘紧贴右肋，左脚向前迈进半步，脚掌撑地，紧靠右脚心成连莲枝步，身亦起立左掌随脚自小腹而置胸前，经右肘傍顺右臂内侧向前推出翻掌，右掌在前，五指掌开，左掌紧贴右手虎口，五指分开，掌根向前，指尖前顶，两肘相向裹肋，肘弯微屈，两眼自两臂中间空隙处前视，用眼角视人，左脚向前进一步，屈膝前弓，右脚在后延伸成左弓右箭步。同时，两掌猛力下按，左掌按至左膝旁，屈肘贴肋，右手后抽，落于右胯根部护裆，然后，左肩下榻前拧，右肩向后微抽，左肱下弦出劲。双掌撑开指尖前顶，掌根向下捺劲，形如虎爪。腹部丹田贯意，以意催气，以气催声，

发出“噫”的一声。称为雷声。其发声大小随内气充沛程度而异，但每次之发声，均以气冲至舌尖平为度，双掌下按时，似抓着天上的把柄，要将天扯塌。心意门中，此称为恨天无把，同时头向前顶，舌顶上腭，口闭齿合，颈项要正直，下颚略内收，从头到右脚须在一条直线上，背不可陷，胸不可挺，腹部凹，臀要实，平视前方，如此收势已成虎扑之势也。

要领：拳谱曰：起手如鹰捉，出手似虎扑。此为心意六合拳之核心，而此式鹰捉紧接虎扑，尤为锻炼捉劲之基本动作。故部该等闲视之，其自外形观之，此把似着重掌之捉劲合广肱之劈劲，其实却是以头之前顶劲为主。

虎观山

承上之式，左脚后腿一大步，承右弓左箭步，同时，左肩背向左后方拧转 180 度，左手趁势沉右，臂膀后撤至右肩窝，于是身续向右转面对正右方，左肩前领，左脚随之前屈，右腿在后延伸，转成左弓右箭步，同时左手自上面下划弧往前斩击，提肘重肱，掌根内外，指尖向下，右手亦同时外翻，经体右侧上提，由脸部摆至左

肩侧上方，迅速往下收至右胯向后斩击，提肘垂肱，掌根向外，指尖向下，头向上顶，下颚里收，平视前方。

要领：此式又名霸王观，以其有猛回头，环顾动静之态，又有霸王胯骓，观察阵势之意其形虽异，而描摹之伸情则一也，学习拳艺，摆姿势易而拿架子得其中劲路难，而且得其神韵更难。习艺者如能于此等处痛下功夫，则拳艺可望大成矣。身向左转时，为身后御敌之法，着重背劲，反身后鼻尖对准，肘尖，脚尖。双目虽未前视而眸子上翻。凛凛霸气意欲伸，静落丹田气无声，审敌虚实而趋其危。

斩捶（或称斩手）

承虎观山之势，右掌变拳往上才击去高与嘴平，右肩前领，臂时垂屈，拳心稍向上，左掌同时顺势上撩，虎口护着右肘弯里侧，垂肘护肋，同时，左脚向前迈进一步，随势起立，足掌抓地战稳，全身重心放在左腿，右脚擦地而起，右腿屈膝上提，以大腿面平直为度，脚尖上翘，于是右拳向前下方砸去低于膝齐，拳端面向下，左手扶护右臂外侧。同时身子下蹲。右脚下错落于左脚前，全身重心踞于双脚之间。两腿成夹马之势，身子挺直不可前俯，不可后仰，左右歪斜。臀勿外凸，平视平方。

要领：练斩捶时，右掌变拳向上提拉击去。必须连肩带背，以右半边身体向前上方提拉，向下要有坐劲，劲向上提，势如旗鼓，落下肘束身下势，右肩臂向前下榻劲。拳谱曰：如虎收山斩手炮，奋击敌手足之拳也，炮者，以喻拳击之猛烈敏捷。

怀抱顽石

承上势，左脚插过右脚前进半步，全身重心移于右腿上，身体依然蹲住，仍以右肩领前，形成倒撤步。同时右拳变掌心，屈肘贴肋，臂变化略成弧形，两掌一齐向左胯落下，上身左转拧劲，于是两掌平伸向左方一抄，两肘屈靠肋际一收，如抄起千斤顽石，托于臂腕间，小腹微用力收缩，提肛吊肚，稍停。右脚向前贴住滑上一步，左脚乃后撤与右脚并拢成莲枝步。右掌在前，左掌在后从腹部抄至嘴前方，掌心向右，抖身而起，向右拧转，左掌顺右臂内侧向前自右掌虎口突出翻掌，右掌在前，五指分开，左掌紧贴子啊右手虎口，五指撑开向上，掌心微向前，左肩前领，成鹰捉之势，两肘下垂，相向裹劲，双目从双臂交叉隙中睨视前方。

要领：此式是为锻炼内劲之法，劲作酷似怀中抱顽石，向天空猛力一抛，其劲路则着重于抖丹田之劲，左脚后撤于后脚并拢，左脚后撤于右脚并拢，左脚须掠地后收。同时抖身而起，肩腰胯一齐向右拧劲，才能抖动丹田之劲而符此把之意。

鹰捉把

虎扑把

虎形盘肘

呈上虎扑把之势，左掌在前，右掌在后，双手先略往前引申，复微微往后一缩，两手合抱着小腹挫劲，丹田后吸，前胸含住，同时左脚向前微提，脚跟离地寸许向前垫步，右腿仍在后蹬直，不可变屈，手脚须一致动作，成欲扑向前之姿势，而左脚垫步落实，左掌由左膝内侧经体右侧向上托起至与头同高，掌心向前上方盖出成虎爪形，肘稍弯曲，右掌从裆际上提到右胸前曲肘，然后，右后脚紧起向前落于左脚后。同时，右肘向前方由上往下砸去。左手外翻，掌心朝上，置于右肘内侧上，三尖相照，三弯要对，平视前方。

要领：练虎形盘肘，其外形似深山老林中的斑斓白额大虎，八面威风，其势吓人，其声如雷。拳谱曰：虎有出山之勇猛。心意拳中之虎形，取虎出山之勇猛，来虎剪扑搏斗之技巧，力量雄浑，外形稳健，肘分左右两拳，它不但促进肋上肢的舒展，并且使上肢的关节肌肉产生了一股争衡的力量。动作起来沉稳扎实有力，无事不到肘不可轻用。

冲天炮

承上之式，右肘往下压，右掌自上往下变拳，顺胸部绕至嘴平，

掌心稍向上，左掌同时顺势护于右肘下，掌心朝右，虎口抵住尺骨鹰嘴，肘与肋侧相距一拳左右。同时，左脚向前迈进一步，随势起立，脚趾抓地站稳，全身重心放在左腿，右脚同时屈膝抬起，脚面垂直，足尖朝下，如金鸡独立之状。右膝不可抬得过高，以右胯同平

握地炮

呈冲天炮之势，右脚落地，屈膝成前弓，左腿在后蹬直，脚跟帖地外扭，成为右弓左箭步。同时，右拳向里，向下翻拧，拳头 猛栽，左掌下落至右臂内侧，平视前方。

要领：练冲天炮，握地炮。是顾法中一种打法，在运用中连环出击，使对方防不胜防，它既能保护自己，又能打击敌方。

反背

承上之式，右拳自下向里收回，顺胸部绕至嘴前变掌撤于右肋下，再变拳。右脚同时起跳落于左脚后，左脚趁右脚起跳时向前跨半步落步。

白虎搜山 1

白虎搜山 2

要领：练反背时，左脚配合要协调，当右脚起跳落于左脚后，左脚趁右腿起跳时向前跨半落步时要站稳，不可东歪西斜。以下接着打出手横拳。

转身挑岭，蹬脚虎扑

承上出手横拳之势，左脚以掌为轴，右脚以后跟为轴，同时踝地，向右后方转体 180 度。右掌置于小腹下，左掌贴于右腮边，右脚尖翘起，前虚后实，含胸拔背，平视前方。

虎扑把

然后，右脚在前成弓步，右脚心悬空，五趾抓地，右掌从下向上呈弧线上挑，手指撑开前顶，手腕要直，肘微垂而裹劲，右肩后收，左掌从右腮边，沿胸前下按置于左胯根部，左肩微微前挺，手指撑向前，身体微微往后一缩，同时悬提右脚向上起跳，左腿趁右腿起跳时，也迅速蹬地跳起，上跳时左脚在前，右脚在后，在身体跃起的同时，右掌从头上方下收至胸前，掌心向右，随之，双手提起，在头上方交叉，右手在外，左手在内，臂伸直。在脚落地的同时，左手靠住左肘，右掌在后，紧靠左臂内侧，右肘抵住右肋。目视前方。

紧接，左脚向前迈进一步，右腿伸直，脚跟贴地外扭，成左弓右箭步，两掌同时循小腹向前钻出，有自下向前，向上扑之意，左肘靠住左肋腰际，手指撑开前顶，掌心内涵，掌根按劲，右手在左手后垂于裆际，肘膀紧靠身躯，掌根着力，向下按劲，头向前顶劲，下颚内收，两眼往上翻，平视前方。丹田结实抱紧，谷道上提，右

胯臀勿翘起，右腿在后延伸，勿使脚跟欠起。从头顶到右胯，至脚跟成一条直线。

要领：练蹬脚虎扑要注意双掌相叠，虎口圆，十指撑开，两手要随身体的下降同时抓下，掌心行前扑出，用意在掌根，两手扑出要同脚的上步落地同时完成，手臂要保持圆弧。三尖相照，三心要实。可以收如伏猫，纵如放虎即此把之意也。

雷声

四把之收势，为鹰捉下落而成蹬脚虎扑之势。练习至此，趁鹰捉下落之势，丹田后收，横膈膜上开，压缩肺气全部外呼，发“噫”音谓之雷声响动，发声时，头顶项竖，舌尖上顶手指前顶。拳谱曰：肺属金，肺动如闪电，气发而为声，声随之发。手随声落，故一枝动而白枝摇，四梢无不齐，内劲无不出矣。

回回十八肘拳法解释

西域天山派拳法，是丝路文化的武学结晶，一千三百年前，由古老的丝绸之路，波斯及阿拉伯商人不远万里来到了中国，他们不但促进了中阿经贸往来，同时也带来了游牧民族马背上的格斗技击武学，当他们到了大唐华夏古国，发现中华武学，更是门派众多，博大精深。杨氏汤瓶盘山肘二十四式从唐朝已形成雏形，后又完善分化出阴阳母子回回肘、回回十八肘等肘法。据恩师义父杨耀钧师伯郭文治所述，相传北宋名将杨继业也称（杨业）的后裔，身居新疆的一代护国将领，杨继明得此肘法的内察觉到此法的途步实战威力，深入为实战加以整合，创建了独特的杨氏阴阳母子回回肘。直到明末清初，杨门后裔，杨明公进一步以口传身带的方式将独特的肘法技能，加以挖掘、整理、完善与传承，汤瓶盘山靠肘二十四式系统的论述肘法的传承，和汤瓶七式拳传承一样，因传承体系严格，只传入门弟子，因此也只能分散掌握在极少数武学弟子手中，并以回传身带的方式，世代相传。而师传非常严谨，严选品德高尚，有武德武学修养的后人来继续，因而能得道演练者，尤为凤毛麟角，少为人知，世上罕见，濒临失传。1989 年我师弟杨华祥率弟子一行三人参加在广西南宁举办的“中国首届传统武术观摩大会”第一次亮相，中国体育报的报道才让武林朋友有所了解。回回一传承肘法，不但可强身自卫，而且更有健身延年之作用，是武学中之珍品。它是习武之人值得深学的武学之一。朝思暮想的华夏武学传承绝技。明一末清初以来武学、医学大家杨明公及后裔杨岭、，穆其太、张志诚、李祯、张聚、买壮图、李海森、丁兆祥、袁凤仪、买鸿宾、袁长青、尚学礼、杨殿卿、卢嵩高、郭文治、杨耀钧、杨祥麟、吕瑞芳、沙忠继、买学礼、买清选、铁志豪、铁国成、孙少甫、居奎、

甘风池、方四等人。主要流行新疆、河南、上海、江苏、宁夏、陕西一带。本人幼年八岁有幸于60年前，拜河南恩师义父杨耀钧处，习得回族三大战场，保家卫国实战拳法，心意六合拳，汤瓶七式拳，回回十八肘法，是我一生缘分，福气，善哉！吾师义父杨耀钧将家传汤瓶肘法传授给我。随着年龄延续，已到夕阳之年，对武学探索研究与理解不断的加深，越来越感觉，吾师义父所传之肘法，精妙绝伦，湯瓶盘山靠肘是由二十四单盘式组成，一招多发，有套路汤瓶阴阳母子肘法。也有对练喂招，拆式。一般先练单式为主，有定式，行式，有搏击格斗，又有连环肘法。分为上中下。下部是七星梅花九宫步，中部是阴阳母子肘，上部是五雷闪电掌。盘打合一，俗话说，硬砸不如巧打，打中有闪，闪中有打阴阳变化，虚虚实实，真真假假，有时候巧打不如硬砸，中门进身，侧身变步，不招不架就是一下见分晓。全身无处不打人，哪里方便用，是明肘，也是暗肘，化肘，闪电肘。歹毒凶狠，残忍如虎豹撕羊，要练成雷鸣内含闪电劲。受击者轻的骨断筋折，重的一命呼呜。不给敌人留一丝机会，一击必杀，太野蛮狠毒可怕，俗话说宁挨十拳，不受一肘。所以世上流传稀少，多是家族性传承。传授者慎之又慎，深恐一时冲动，害人又害己。就像上海心意六合拳开山鼻祖，前辈临终前对郭文治师伯所说，大哥，我这一辈子遗憾没跟师父学汤瓶七式拳。

回回十八肘拳，步法是七星梅花九宫步。奔步、小跳步、坐盘步、十字步、马步、快步、慢步、寸垫步、滑步、倒插步、三角步、地震步。肘法以挑、沉、压、砸、托、滚、扫、顶、撞、化、夹、为主。劲法有崩、点、抖、拧、展、撕、身法，束长，进退，翻身，吞吐，螺旋，闪战，捷跃，正面，斜面，刚柔，畜力为主。肘式有，汤瓶壶把肘，依玛尼晃肘，拨郎外摆肘，天山雪莲肘，横扫千军肘，狸猫上冲肘，后抽连环肘，老虎双夹肘，黑熊双推肘，如影随形肘，蝴蝶双分肘，猿猴起落肘，闪电穿心肘，左右翻浪肘，偷步捣拐肘，凌空劈砸肘，拨云托天肘，霸王拉弓肘，盘山靠打肘，闪门接打肘，蛟龙翻山肘，白蛇吐芯肘，接臂破命肘，阴阳母子肘。

Explanation of Hui Nation Eighteen Elbow Boxing Method

Western Region Tianshan School Boxing Method is the crystallization of martial arts of the Silk Road culture. 1,300 years ago, along the ancient Silk Road, Persian and Arab merchants came to China from a great distance. They not only promoted economic and trade exchanges between China and Arab countries, but they also brought the martial art of nomads fighting on horseback . When they arrived in the ancient China of the Tang Dynasty, they discovered that Chinese martial arts had many schools and profound knowledge. Yang family Tang Ping (soup bottle) Panshan elbow 24-form took shaope during the Tang dynasty. Later, the Yin-Yang mother and child elbow, Hui nation 18 elbow-on-elbow method was perfected. According to Yang Yaojun and his foster father Guo Wenzhi, according to legend, the Northern Song Dynasty general Yang Jiming (also known as Yang Jike, a descendant of Yang Ye), was general living in Xinjiang. Yang Jiming realized the power of this method in actual combat, and integrated it into actual combat to create a unique Yang family Yin-Yang mother and child Hui nation elbow method. At the end of the Ming Dynasty and the beginning of Qing Dynasty, Yang school descendant Yang Minggong further developed, organized, perfected and passed on his unique elbow skills by means of oral transmission. Tang Ping Panshan twenty-four elbow form as a systematic exposition for passing on elbow skills is in the same heritage as Tang Ping 7-form boxing. Because of the strict inheritance system, only disciples were introduced, so it was spread in the hands of only a very small number of martial arts disciples, and

passed on from generation to generation only within the Hui nation. The teacher passed on very rigorous, carefully selected and noble morals, and though the accomplishment of descendants in martial arts training continues, those who can follow the way are very rare, seldom known, rare in the world, and on the verge of being lost. In 1989, my younger brother Yang Huaxiang led a group of three students to participate in the "First Chinese Traditional Wushu Study Conference" held in Nanning, Guangxi. The report in China Sports Daily was the first time that martial arts friends had become aware of it. Hui heritage elbow method not only strengthens self-defense, but also promotes fitness and prolonging life. It is a treasure amongst martial arts, and one worthy of further study by those who practice martial arts. From the end of the Ming Dynasty and the beginning of the Qing Dynasty, it has been practiced by master of martial arts and medicine Yang Minggong and his descendants Yang Ling, Mu Qitai, Zhang Zhicheng, Li Zhen, Zhang Ju, Mai Zhuangtu, Li Haisen, Ding Zhaoxiang, Yuan Fengyi, Mai Hongbin, Yuan Changqing, Shang Xueli, Yang Dianqing, Lu Songgao, Guo Wenzhi, Yang Yaojun, Yang Xianglin, Lu Ruifang, Sha Zhongji, Mai Xueli, Mai Qingxuan, Tie Zhihao, Tie Guocheng, Sun Shaofu, Jukui, Gan Fengchi, Fang Si and others. Mainly popular in Xinjiang, Henan, Shanghai, Jiangsu, Ningxia, Shaanxi. Sixty years ago, when I was eight years old, I had the honour to worship Yang Yaojun, my mentor from Henan Province, learned the three major battlefields of the Hui nationality, the actual combat methods of defending the home and the country, Xinyi Six Harmonies Boxing, Tang Ping 7-form Boxing, Hui nation 18 elbow method, it was my destiny, blessing, kindness! My teacher and foster father, Yang Yaojun, taught me the family Tang Ping elbow method. As I matured and reached old age, my exploration, research and understanding of martial arts continued

to deepen, and I felt more and more that the elbow method taught by my teacher foster father was exquisite and beyond compare. Tang Ping Panshan elbow method comprises of twenty-four single moves, each move had multiple applications, forming the Tang Ping Yin-Yang mother and child elbow method. There is also pair-wise sparring. The first part is the seven-star plum blossom nine palace steps, the middle part is the Yin-Yang mother and child elbow method, and the final part is the five thunder and lightning palm. Combining moves, as the saying goes, hard strikes are worse than clever strikes, there are dodges in strikes, there are strikes in dodges as yin and yang cycle, false and real, true and false, sometimes clever strikes are worse than hard strikes, enter the middle door and step to one side. If only you try, you will see the difference at a glance. There is nowhere in the whole body where it is not convenient to strike with the elbow, bu the elbow is hidden and fast as lightning. Vicious and cruel, like a tiger or a leopard tearing a sheep, you must achieve rolls of thunder with lightning strength. The light bones and tendons of the victims are broken, and the heavy ones crushed. Don't leave the enemy a chance, one blow will kill, too savage, vicious and terrifying, as the saying goes, it's better to receive ten punches than one elbow strike. Therefore, it is a rare skill in the world, and most learn it through family inheritance. The master is deeply cautious , afraid of impulsiveness and the risk of harming others and self. So the originator of Shanghai Xinyi Six Harmonies Boxing, said to Guo Wenzhi before his death, "Elder brother, I regret that I never learned Tang Ping 7-form boxing from my Master."

In Hui nation eighteen elbow fist method, the footwork is the seven-star plum blossom nine palace steps. Running step, small jump step, sitting cross step, cross step, horse step, fast step, slow step, inch step, sliding step, reverse step, triangle step, earthquake step. The power

techniques include collapse, point, shaking, twisting, stretching, tearing, whole-body method, long grip, advance and retreat, overturn, gather and expel, spiral, dodge, quick leap, direct, oblique, firm and soft, and animal power. Elbow techniques include Tang Ping soup bottle pot handle elbow, light of Mani shake elbow, pull outside elbow, Tianshan snow lotus elbow, sweeping elbow of one thousand soldiers, leopard raises elbow straight ahead, draw chain back elbow, tiger double press elbow, black bear double push elbow, shadow follows body elbow, butterfly split elbow, ape lifts and lowers elbow, lightning pierces heart elbow, elbow turning left and right, steal step and smash elbow, volley smash elbow, sweep aside cloud to grasp heaven elbow, overlord draws his bow elbow, circle mountain elbow strike, dodge entrance to strike elbow, dragon overturns mountain elbow, white snake spews elbow, catch and break arm elbow, Yin-Yang mother and child elbow.

汤瓶七式拳
Tang Ping 7-form Boxing

杨氏汤瓶七式拳又称“西域天山派荡平七式拳”，是由河南孟县武术及回族医学大家至明末清初，世代相传延续至今。在传承过程中，经不断吸取中华传统流派有效击技防身技法，养生法使汤瓶七式拳，在拳法招式上进一步得到完善。汤瓶七式拳后因杨氏家族从河南孟县迁移至周口，并和买氏心意六合拳传承人买壮图一脉结为姻缘，因是同族，群内所传承并被称为“西域天山流派”。同时和其他武术有了更多交流与融合。特别是解放前期从河南周口移居至上海的汤瓶七式拳一代先贤郭文志师伯和著名“心意六合十大形”上海传承泰斗大师卢嵩高老先生为更好地促进两拳种的交流与团结。同时，我的恩师杨氏汤瓶七式拳与汤瓶盘山靠肘，第六代传承人受过正统私塾教育并于一九二一年就参加由早期共产党所发起的革命运动，并 1926 年加参伟大的中国共产党，离休后经周恩来总理特批投亲大女儿定居上海，我的恩师杨耀钧先生，也是“买氏心意六合十大形”的传承人之一，当时他们三人在沪上被称为“心意汤瓶门”。河南派三杰。由恩师杨耀钧义父的配合，先贤们将两种回族内家拳种的精华技法与养生融为一体，总结创编了；具有育气强内功，及实战技击和强身健体的综合套路，先贤们称之为“七心套子”又称心意七式拳。“七心套子”共分三大路与七小套路。一大路心意拳为主其他为副，二大路七式拳为主其他为副，三大路回回肘为主，其他为基础。七小路是分解小段。形成了更有现代实战技击强身健体的综合格斗套路《汤瓶盘山靠肘二十四式》的传承，我与上海两拳派中部分入门弟子，有幸得到恩师的传授。此肘法，招法凶猛灵

活，头肩，脚腿掌肘合一并用，对手眼身法，进退起落，吞吐沉浮，散展技击，有实战性技能，只是此肘法，一定要有两拳法功底的弟子才能更准确掌握演练出惊天动地，地震山摇，威风八方。是对肘法的提炼与总结。此肘法因运动强度要远比单式，更耗体能。只适合于十八至五十岁内，身体强壮的传承弟子演练。

Yang family Tangping 7-form Boxing, also known as "Western Tianshan School Dangping 7-form Boxing", has been passed down from generation to generation from the Hui martial arts and medicine masters of Mengxian County, Henan Province since the end of the Ming Dynasty and the beginning of the Qing Dynasty. As it was passed down the generations, gradually absorbing the defensive techniques of traditional Chinese schools, the health-preserving aspects of Tang Ping 7-form Boxing were further improved. Later, when the Yang family moved from Mengxian County to Zhoukou in Henan Province, and married into the family of Mai Zhuangtu, the inheritor of Mai family Xinyi Six Harmonies Boxing, Tang Ping 7-form Boxing was absorbed into this group and was called "Western Regions Tianshan School". At the same time, there was much communication and integration with other martial arts. In particluar, in the early days of liberation, Guo Wenzhi, a master of the Tangping 7-form Boxing who moved from Zhoukou of Henan to Shanghai, and Mr. Lu Songgao, the famous "Xinyi Six Harmonies Ten Great Forms" Shanghai heritage master, joined together in order to better promote the exchange and unity of the two types of boxing. At the same time, my mentor, sixth generation inheritor of the Yang family Tang Ping 7-form Boxing and Tang Ping Panshan elbow strike, received an orthodox private education and participated in the revolutionary movement initiated by the early Communist Party in 1921, and in 1926

joined the great Communist Party of China. After he retired, Premier Zhou Enlai approved the request of his eldest daughter that my mentor, Mr. Yang Yaojun, also one of the inheritors of "Buy's Mind Six-in-One", should settle in Shanghai. At that time, the three of them were known as the "Xinyi Tang Ping School" of Shanghai. Three masters of Henan were sent to join them. With the co-operation of my mentor and foster father Yang Yaojun, the masters integrated and summarized the essence of the two types of Hui internal boxing and health preservation techniques. They produced a comprehensive routine for cultivating qi and strengthening internal power, as well as actual combat and physical fitness. The masters called it "Seven Heart Set", also known as Xinyi 7-form Boxing. "Seven Heart Set" is divided into three great and seven small sets. The first great set focuses on Xinyiquan, the second great set focuses on 7-form Boxing, and the third great set focuses on the Hui nation elbow method. The seven small sets form sub-sections of these. This became the "Tang Ping Panshan 24-form elbow strikes", a comprehensive fighting routine with more modern combat skills and physical fitness. I and some of the beginner disciples of the Shanghai Two Boxing Schools were fortunate to be taught by our mentor. This elbow method is fierce and flexible, with the head, shoulders, feet, legs, and elbows being used together. While the opponent's eye and body movements, advance and retreat, rise and fall, lift and drop, all have practical combat applications, in this elbow technique, disciples must have a solid foundation in the two-fist technique more accurately to master earth-shattering power in all directions. This is the essence of the elbow method. This elbow method consumes more energy than others due to its exercise intensity. It is only suitable for practice by strong inheritance disciples between the ages of 18 and 50.

汤瓶，二把半是汤瓶古法心意拳之中秘传套路，全套虽只有数式，但其势，惊天动地，天翻地覆恨天无把，恨地无环，出招凶猛狠快，劲势雄伟，极具爆发内劲，汤瓶二把半共二趟 10 式，由西域古法心意拳始祖杨明公，五代杨殿卿，杨瑞堂，河南周口人回族传杨耀钧，杨祥麟。恩师义杨耀钧老先生，河南周口人。系心意泰斗巨匠买壮图孙女婿，殿卿之侄，传义子董纲成、长子杨华增、次子杨华祥、李亮、阚罗祥。宁夏女婿蒋红岩、于承惠、杨金柱等人。汤瓶二把半盘练法。熊出洞；左脚在前，身向右侧整体下蹲，两腿弯曲，前后相套，左掌置右腮处。掌心向里，右掌置右胯处，掌心贴胯，目视前方。图 1。

接把左转身，上右脚卷地风，同时右掌握拳由下向上撩击，高至腹部，左掌从右腮向下朝前击出，高同肩平，回左掌拍右腕。图 2。

鹰捉虎扑，双掌交叉上举，掌心向内，左掌在右掌虎口上，同时上右脚卷地风，双掌前撞，翻掌拍按左脚上前一大步成牮柱式，指的庙里斜着支撑的柱子，同时双撑撕拽而下，左掌靠左膝内侧，指尖朝前，右掌置裆部，护裆。图3。

横拳；右手握拳，拳眼向上，左掌五指张开贴在右拳上，同时起身，右脚上前半步，震脚，双手由下向上划一弧形收至腹部，左脚上前一大步成牮柱式，双手由下的上撩击高与胸平，目视前方。图4。

转身挑岭阴阳势，全身整体下蹲，右掌下插至左胯旁，左手提至右腮旁，右合转身，右脚上步右掌上挑，高过头顶，全身起立，左掌下按至裆前，左脚上半步，重心落在右脚上，左脚跟着地，脚尖翘起。图5。

沉劈，左脚垫步上右脚脚尖翘起，全身下蹲，同时右掌尽力下劈，至裆前手背靠右脚心，左掌上提至右腮旁，掌心向内。图 6。

挑岭，左脚猛蹬，右脚上一大步成犁柱式，同时右掌由下向上朝前发崩抖劲挑起，置头部前上方，掌心向里，五指张开，左掌下按至裆部护裆。图 7。

并步单掌，左脚上一步和右脚并齐，左掌扶石掌腕部向前击出，高于肩平。图 8。

转身鹰捉虎扑，狸猫扑鼠左后转身，双掌交叉上举，掌心向内左掌在里，右掌在外紧贴右手背，同时上右脚卷地风双掌前撞翻掌拍按，左脚上一大步成犨柱式，同时双掌撕拽而下，收至腹部，随着左脚前落双掌向前击出至左膝前，狸猫扑鼠雷声收势图 9。弓步变马步随转伊玛尼，汤瓶壶《式》。

穆氏汤瓶七式拳天山派汤瓶七式拳

（也称天山派回回门汤瓶功七式拳）
又称：荡平七式拳天山派

作者　董纲成

穆氏汤瓶七式拳天山派汤瓶七式拳（也称天山派回回门汤瓶功七式拳）又称：荡平七式拳天山派.创始于南宗光宗赵惇绍熙元年（公元1190）至今八百多年。

祖师杨继明北宋名将，杨继业之后他幼时于太行山从师于晋葛真人所创丹鼎派丽九代传人，王世光真君，后由于南宋衰落。金兵进犯，连年战事，元兵兴起，遂远遁西域（今新疆维吾尔自治区天山山脉博格达山区）隐居，习练武功，修心养心，参悟玄玄。

祖师杨继明之子，杨延天和同隐天山之神霄派王文卿之徒萨守坚真君同修参悟，一起创派并制规，因地而名为“天山派”因杨继明祖师和萨守坚真君诞辰为阴历九月二十三。

天山派开山日也即阴历九月二十三。天山派武功法以丹鼎派为内功基础，并融汇了神霄派之心法。杨氏家传之武功，讲求内养心神，外练身形，以外补内，玄人天一。

杨延天祖师之女，萨守坚真君之徒渡烟神君（亦称了空神君，后称孤独氏）为第一代。

第二代传人系渡烟神君，后称孤独氏之徒“八臂神猿”铁肩道长。

第三代张志平，原从师于全真道第二代传人之一“华山派”创立者郝大通真人，后加盟天山派，其号“担风道长”，担风道长将天山派武功法融合了“全真道”之教义，增立了山林制度越加完善了天山派的功法和派规。

第四代传人系维吾尔族，是伊斯兰教大阿訇阿不都沙吾提之女阿母姑。因西域政变，其父遭难，难中遇担风道长救助，并收为徒，阿姆系侠天山南北，从维吾尔族习俗，头戴红巾，因攻得名飞红巾“道号”“日红神君”天山牌无功法中又增进了伊斯兰教之某些教规和修炼法，飞红巾曰红神君后定居天山山脉南高峰托木尔山区。四川“岷山派门赤城子于元朝中叶游历西域，加盟天山派，担风道长收为徒，号为“日郎道长”后定居天山山脉北高峰博格达山区，因天山山脉蜿赦千公里，北高峰博格达山区与南高峰托木尔山区相隔一千多公里。路途遥远，多有不便之处，日郎道长与日红神君分于南北两高峰授徒，天山遂分为南北二宋，支派又有“萨神派”萨真君西河派等，直至第十六代传人，化音道长承继掌门，南北二宋才告合并。

天山派传至今日，经历了六个朝代八百多年，历代传人于武当，少林，青城、峨嵋、崆峒、昆仑等诸派均有交往接触、吸收了众家之长，形成了天山派武功、功法特有的武功功法体系。

汤瓶七式拳（亦称回回门汤瓶拳，七式拳）是中国回族武术重要拳术之一，因拳术动作形似回族所用的汤瓶而得名，后又称“荡平七式拳”起源于“妥勒盖修练法”汤瓶的命名源于唐朝，当波斯中东穆斯林对中国经济的繁荣，商务交流，外交来往，有所贡献的时候，唐王李世民为了给于表彰，按照穆斯林的习俗打造了一只瓶壮的“洗壶”命名为“唐壶”随着朝代的演变，“洗壶”是穆斯林用于洗阿布代斯的器具，其意为幕幕穆斯林“洗大净”和“小净”的水壶为使之清洁肌肤、净化心灵，壶内装有热水，古代人“热水”称为汤故易名为“汤瓶”汤瓶是穆斯林具有代表性的专用器具。因此，跟穆斯林相关的文代，商标都以“汤瓶”命名，汤瓶拳因此得名。诗云，汤瓶七式世间稀，此拳艺术使人迷，

君如知其中奥妙？必有名师亲指点。

雄鹰不怕大山高、海燕不怕暴风雨。

苦练三伏与三九，十年八载满间归。

杨氏家族是在明末清初，其祖父杨明公系北宋名将杨继业，天山派祖师杨继民、杨延天之后，他幼时于掌握杨氏家传之武功，后开始承袭运用。杨明公精通医道教门颇深，对中国古代的易学和内经学，潜心研究，习练武功，功法，修心养性，强身健体，参悟玄玄，并以口传心授，言传身教，传给后人。

汤瓶功、汤瓶拳、发展到清朝初期已经是具有一定规模，明公之子杨振山诗书皆伏、曾应之武中举，欲效法明公中第即返乡，深研医道，教道和中华本士文代中的阴阳（周易）五形与中医经络学说，一心以继承父志为大业花甲以后因明公年迈，方开始接管杨武馆，在乡里族内授徒传功，此间依然恪守族规，人回族弟子习武者但有心志与内质，均可随振山练习汤瓶功、汤瓶拳。振山同时广泛义诊，医德武得均深获赞誉，然后，振山毕竟系一介书生、其继承汤瓶功，汤瓶拳只是为了不被失传，对拳法、功法本身而言并无发展，正是由于这一点，明公无奈又传汤瓶功、汤瓶拳于河南籍外姓回族子婿穆其太、穆其太系“天山派第四代传人我维吾尔族是伊斯兰教大阿訇阿不都沙吾之女阿姆姑后人。其太不负泰山重望，力担责任。将汤瓶功、汤瓶拳发展几达顶峰、中年时已经是“ 汤瓶拳”汤瓶七式之高手，并将此七式中的硬七式传于外界，据说其太曾三次独赴少林寺切磋武技获“铁罗汉”之赞。

传说，他独闯少林寺时，一位武功高手对他说“少林寺高手如云，武振天下，你去闯必吃大亏”，穆其太说，我非要试试看那人便说：“你打得我再去不迟否则你白白的送死，言后两人比武，各显神通，拳脚生风，猛如飞虎，你来我去，打得天昏地暗，其太获胜那人辑说，你不愧是杨氏家族武功高手，得到杨氏家传之武功。但我劝你还是别去，有多少武林名家高手，有去无返，血气方刚的穆其太来到了少林寺后，他看到一个小和尚在大殿柱子旁劈柴烧水，他从高墙轻轻跳下走到小和尚后面，左手掂 住小和尚衣服下方、右手抱住柱子，来个鲁子深倒拔杨柳往上一提，把小和尚衣服压倒柱子下，随后走

到小和尚面前，左手拿柴，右掌劈柴，然后把柴丢进火炉里，小和尚一见之景，眼前这陌生人，就大声叫喊有“刺客”。出来方丈一见此景，便知高手来临、蹬的一下，穆其太闪在方丈面前、双手辑说方丈你好，晚辈前来讨教学艺，请赐教，方丈微微一笑，便命人在地上洒下豌豆一路，这豌豆又光又滑，没有高深的功夫难以越过，只见方丈呼声一动，拿出轻功古书多有记载沈括在《梦溪笔谈》卷二十《神奇》中就记述了一履木叶而行的轻功故事熙宁（1074）嘉兴有僧人名道亲号通照大师为秀州僧，正有次在温州激雁山打从龙湫 回来快到瑞應院时见一位不知名姓身着布福的隐者，行于山涧之上身轻如飞踏一片木叶而过叶皆不动，身轻若此现这位隐者的轻功功夫大有飘然凌云之仙气，只见其太微微一笑，他以躬腰来了个“敬德打虎三斜式”其招法是汤瓶七式、二十四破法、其中一式，将内气沉于双脚刷刷地从豌豆上穿过，方丈回头一看，大吃一惊，凡穆其太走过的豌豆全被辗成粉末，他不仅赞叹“真乃铁罗汉穆其太也，而且获得少林寺练功秘本真谛，有人称他为“穆氏汤瓶七式拳始祖。

作为明公保留的中国伊斯兰汤瓶功的嫡亲杨传人则有杨振山（第一代）后有义子其女婿回族武术气功家穆其太得汤瓶功、汤瓶拳之真传，习练汤瓶七式拳且又收徒传功，使汤瓶拳、汤瓶功几达盛期，杨万运（第二代）杨岭远（第三代）杨瑞堂（第四代）杨耀均（第五代）杨华祥 董纲成（第六代）马泰鑫 马原子 童嘉昊等（第七代）流行于新疆、河南、山东、湖北、上海、宁夏、青海、甘肃、江西、安徽等地。

现在流行的汤瓶七式拳，多由河南周口、淮阳、开封、回族袁青山、 袁老弟、郭文治、方四、我师杨耀均等人传出。该拳功法有两种共分文武二式，文修于内、武修于外。武式硬汤瓶，包括技击、散打点穴、凌空飞跃、腾闪，此外还有根基功夫，如轻工、重功、软功、硬功、柔功、铁沙掌、硃砂掌、鹰爪功、金刚指、金刚锤等 硬汤瓶习练武功。文式、软汤瓶、包括站、静、坐、仰卧内劲阴阳五指功是用来养生治病的一种功夫，此功法又称中国伊斯兰汤瓶功、

具有明显的回族宗教礼仪色彩、某些教规和修炼方法，取意于穆斯林礼拜前洗阿布代斯（净身）过程中的虔诚，严肃，归心，等各种动作组合，形成一套功法。并分为初、中、高三级。其中包括修性养身内含大力功、八大布气法。武术气功、通过锻炼可以健身治病，锻炼相当程度。还可以利用内气功力、冲力、热力远于全身或手掌、手指、内劲外发、可以为他人治病。行功特点无须意念、循其自然。所谓静心安真元，底桩 盘古根、明同相传功到艺自成、意传内气行，手疾眼快更明静如海中礁、动如雷轰鸣。

河南开封一带等地方习练属于七式共有 108 招，而河南淮阳沙庄一带流传的是原本七式，汤瓶七式拳，以回族洗净小净（阿卜代斯）装水用的汤瓶标记，相继流传至今，其汤瓶拳共分七大式，每个式可化分七个架式为一势。

一式是汤瓶式（荡平式）二式是抓，三式是盖捶，四式是切，五式是崩，六式是荡（挡）七式是撕，七七四十九式除拔郎鼓外共分阴阳两类，阴为破、阳为打。

二十四破法如下：

1) 原始七式身战招 2）翻身调打武艺高，

3）七星架子劈心式 4）袖肋专扎肺物炸

5）双手分掌斩乌龙 6）闪门就怕摇切打

7）二女争夫并相连以下从略此处不谈。

二十四打法如下：

1）金探起架势难防 2）左开右进探心掌

3）合手杀下千斤隧 4）隔臂打耳破命伤

5）蔽手合掌掐喉咙 6）连打一着并相同

7）疾手又打盖面掌

以下从略此处不谈。

七七．四十九，赦中有术，术中赦 、阴阳变理、艺在其中，艺不可没，没则不中。除破法、打法还有若干小手，其中有上七手、

中七手、下七手等 暂从略不谈。

架式可分硬架子、软架子，死架子、活架子、高架子、平架子、低架子，大架子、中架子、小架子，这些架子是在平时个人锻炼、双人或者多人技击、散打、搏击、点穴等对练中运用。

破发，顾法为主，“打法为进法”以后发制人的自卫性拳术，出土的唐拳击涌＂汤瓶式为佐证，门户谨严，秘不外传，有传子不传女、艺不外传俗规。

二郎担山拔郎是汤瓶七式拳的基础（练松节功）腿法，此式要求“四平马步、头往上顶，两臂屈肘，两拳撑腰，两肩下沉、直眷立腰、磕膝里扣敛，大腿外翻屈膝下蹲，大腿与小腿成 90 度，双足五趾抓地“落地生根、呼吸自然尤如瓶壶、在运动中要求两足如磨心，先开后关，左右转身荡摆”尤如蟹横行，顺逆成线，前进一丈五尺，后退一丈五尺，左闪右晃又是一丈五尺，在技击运动中磕胯捷跃，闪战阵夺，吞吐沉浮，探捞牵挂，这十六字说的是十六种技击法，要在其它练功基础上练熟后，才能运用自如。自称为“巧打捉拿笨办法”，它的特点在战略交手中“审敌虚实而去其危”能而示之不能，用而示之不用，示弱迷惑对方，战术中把对方分左侧门，中门，右侧门，上、中、下。防守反击性强，善于捕捉战机，战术灵活机动，它不但腾得高而窜得远，身法低，步法轻快，手法巧很，而要求贴地而起多变，一眨间出手，也就是出手一种打法或破法有六个小手法相互配合，尤如暴风骤雨，万钧雷霆，地震山摇。相似机枪架大炮。使对方顾上，顾不了下，顾中顾不了右。顾右顾不了左等 无法应付，被击中者犹如离弦之箭 脱网之鱼，惊弓之鸟，又好似被强电流去中一样实可谓“神妙绝技”。

已故卢篙高老师，临终时之前，曾经说，心意六合拳比较狠毒，无事不到，头肘膝不可轻用，又说我一身遗憾的是没有学到“汤瓶七式拳”因为它是回族真正内家拳的看家拳。

常人习武练拳只知一套或一种,不知一套一种尚有高平低三种。

汤瓶七式拳架子可分三种，以各人体质，高低和毅力而任，初习时练为高架子，次习平架子后习低架子，而三种架子之中又分大、中、小，大架子求势开展，在遇敌交战中远距离运用，中架子求各势动作合手中庸之道。遇敌交战 中距离运用，小架子求各势紧凑动作灵敏，而迅速遇敌交战，近距离运用，授若此三种之中以不架为最难每一势一式一招丹田吐力、背发寸劲，尺劲 敌前进、后退左闪右避步法甚手法肩腰腿必须一致，学会三种架子决非一年半载，冰冻三尺非一日之寒。而能藏初习者只能每日学习一手，须练得相当、纯熟，才传授下一式，宜因人材施教 不可贪多蛮练必有名师指点，因过多姿势不能？？，后易人于油滑之途，有失汤瓶七式拳之威。

穆氏汤瓶七式拳，练习时要求，动中有静，动中求静，由动入静、静中求动，外静里动、动静相兼。其特点充分发挥意识中假借和内视引导作用。在练习中主导作用上采取连贯园活方刚肢体运动。采用“呼吸精气”练精化神，练神还虚、能起到疏通经络，调理气血外强肢体内壮脏腑的作用，以达到预防疾病增强体质、强身仿敌的目的。古人云。得神者昌、失神者亡，谱云，“外练经骨皮内练精气神，亦即不仅外动，而且注意内气的畜养与引导，功夫练到一定火候可使身体练得”软如锦花“硬如钢铁，轻如鸿毛，重如泰山。此艺在旧社会保守过甚，传媳妇不传闺女，知者不多，传者极少，故不如其它拳术流传广泛，有宁带手传，不带口传，宁口失传，艺不轻传向无拳谱流传。

第五章

汤瓶八诊介绍

不忘初心 传承有序

后记

西域天山派武学秘籍

汤瓶八诊介绍

唯一一个由省级政府出资办学的培训项目

宁夏医科大学
汤瓶八诊培训学院

由于当下政策因素，非医疗人员无法从使针灸工作，养生馆美容院无法从使针灸业务。

汤瓶八诊乃国家非遗项目，依据《中华人民共和国非物质文化遗产法》，传承人可以在“传承机构”从使“传承针法”。这是一种法律特许，非医疗人士通过培训取得传承人资格证；美容院、养生馆通过加盟取得传承基地资格。为合法经营铺平道路。

神奇的湯瓶八診
来自1300年古丝绸之路上的记忆
微信号: tangpingbzhen
一带一路共分享　千年传承保健康
民族瑰宝汤瓶八诊

世界唯一　中国独一
《汤瓶八诊传承谱系》
第一代传人（1710年—1850年）
第二代传人（1744年—1844年）
第三代传人（1780年—1879年）
第四代传人（1825年—1928年）
第五代传人（1863年—1950年）
第六代传人（1903—1991）
第七代传人：杨华祥（1952— ）
第八代传人（1977年— ）
杨华祥教授简介
杨华祥，国家非物质文化遗产——汤瓶八诊第七代传承人，传统医学教授，中医副主任医师，宁夏自治区第五届、第六届政协委员，东盟工商总会顾问，世界中联一带一路标准与健康产业联盟第一届理事会副理事长兼健康丝路专家指导委员会副主任。
杨华祥教授少时家教甚严，从父修武习文，夏练三伏，冬练数九，继承家学，持之以恒，矢志不渝，用家学绝技、祖传秘方为众病黎施治，杨教授一直潜心研究汤瓶八诊内病外治，非药物疗法，主张以善为本，以量为度，以德为高，以诚为荣，近些年来，随着杨华祥教授在马来西亚等世界各地传播医学大放异彩，并将祖传秘方用现代科学技术进行萃取和提炼，经过大量的实验研究，开发出汤瓶八诊系列成药和保健食品，与之前药方相比服用更方便，更安全有效，一经推出即收到汤瓶八诊新老病友的广泛好评。
多年来，为宣传祖国、宣传宁夏，杨教授以汤瓶八诊为桥梁，为宣传宁夏做出了很大贡献，宁夏政府授予"情系宁夏爱洒回乡"牌匾予以表彰，并被马来西亚及宁夏政府冠以"民间大使"的光荣称号！

千年传承 古老传奇
《汤瓶八诊历史渊源》

唯一一个由国家出资出版的系列丛书
湯瓶八診
奇效療法
七代名
回医汤瓶八诊疗法
微信号: tangpingbzhen

国家非物质文化遗产

汤瓶简要

汤瓶的命名源于唐朝，当波斯、中东穆斯林对大唐王朝的经济繁荣、商务交流有所贡献的时候，唐王李世民为了给予表彰，按照穆斯林的习俗打造了一只瓶状的“洗壶”，命名为“唐壶”。“唐壶”内装有热水，古时“热水”称之为“汤”，故易名为“汤瓶”。

八诊简要

明末清初，杨氏家族第一代传人杨明公，潜心研究中国古代易学和中华医学，在“末梢经络根传法”的基础上，在长期的实践中逐步形成了较为完整、有主次的八种诊疗方法被称之为汤瓶八诊疗法：头诊、耳诊、面诊、手诊、脚诊、骨诊、脉诊、气诊。

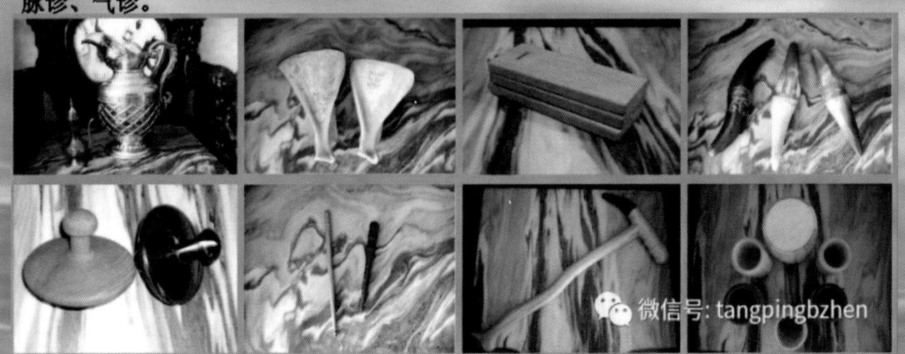

头围 颈围 腰围行针示意图

每侧由前向后分6个纵区

1、2、3区在前面

4、5、6区在后面

以横膈为界，将6个纵区分成上下两半

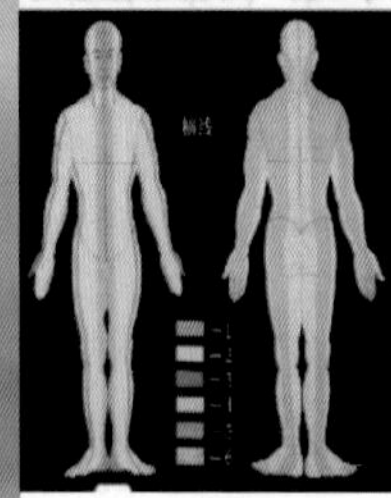

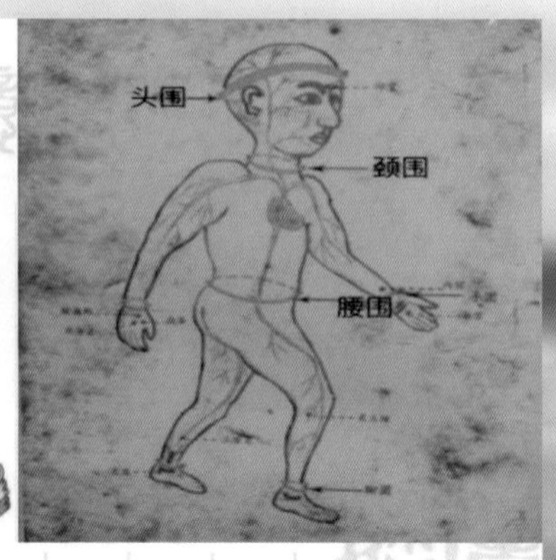

- **各种痛症：**如各种急性扭伤、手术后疼痛、换药疼痛、痛经、人流疼痛、肾绞痛等。
- **某些神经精神疾病：**失眠、焦虑、抑郁、高血压等。
- **其他各科的一些病症：**内科、外科、妇科。

欢迎走进汤瓶八诊
共享健康人生

不忘初心 传承有序

师父 师母 留影

杨华祥教授在泰国一带一路高峰论坛

杨耀均与徒弟董纲成

董纲成头顶开石

董纲成双耳开石

董纲成徒弟表演嘴咬台子

董纲成弟弟董玉宽表演踩砖

董纲成与弟弟表演双人开石

杨耀均与徒弟董纲成、董玉宽

杨耀均与徒弟董纲成

董纲成弟弟董玉宽表演

中国武术协会
CHINESE WUSHU ASSOCIATION

中阿传统医学交流的结晶

来自1300年前丝绸之路
湯瓶
国家非

PORSCHE DESIGN
HUAWEI Mate 10

民族的就是世界的

扬我国粹 龙腾阳
武

江苏百超

江苏百超投资有限

扬我国粹 龙腾阳湖
武

主办单位： 中国老龄事业发展基金会
江苏百超投资有限公司

2009
国银行全民健身奥体嘉年
FITNESS OF THE NATION CARNIVAL 2009

身怀氣功絶技
无私传授神功

西域
天山派

西域天山派武学密籍系列(三)
西域天山
龙头大铡刀

中华武魂
1期
封面人物
高海形意拳名家孔门拳传承人
马泰鑫
6 937147 252044
2020年03月

西域天山派武学密籍系列(一)
西域天山
追魂密肘
《中华武魂》民间传统武术珍珠古籍

西域天山派武学密籍系列(四)
西域天山追魂刀
《中华武魂》民间传统武术珍珠古籍

西宁市非遗代表性
承人培训班
暨第三批传承
牌仪式

青海省第五届少数民族传统体育运动会
比赛
08/08/2013

第三届全国武术运动大会
武术科学大会

2020年 第1期
www.zhwhzzs.com
中华武魂
中国昆仑派天宗门第十九代传承人
马原子
武
18215070622
青海形意拳及苗刀主要传人
馬泰鑫：武林传奇 传承使命

西域
天山派

武魂
封面人物：马原子
SEPTEMBER 2013. 11
ISSN 1002-3267

临夏武术志
主编：马志勇 马原子

八门统备武艺
BAMENQUAN SHUZHEN
金泉 马原子 编著
八门拳非物质文化遗产传著解译

当代西北武林人物风采
当代西北
武林人物风采

西域
天山派

中华武魂
西域天山派26代传承人
童嘉昊
1期
2020年03月
6 937147 252044

后记

今年是2020年庚子年，1989也就是30年前，我应在塞上江南宁夏首府中国宁夏伊斯兰气功医疗康复中心既宁夏第一家回民医院任主任兼院长的师弟杨华祥邀请、赴宁夏探望在医院任顾问的义父杨耀钧，同时为支持师弟杨华祥的气功医疗事业、将所学武医气功用于临床。后又应宁夏武警总队特警队的特邀任气功、武术、总教练。那一年我未及不惑，才38岁。这一次我来南京，六朝古都，我已逾古稀，南京民国时期，中央国术馆1928年开馆时，天下武林高手聚集地。在这里，我想完成一生愿望，把我在60年前拜河南杨氏家族，西域古法心意拳，杨氏汤瓶七式拳，杨氏阴阳母子回回肘，俗称回回十八肘。第六代掌门传承人，义父杨耀钧老先生，所学武功秘绝书稿整改出来，准备出版。30年前，我任宁夏武警总队，武术总教练时期，我写得“西域古法心意拳”书稿。由于历史因素，老一辈得来东西不易，没有出版。今年12月1日是我义父杨耀钧老先生诞辰120周年，为了纪念他，我写了“西域古法心意拳”书稿。从新拿出来，整理修改，即将出版。在很早年前，我就关注，杨明公他是北宗名将杨继业，杨家将后裔。心意六合拳，汤瓶七式拳，回回十肘。新时代，改革开放，促进了经济的发展，带来了传统文体繁华，到处可以看到，心意拳武馆，俱乐部，研究会，心意拳博物馆。该拳走进高等学府，大学，中学，小学，有的地方市、区、都在开幕一年一次表演大赛。吸引外资，并传播到国外，成为世界文化交流项目。同时选入国家非物质文化遗产保护名录。在网络视频中许多人自称心意六合拳，汤瓶七式拳，回回十八肘，第某某代掌门人，嫡系传承人。表演，解读，论续，教授诠释。沸沸扬扬，百花开放。然而，这些解读论述教授和我恩师杨耀钧老先生传给我的几乎不一

样，没有共同之处，这促使我必须写出还原历史本真。我曾经看过许多武林书籍，年轻时，以武交友，走遍了大半个中国，深山寺庙，见到过无数高手。也曾经仔细反复看过，心意六合拳，武林大会表演比赛。事后感到十分纠结与痛心，因为其中没有心意六合拳的真髓。只能练身健体，表演玩玩，做做武术体操。跟(心意拳谱)中明确阐述要求大相径庭，相距甚远。西域古法心意拳，是一种家族性传承保守，神秘威力强大的“教门拳”，是回族人民自创具有独特民族风格的拳种，至今外人难窥其径，有人说，传统武术与中医传承有不谋而合的地方。可以用留一手，形象来比喻，因为中国封建社会传统理念早已根深蒂固，导致在传统传承上认识不足。为了防止家传秘籍被盗取，都会在传教中留一手，将武学医学中最精华的东西带到神秘中去，这样代代相传，其保守的思想代代生根，国学精华代代流失，直至今日，好的东西只有掌握在极少数人手里，他们视物似命。不轻易教徒。西域古法心意拳，杨氏汤瓶七式拳，杨氏阴阳母子肘，(俗称回回十八肘)它由明末清初，杨家将后裔始祖杨明公所创！“汤瓶式”而完善了“杨氏汤瓶七式拳””，西域古法心意拳“杨氏阴阳母子回回肘”俗称回回十八肘。杨氏家族，历来都和心意拳名匠巨手们来往交流总结，三大古战场保家卫国拳法。传统武术博大精深，蕴含深厚的哲学文化，难在短时间内有所成，而现在社会发展速度飞快，人更适应快速接受新事物，短时间有成效的运动，所以我认为以三大古战场，保家卫国拳法为基础，与古代老子哲学的思想统领“大物无形””大音无声”结合。有形则易行，无形则难修，它融会贯通进拳法，表现为要气血发力，手脚出击，飞速生风，快捷无形，主张形骼操练不以形，有形而破体，无形则居气。创始中华无形道。我曾任宁夏武警总队特邀武术总教练。身怀西域，天山派，汤瓶门武功的绝技。深深担心拳法断层，为中华武术源远流长着想，习武者必须打破门户之见，搏采众长，要有海纳百川胸膛，勿使前辈之遗失于我手，勿使国之精神止于我

身，我们这一代有历史使命，要把这门国粹一定要发扬光大，走向世界。

董大师至今 72 岁弟子无数，简单提几位不同阶段，有影响的徒弟：馬泰鑫、马原子、童嘉昊、杨庆宝、张吉生、洪新忠、朱光华、杨俊峰、赵华、刘胜利、刘旭晨、盛友春、袁小建、古小辉、海洋、朱向东、孙文、王学军、张青路、李培青。家父在宁夏除全面传授我与蒋红岩外也曾传授过：王新武、张全乐、张新乐、于承慧、袁济生、杨建军、吴尚文、杨金柱、杨俊峰，这些人主要是由我代父传承的。

Postscript

This year is 2020. 30 years ago in 1989, I was invited by my younger brother Yang Huaxiang, who was the director and dean of the first Muslim hospital in the capital of Ningxia province, the Ningxia Islamic Qigong Medical and Rehabilitation Center, to viist my foster father Yang Yaojun, who served as a consultant at the hospital, and used the martial arts qigong he had learned to support my younger brother's qigong clinical career. Later, I was specially invited by the special police team of the Ningxia Armed Police Corps to serve as head coach of qigong and martial arts. I was then 38 years old. Now I have come to Nanjing, the ancient capital of the Six Dynasties, and I am more than seventy years old. During the Republic of Nanjing, when the Central Guoshu Museum opened in 1928, it was a gathering place for martial arts masters from all over the world. Here, I want to fulfill my lifelong wish to worship the Yang family of Henan Province, the Western Regions ancient method Xinyiquan, the Yang family Tang Ping 7-form Boxing, the Yang family Yin-Yang mother and child Hui nation elbow method, commonly known as the Hui nation 18 elbow-on-elbow method. the sixth generation of inheritor, foster father Yang Yaojun, the manuscript of the secret masterpiece of martial arts he learned was rectified and prepared for publication. The manuscripts of the secret martial arts from which sixth generation master, my foster father Yang Yaojun, learned have been corrected and prepared for publication. Thirty years ago, when I served as the head coach of martial arts of the Ningxia Armed Police Corps, I wrote the manuscript of "Xinyiquan". Due to historical factors, it was not easy for the older generation to get materials, and it was not

published. December 1st this year is the 120th anniversary of the birth of my foster father, Mr. Yang Yaojun. To commemorate him, I have reproduced my manuscript on "Xinyiquan", corrected and revised it, and it will soon be published. For a long tome, I have been interested in Yang Minggong, descendant of Yang Jike, a famous general of the Northern Zong. Xinyi Six Harmonies Boxing, Tang Ping 7-form Boxing, Hui nation 18 elbows. In the new era, reform and opening up have promoted economic development and brought prosperity to traditional styles. You can see Xinyiquan martial arts museums, clubs, seminars, and Xinyiquan museums everywhere. Boxing has been introduced into institutions of higher learning, universities, middle schools, elementary schools, and some local cities and districts hold an annual open competition. It has attracted foreign interest and been spread abroad, in a world cultural exchange project. It has also been selected for the National Intangible Cultural Heritage Protection List. In the online videos, many people claim to be direct line descendants of the originator of Xinyi Six Harmonies Boxing, Tang Ping 7-form Boxing, Hui nation 18 elbows, performing and interpreting the continuation of their teacher's interpretation. However, these interpretations are almost always different from what my mentor Yang Yaojun passed to me. They have nothing in common with it, which prompted me to write my manuscript to restore its true history . I have read many martial arts books. When I was young, I made friends with martial artists, and travelled throughout China, to temples deep in the mountains, to meet countless masters. I have also carefully and repeatedly watched Xinyi Six Harmonies Boxing martial arts performance competitions. Afterwards, I always felt very confused and distressed, because there was no essence of Six Harmonies Boxing in it – merely physical fitness, performance and play at martial arts gymnastics. This

is very different from the requirements clearly stated in the Xinyiquan chart. Western Regions ancient method Xinyiquan is a family tradition and conservative, mysterious and powerful boxing sect. It is a unique national style of boxing created by the Hui people. Because of its familial nature, it is difficult for outsiders to follow. It is difficult for outsiders to see its path. Some people say the heritage of traditional martial arts and traditional Chinese medicine coincide. Metaphorically, it is like holding a single image in one's hand, because traditional ideas of Chinese feudal society have long been ingrained, leading to insufficient understanding of traditional heritage. In order to prevent family secrets from being stolen, they will hold back the best things in martial arts and medicine. In this way, the conservative ideas will take root and be passed from generation to generation, and the essence of Chinese learning will be lost. Today, good things are only in the hands of a very small number of people, who see this as their fate – not easy to become a disciple. Western Regions ancient method Xinyiquan, Yang family Tang Ping 7-form Boxing, Yang family Yin-Yang mother and son elbow, (commonly known as Hui nation eighteen elbow) was created by Yang Minggong, the ancestor of the Yang family in the late Ming and early Qing! The "Tang Ping Style" is a refinement of the "Yang family Tang Ping 7-form Boxing". The Western Regions ancient method Xinyiquan's "Yang family Yin-Yang mother and son Hui elbow" is commonly known as Hui nation 18 elbow. The Yang family has always interacted with the masters of Xinyiquan on the three ancient battlefields in order to defend the home and the country. Traditional martial arts are a broad and profound philosophical culture. It is difficult to achieve success in a short period of time. Nowadays, society is developing rapidly, and people are more adaptable, quickly accepting new things and wanting rapid progress in sports. Therefore,

I think the three ancient battlefields on which we protect the home and the country must be combined with the ancient philosophy of Lao Tzu, which governs "great things are invisible" and "great sound is silent". The tangible is easy to perform, the intangible is difficult to cultivate – this is integral to boxing technique, manifest in the importance of qi and blood to exert force, attacking with feet and hands with forceful exhalation of breath, fast and intangible, it asserts that the appearance of the form is not the form. This is the basis of China's formless way of Taoism. I used to be the head coach of the special police team of the Ningxia Armed Police Corps, conveying Western Regions, Tianshan School, Tang Ping style martial arts skills. For a long time I have been deeply concerned about faults in boxing techniques, for the sake of Chinese martial arts, martial arts practitioners set aside their opinions, try to learn from others, and be open-minded, don't let our ancestors skills be lost in our hands, and don't let the spirit of our country end in our bodies. Our generation has a historic mission, and we must carry forward this national quintessence to the World.

Master Dong has countless disciples at the age of 72, and briefly mentions several influential apprentices at different stages: Ma Taixin, Ma Zhizi, Tong Jiahao, Yang Qingbao, Zhang Jisheng, Hong Xinzhong, Zhu Guanghua, Yang Junfeng, Zhao Hua, Liu Shengli, Liu Xuchen, Sheng Youchun, Yuan Xiaojian, Gu Xiaohui, Haiyang, Zhu Xiangdong, Sun Wen, Wang Xuejun, Zhang Qinglu, Li Peiqing. My father taught me and Jiang Hongyan in Ningxia, and also these people: Wang Xinwu, Zhang Quanle, Zhang Xinle, Yu Chenghui, Yuan Jisheng, Yang Jianjun, Wu Shangwen, Yang Tianzhu, Yang Junfeng.

西域天山派秘籍书籍

西域天山派武学秘籍（一）西域古法心意拳
西域天山派武学秘籍（二）中华南北心（形）意拳
西域天山派武学秘籍（三）西域天山扬家汤瓶七式拳
西域天山派武学秘籍（四）西域天山扬家阴阳母子回回十八肘
西域天山派武学秘籍（五）西域天山扬家董氏六合大枪
西域天山派武学秘籍（六）西域天山汤瓶阴阳母子剑
西域天山派武学秘籍（七）西域天山杨家乌纱双捧
西域天山派武学秘籍（八）西域天山荡平元霸阴阳母子双锤
西域天山派武学秘籍（九）西域天山杨家阴阳母子鸳鸯点穴凿
西域天山派武学秘籍（十）西域天山五大绝技
西域天山派武学秘籍（十一）西域天山 追魂长刀
西域天山派武学秘籍（十二）西域天山追魂密肘
西域天山派武学秘籍（十三）西域天山龙头大铡刀
西域天山派武学秘籍（十四）西域天山双手长剑
西域天山派武学秘籍（十五）西域天山春秋大刀
西域天山派武学秘籍（十六）西域心意鞭杆

西域古法心意拳

董纲成　编著

书　　号：ISBN 978-988-75077-7-2
出　　版：香港国际武术总会出版
发　　行：香港联合书刊物流有限公司
代 理 商：代理商：台湾白象文化事业有限公司
香港地址：香港九龙弥敦道 525-543 号宝宁大厦 C 座 412 室
电　　话：00852-98500233 \ 91267932
深圳地址：深圳市罗湖区红岭中路 2118 号建设集团大厦 B 座 20A 室
电　　话：0755-25950376 \ 13352912626
台湾地址：401 台中市东区和平街 228 巷 44 号
电　　话：04-22208589
印　　次：2021 年 11 月第一次印刷
印　　数：5000 册
总 编 辑：冷先锋
装帧设计：明栩成
设计策划：香港国际武术总会工作室
网　　站：www. hkiwa.com　Email: hkiwa2021@gmail.com